N. DE M.

ABOUT THE AUTHOR

Gerald M. Best is an avid and active railroader, and in this book has been able to put to use some of his vast collection of negatives and prints of steam and narrow gauge in North America.

For the past two and one-half years he has been a technical advisor to the National Park Service, and in that capacity has been working for the 1969 Centennial of the Golden Spike Ceremony at Promontory, Utah.

Mr. Best's previous books for Howell-North have been SHIPS AND NARROW GAUGE RAILS, SNOWPLOW and NEVADA COUNTY NARROW GAUGE, although he has written on many other railroad subjects also. His collection of short histories of various railroads has burgeoned into a large reference library in the 40 years he has been at it. His railroad author friends are indebted to him for his generous sharing with them of his pictures and his very accurate locomotive rosters.

A retired sound engineer, he travels now, recording the last of steam all over the world. His affection for railroading and his systematic approach to recording its history, make his contributions in this field a true and valuable benefit.

It is a sunny afternoon on a field in Morelos state, with Popocatepetl's monumental 17,887-foot peak soaring above the clouds in the center. Two donkeys, traditional Mexican motive power, stand in the foreground, ignoring the distant passenger train steaming toward Mexico City on the first Mexican-built narrow gauge railroad. *(Gerald M. Best)*

MEXICAN NARROW GAUGE

By Gerald M. Best

Berkeley California

MEXICAN NARROW GAUGE

Printed and bound in the United States of America

Library of Congress Catalog Card No. 68-57487

TO
EDWIN W. LOHR
AND
LEONARD T. HAUG

Published by Howell-North Books
1050 Parker Street, Berkeley, California 94710

Acknowledgments

The writer is indebted to a number of friends on both sides of the border for assistance in preparing this book. Handicapped as I am by insufficient knowledge of Spanish to write letters in that language, my friends in the management of the National Railways of Mexico have been particularly indulgent by replying to my requests for information in English. Of particular assistance in recent years has been Mr. Jose I. Vasconcelos, General Agent for the Mexican Government Railway System in the United States. Many of the historical archives of the railways of Mexico were destroyed during the disturbances of 1911-1916, particularly the early motive power lists. Fortunately, the annual reports of the Secretaria de Fomento, and later the Secretaria de Communicaciones y Obras Publicas (S.C.O.P.) were sent to various libraries in the United States and today are available to historians. The American and British companies which built most of the early Mexican railroads published their annual reports in the United States and Great Britain, and these frequently contain information which was lost from the Mexican archives during the revolution.

The DeGolyer Foundation and Mr. Everett L. DeGolyer, Jr. of Dallas, Texas have been of great assistance through the loan of pictures and of the secretarial reports of the Mexican Government. Mr. DeGolyer's profound knowledge of Mexico through having lived there from time to time in his earlier days has been invaluable in many ways. For the use of photographs I wish to thank C. W. Witbeck of Hammond, Louisiana, with whom I shared weeks of travelling around Mexico, photographing locomotives and trains on the railroads; the late Edwin W. Lohr, retired Jersey Central engineer who spent his winters in Mexico riding and photographing the narrow gauge; Paul Darrell of Richmond, California, for the loan of pictures from the collection of the late Leonard T. Haug; Jim Shaughnessy of Troy, New York, for his splendid action shots made in the latter days of steam on the Mexico City-Cuautla line; Stan Kistler of Pasadena and Donald Duke of San Marino, California, for narrow gauge action photos, and to Mr. Herbert L. Broadbelt of Morrisville, Pennsylvania, for Baldwin builders' photos. Pictures not otherwise credited are by the author or from his collection.

My special thanks to Mr. Harold L. Stewart of Pasadena, California, for photos of the electric railroad at Chihuahua and his many fine action photos of steam operations at various places in Mexico. His recent and accurate reporting of narrow gauge operations as they are in 1968 has made it possible to bring the text up-to-date.

GERALD M. BEST

Beverly Hills, California
June, 1968

Articulated No. 368 hauls the Mexico City-Acambaro passenger with ease up the grade out of the Valley of Mexico, in the last year of narrow gauge on the Acambaro line. *(L. T. Haug)*

Contents

Preface

During the past two decades Mexico has been invaded by visitors from the United States, Canada and even far-away Australia whose primary purpose was to ride on the narrow gauge railroads which at the beginning of this era comprised over 1500 miles of track. Of this mileage, three-fourths was operated by the National Railways of Mexico; the remainder consisted of isolated lines, none of them connecting with the National Railway's narrow gauge network. The latter had frequent passenger service, with sleeping cars on the long runs and represented a much higher development of narrow gauge to handle heavy traffic, than was displayed by the few surviving narrow gauge lines in the United States.

On my second visit to Mexico in 1953, I rode from Puebla to Mexico City on a narrow gauge passenger train which required ten hours, fifteen minutes to cover 243 miles. It made frequent stops and seemingly was doing a thriving business as there was never an empty seat on the train, with plenty of standees filling the aisles and platforms of the second-class coaches. The highway connecting the two cities, though it was narrow and winding as it crossed the mountain range, was less than a hundred miles long and could be negotiated in about three hours at that time. Another standard gauge line extended north from Puebla through San Martin and San Lorenzo, then south along the western slopes of Ixtaccihuatl volcano through Texcoco to Mexico City, a distance of 130 miles. Passenger trains on this line covered the route several times daily in four hours, fifty minutes.

A friend from the States accompanied me on this trip and remarked that the people riding the train must be crazy to consider it as a means of riding from Puebla to Mexico City when it could be done by bus or the train around the northern route in less than half the time our train would require. My answer was that anyone who rode this train from terminal to terminal *was* crazy and there were just two such people on the train—ourselves! The conductor on this train good naturedly regarded us as out of our minds, voluntarily to endure the long, dusty ride when we could use other means of transportation. Of course he knew we were out to see the marvelous scenery, to experience the thrill of riding behind steam locomotives which were fast disappearing in our own country, and we did not mind the long ride; in fact we loved every minute of it.

My friend's question, repeated by many others within my hearing is easily answered. This particular railroad was never intended to be a through route between the two big cities. It was built under two separate charters, one to provide a railroad from Mexico City to Acapulco and the other to extend from Puebla to Acapulco. They began as independent projects and both failed of their ultimate objective, Acapulco. Many years later a connecting link of 39 miles joined the two dead ends together. The many patrons of the train then as now, were riders for short distances only. Those who boarded at Puebla had all left the train when it reached Atencingo, their places taken by more passengers who seldom rode west of Cuautla. After the train left the latter town, it filled up again with passengers going from the villages in the back country to the public markets in the big city, carrying their wares with them. Though occasionally a few carloads of freight are hauled from one terminal to the other, the bulk of the business originates in the great valley of which Cuautla is the center and goes either east and north to Puebla, or west and north to Mexico City.

The section from Cuautla to Mexico City is one of the oldest railroads in Mexico and certainly the oldest narrow gauge railroad of any importance.

One of the work horses of the Cuautla line is being turned at the 80-year-old San Lazaro roundhouse in Mexico City. *(Jim Shaughnessy)*

That it should be the last surviving narrow gauge part of National Railways of Mexico is probably due to the fact that it is now of secondary importance to the company. Some of the divisions may not be worth standard gauging. Those which are retained will certainly become standard gauge in the near future. Even in these latter days of narrow gauge with steam operation, locomotives only recently retired bore the initials of railroads long since absorbed into the Mexican Government Railway System. This book is intended to outline the history of the individual railroads, their purpose in the development of the country and to list their equipment, some of which is still in use. Included in the text are short histories of the principal short lines and industrial railways which were narrow gauge, with lists of their motive power.

Before detailing the history of the four major projects involving narrow gauge trunk lines in Mexico, all promoted by British or U. S. groups, a short review of the status of the railroads in Mexico in the year 1880 is important to the general Mexican Railway (Ferrocarril Mexicano), built picture. Until then, the only large railroad was the by British engineers under various concessions between 1864 and 1873. This standard gauge line in 1880 extended from the port of Vera Cruz on the Gulf of Mexico, to Mexico City, a distance of 264 miles, with a branch to Puebla from the main line station of Apizaco. Most of the country's exports or imports overseas had to pass over this railroad and its British owners had in effect a monopoly on rail transportation. Complaints of indifferent service and high freight rates reached the ears of President Porfirio Diaz; he became receptive to proposals for concessions to build competing railroads, particularly those which would either parallel the F. C. Mexicano or connect the heart of the country with another seaport, preferably one located on the Pacific coast. There had been a strong prejudice in Mexico against railroads connecting the United States with central Mexico, for the memory of the invasion of the country from Texas in 1845 was still fresh in the minds of the older generation. Granting the validity of this fear, and sharing it to a certain extent, Diaz nevertheless felt that one or more railroads connecting the rapidly growing network of railroads in the United States with the largely undeveloped part of Mexico north of Mexico City would benefit his country more than harm it.

In 1880 the owners of the Atchison, Topeka & Santa Fe had advanced their railhead well into the state of New Mexico, past the capital city, and expected early the next year to connect with the Southern Pacific at Deming. (This event occurred March 8, 1881.) They were also determined to build an extension from the Santa Fe-Deming line to El Paso, Texas and from there to Mexico City, with the Mexican government's permission. Early in 1880 a group headed by Thomas Nickerson, Santa Fe's president, formed the Mexican Central Railway (Ferrocarril Central Mexicano) and through their agent in Mexico, Robert R. Symon, asked the Diaz government for permission to transfer to the new company an 1874 concession for a railroad from Mexico City to Leon. They would then build a standard gauge railroad to the capital from Paso del Norte, now Ciudad Juarez, on the border opposite El Paso. Diaz approved this plan on condition that a branch would be built to Guadalajara, with another to the port of Tampico on the Gulf of Mexico. This concession was granted on April 3, 1880, with a subsidy of $15,000 per mile of railroad built, the balance to be paid by the U. S. company. Construction of the Mexican Central began in Mexico City on September 15, 1880 and early in 1881 from Paso del Norte. With ample capital and the will to see the project through as quickly as possible, the Mexican Central was opened for business April 10, 1884. It was a first class railroad, 1224 miles long and was operated and maintained according to the high standards the Santa Fe had set up for its own properties in the United States. The route from Kansas City to Mexico City over the completed system was a circuitous one of over 2400 miles and required five days for a passenger to complete the journey. It provided the first direct rail service between Mexico City and the principal cities of the United States and was built without failure of any of the contractors or companies involved. Its owners had high hopes for a large volume of traffic over the new railroad. That this was not to be is not pertinent to this story.

The equipment used on the railroads of Mexico regardless of the different gauges was largely built in the United States, although some for railroads built and owned by British investors was built in England. As this rolling stock wore out, it was replaced by the less sophisticated but more durable American equipment, and it is safe to say that 95% of all the rolling stock on the railroads of Mexico was built in the United States prior to World War I. Later, Mexican industry acquired the "know-how" to fabricate freight cars of the same quality as those purchased outside the country, and today all new freight cars in Mexico are made locally. Only three steam locomotives, two of 3-foot gauge and one standard gauge were ever built in Mexico. Hence the motive power was especially interesting to students of U. S.-built locomotives. It is largely for these hobbyists that this story has been written.

1

Major Narrow Gauge Systems

THE MEXICAN NATIONAL RAILWAY (F. C. NACIONAL MEXICANO)

This railroad was the brainchild of General William J. Palmer, builder of the Denver & Rio Grande Railway and strong advocate of narrow gauge railroads as a means of reducing the high cost of standard gauge construction, especially through mountainous terrain. General Palmer won his battle to keep the Santa Fe from building through the Royal Gorge and thence south to Santa Fe, but the wily group from Boston who built the Santa Fe Railway outsmarted Palmer by building south from La Junta in Colorado, through Raton Pass and across New Mexico to a junction with the Southern Pacific at Deming, thus providing another transcontinental route. General Palmer was determined to reach the Rio Grande somewhere along the Mexican border and to build a railroad from there to Mexico City, if for no other reason than to compete with the announced purpose of the Santa Fe to finance and build a railroad from the Texas border to Mexico City.

Acting through his agent, James Sullivan of Mexico City, Palmer asked for a concession to be granted to the Mexican National Construction Co. (Cia Constructora Nacional Mexicana), to build a 3-foot gauge railroad from Laredo, Texas through Monterrey, Saltillo, San Luis Potosi, Celaya, Acambaro, Maravatio and Toluca to Mexico City, a distance of 840 miles. Through a connection with the International & Great Northern, then building between Austin, Texas and Laredo, Palmer would have a shorter route to Mexico City from Chicago and Kansas City than the line planned by the Santa Fe. Simultaneously, Palmer organized the Mexican National Railway Co. (Ferrocarril Nacional Mexicano), which was to take over each section of the railroad as it was completed by the construction company, and to operate it. Application was also made to build a branch from the main line at Acambaro to Guadalajara, Colima and the Pacific seaport of Manzanillo. Other branches would run from San Luis Potosi west to Zacatecas and Guadalupe Hidalgo, to El Salto from Mexico City and from Monterrey to the seaport of Matamoros on the Rio Grande, across the river from Brownsville, Texas. This concession was granted to Palmer and Sullivan on September 13, 1880, two days before the Mexican Central began construction in Mexico City. Subsidies in various amounts were granted depending on the topography of the country, but under a subsequent revision it averaged $11,270 per mile of completed track. To pay for the balance, the company issued $25,000 in stock and an equal amount in bonds per mile of railroad completed.

An entrance into Mexico City was already available through purchase of a partly completed railroad called the Mexico, Toluca & Cuautitlan, a 3-foot gauge line which had been granted a concession to build north from Mexico City to Cuautitlan, 18 miles, and to Toluca, 45 miles west. The railroad had reached Cuautitlan in 1880, but little had been done west of Tacuba Junction, three miles north of the terminal. Its owners transferred their concession to the Mexican National late in 1880, providing Palmer with an entrance into the heart of Mexico City. Known as Colonia Station, it was on the Paseo de la Reforma on a site now occupied by a public park, less than a block from the statue of Cuauhtemoc. Since the Mexico, Toluca & Cuautitlan had been laid with 35-pound rail, too light for the traffic load planned by its new owner, it was relaid with 45-pound rail as soon as construction work began.

After the concession had been ratified by the Mexican Congress, General Palmer's group ordered large quantities of supplies, including 35 locomotives from the Baldwin Locomotive Works

'he twin volcanoes Ixtaccihuatl and Popocate-etl form an impressive backdrop for the Puebla-Iexico City daily passenger, at left, as it ap-roaches Chalco. *(H. F. Stewart)*

and thousands of tons of 40 and 45-pound steel rail to be delivered at both ends of the project. Construction was first begun by relaying the rails out of Mexico City, for the company had acquired five Baldwin locomotives with the Mexico, Toluca & Cuautitlan which proved very useful in getting the work started. As soon as a large supply of rail had arrived, tracklaying began on the grade of the unfinished Toluca line. At Nuevo Laredo, across the Rio Grande from Laredo, Texas, track construction began in the summer of 1881 and progressed rapidly south through open country in the State of Nuevo Leon, at a gentle rise of ten feet per mile, the railhead reaching the city of Monterrey in September 1882, 168 miles from Laredo.

Construction work west of Mexico City proved to be extremely difficult, as the line climbed from an elevation of 7700 feet at Mexico City to 10,000 feet at Salazar, 25 miles west, for an average climb of nearly a hundred feet per mile and in many places grades of 4% were encountered. The first ten miles had been in the valley of Mexico, thus concentrating all of the heavy grades in a section less than 15 miles long. In spite of these handicaps the line from Mexico City to Toluca was accepted by the Mexican National from the construction company on September 4, 1882. The work was much easier north and west of Toluca as the line progressed down the valley of the Rio Lerma and the line was opened for traffic to Acambaro, 177 miles west of Mexico City in May 1883. Work on the branch from Acambaro to Manzanillo was begun from both ends and on September 12, 1883 the first locomotive steamed into the city of Morelia, causing wild excitement as the populace gazed on the iron horse for the first time. From

The gold leaf and fine-line artists at Baldwin were at their best when the tender of the TLALNEPANTLA and its mate, the BARRIENTOS were lettered for the Mexico, Toluca & Cuautitlan.

Mexican National Construction Co. No. 10 by Baldwin was used on construction trains. *(Left and opposite below: Herbert L. Broadbelt collection)*

Manzanillo, track was laid east to Armeria for a distance of thirty miles during 1883 under the greatest possible difficulties. Rail, a locomotive and flatcars and other supplies had to be shipped from San Francisco by water, and labor was hard to find in a region given over primarily to fishing. When the supplies were exhausted late in the year, all construction work east of Manzanillo ceased.

The 68-mile section south from Monterrey had an average grade of 50 feet per mile ascending the lower slopes of the Sierra Madre Oriental mountains, reaching an altitude of 5300 feet at Saltillo, approximately that of Denver, Colorado. Work was slow due to the great amount of excavation required and a year passed before the first train ran from Laredo to Saltillo, 235 miles, on September 5, 1883. Another crew of the construction company had completed a part of the branch from Zacatecas towards San Luis Potosi, reaching Ojo Caliente in the fall of 1883. Supplies had to be brought to Zacatecas over the rival Mexican Central, and two locomotives were assigned to this branch for construction train service. Still another construction gang of five hundred men began work from Matamoros, across the Rio Grande from Brownsville, Texas, towards Monterrey, making a total of six groups working on various sections of the project at one time.

All of the grading, excavating and fill work was done by the pick and wheelbarrow method, none of the modern excavating machinery we are accustomed to today being available. The crew on the main line alone totalled 8000 men, all peons or members of the various Indian tribes of the districts through which the line was to run. A letter from a newspaper reporter who interviewed John Scullin, general manager of the construction company is very revealing as to conditions under which the American engineers worked. Scullin stated that the peons were as good railroad builders as any he had encountered in the United States. Graders were paid 30¢ (U.S.) per day, rock workers 36¢ per day and overseers got a dollar a day. The cost of living for the workers was 25¢ per week, the principal food items being frijoles (beans) and tortillas (corn meal pancakes). A reporter for the *Railway Gazette* saw 5000 of the workers paid off on a Saturday and said there were no drunks or any fighting as had been the usual thing on such construction jobs as he had seen in the western part of the United States. He said the workers went to their homes on Sunday if they were near enough to get there on foot, and were back on the job early Monday morning. Scullin was quoted as stating that the work in the Laredo-Saltillo section had cost only $18,000 a mile, although he agreed it was much higher in the mountainous section from Mexico City to Acambaro.

The year 1883 ended with the railheads at Celaya and Morelia on the southern end, San Miguel from Matamoros towards Monterrey, a completed line from Mexico City through Cuautitlan to El Salto and the northern railhead was two miles south of the city of Saltillo. A total of 698 miles of 3-foot gauge line had been built, and to this was added the Texas-Mexican Railroad, a 161 mile narrow gauge line from Laredo to Corpus Christi, Texas on the Gulf of Mexico. This railroad was a separate project and was leased to the Mexican National. Though the Mexican Government had paid the construction company a total of $9,250,000 for mileage completed to the end of 1883, it was but a drop in the bucket as compared to the costs Palmer's group had obligated themselves to pay. The bond interest on the 24 millions of 6% bonds was nearly a million and a half dollars, and though trains ran on the completed sections and produced a revenue of over a million dollars in 1883, it did not even pay operating expenses. There still remained a gap of 385 miles of main line to be built, before through trains could be run and the crews of the rival Mexican Central were within two months of tying together their two railheads in one unit extending from Juarez to Mexico City.

On April 1, 1884 Palmer announced that the bond interest payments would not be made for three years, but in order to avoid receivership, contingent 6% bonds to the amount of the interest due, would be paid to the bondholders. All construction work was ordered to cease except to lay track on the completed grade from Zacatecas to Ojo Caliente, and for over two years nothing was done to complete the railroad although Palmer and his associates struggled desperately to raise additional funds. Palmer was finally successful in obtaining money abroad, but at a price. On September 30, 1886 he signed an agreement with the London firm of Matheson & Co., which guaranteed a new issue of bonds which would provide the money to close the gap between the north and south railheads and enable the railroad to become self-supporting. On May 23, 1887 the Mexican National Railway was sold under foreclosure agreement with the bondholders, the Mexican National Railroad Co. emerging as the new owner. W. G. Raoul, first vice-president under General Palmer became the president of the new company; though Palmer remained on the board of directors until 1891, he no longer directed the destinies of the railroad he had started with such high hopes in 1880 and retired to remain the head of his Colorado and Utah empire for many years to come.

Construction work was resumed south of Saltillo in September 1887 and in December, tracklaying began on many miles of completed roadbed north of Celaya. In the 24 miles from Saltillo to the summit of the Sierra Madre at Carneros, the line went from the mesa of Ojo de Agua, up the rocky slopes at a uniform grade of 100 feet per mile, passing Buena Vista, site of the great battle between U.S. forces under General Taylor and the Mexican armies of General Santa Anna in 1847. The tracklayers reached the summit at Carneros, 7300 feet above the sea and approximately the altitude of Mexico City in March 1888. Descending into the great arid desert of El Salado, reminiscent of the Mojave Desert in California, with its many varieties of cactus, progress southward towards San Luis Potosi was rapid, as was the work north of Celaya. In one year a total of 385 miles of railroad was built and placed in operation. On September 29, 1888, over four years after the Mexican Central had been completed, the Mexican National Railroad was opened for business from Laredo to Mexico City.

General Palmer's dream was realized at last, although he had nearly become bankrupt in the process, losing most of what he had personally invested in the road. Palmer, and Raoul who followed him, achieved the primary purpose of building from the Rio Grande to Mexico City but failed in the secondary objectives to a large extent. When Palmer's company ceased construction work in 1884, Porfirio Diaz cancelled the concession for the branch from Celaya to Guadalajara and gave it to the Mexican Central. The Manzanillo line towards Guadalajara was extended from Armeria to Colima in 1888 but was retained by the construction company as a sixty mile orphan road, as was the Zacatecas branch towards San Luis Potosi, which had laid 19 miles of track towards Ojo Caliente and completed the roadbed to that town in 1884. Track was laid on the roadbed to the latter town in 1888 and there the line ended.

Additional locomotives and rolling stock were purchased in 1888, and to provide for the comfort of through passengers a number of new Pullman sleeping cars were ordered, besides six Pullman sleepers released by the Denver & Rio Grande in 1890 when its main line had been standard gauged. These latter were rebuilt for use on the long Mexican runs, though most of them retained their Colorado names. To handle the through trains, forty Ten-wheel passenger engines weighing 35 tons each were ordered from Baldwin, and they were soon at work hauling the through trains on what was then a very fast schedule for a narrow gauge railroad. The trains covered the 840 miles in 41 hours, 50 minutes for an average of 20 miles an hour, with 109 stops en route. The rival Mexican

Of the two 0-6-0 engines on the Mexican National's 3-foot gauge, the last survivor is shown as it looked in 1929 at the Acambaro Shops.

A local train in the early days of Mexican National operation stops at the foot of the cliffs at El Salto de Medina, right. When the Denver & Rio Grande main line became standard gauge in 1890, the ESPANOLA was one of eight narrow gauge sleepers transferred to the Mexican National. *(Below: Arthur Dubin Collection)*

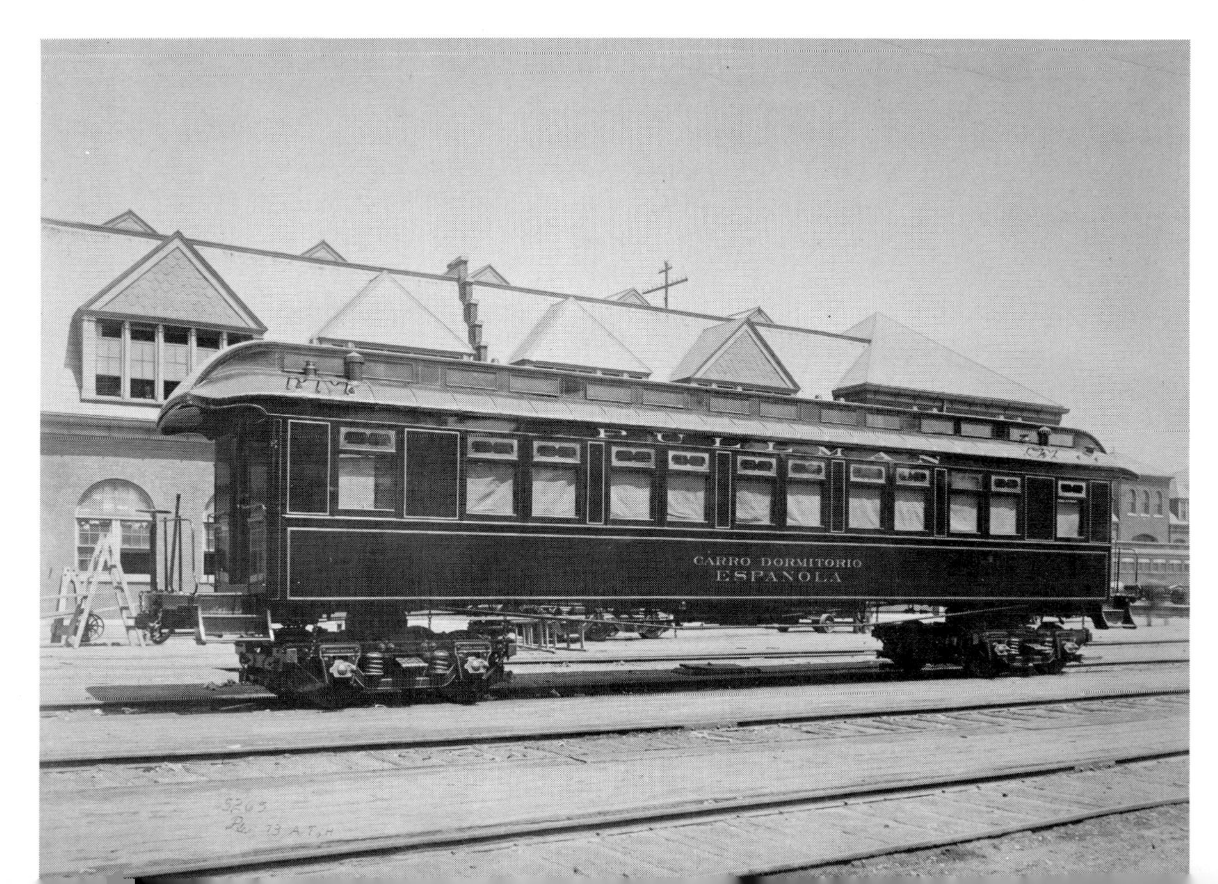

General William Jackson Palmer was founder of the Mexican National and the Denver & Rio Grande railroads. *(Denver Public Library, Western collection)*

Central made the 1224 miles between El Paso and Mexico City in 59 hours, 40 minutes, also at an average of 20 miles an hour, with 114 stops along the line. Using Chicago as a starting point, the running time of the Santa Fe to El Paso was 65 hours, with a four-hour layover there before departure of the Mexican Central train. The fastest and most direct train service from Chicago to Laredo, with a change of trains in St. Louis, could be made in 45 hours, with a two-hour layover in Laredo. Thus the narrow gauge Mexican National was providing 88-hour through service from Chicago to Mexico City, whereas the Santa Fe required 128 hours, nearly two days longer. It was no wonder that by 1892 the Santa Fe was toning down its advertisements of through service from Chicago to Mexico City and had discontinued the through Pullman sleeping cars over this route. There were no sleeping cars on the El Paso branch of the Santa Fe by 1892, thus requiring two changes of trains en route.

Though the Mexican National had the fastest passenger service to Mexico City, there was still the vexing problem of the transfer of freight between standard and narrow gauge at Laredo. Shippers complained because of the delays at the transfer platform and damage to fragile shipments due to the additional handling. The same problems which had beset the Denver & Rio Grande and caused it to convert its main line to standard gauge were presented all over again on a much larger scale. Arguments for standard gauging the Mexican National were soon appearing in the press and in trade publications, though in 1897 President Raoul told reporters for the latter that the company had no intention of standard gauging the railroad. As if to prove his point he authorized additional construction towards the Pacific from Patzcuaro and on March 19, 1899 the first train entered Uruapan, 143 miles from Acambaro. This was the last piece of narrow gauge construction by the Mexican National.

In connection with the development of mining and lumbering industries, various short lines were built between 1890 and 1900 at points along the Mexican National and it was quite logical that these should all be narrow gauge. Some of them were soon leased or absorbed into the Mexican National, the most notable being the Michoacan & Pacific, 57 miles between Zitacuaro and Maravatio on the Uruapan branch, leased August 1, 1900; the Guanajuato, a San Luis de la Paz y Pozos Railroad, built between Rincon on the main line, to Pozos and purchased outright in 1901, and the Vanegas, Cedral & Rio Verde Railroad, running from Vanegas on the main line to the silver mining district of Matehuala, also purchased outright in October 1902. There were a number of other short lines or industrials along the Mexican National which acted as feeders but were not taken over, remaining narrow gauge to the end of their days.

In the annual report of the Mexican National for 1900, President Raoul stated that standard gauging of the railroad, though of obvious benefit to the company, was still some years away. He admitted that the original rails and rolling stock were wearing out, necessitating replacement with heavier steel rail from Mexico City to Toluca and Monterrey to Laredo. Even with the handicap of transferring freight at Laredo, business was steadily increasing and the existing roadbed would soon be unable to handle it. Net earnings after operating expenses were paying all the bond interest and deferred coupons on the old issues, and a small surplus was being added each year to the fund for improvements, but nothing for extensions or standard gauging. The Mexican Government, in understandable rage cancelled the concessions on

Acambaro station and engine house in the above photo were busy places in the days when it was a division point on the Mexican National main line. Engines, like No. 131, right, and No. 151, shown below at San Luis Potosi, were heavy main line power in the 1890 period. *(Top and bottom: E. L. DeGolyer, Jr. collection)*

F.C.I. No. 8, last surviving ten-wheeler of that road, is ready to leave Puebla on the morning passenger train for Mexico City in the 1948 photo at the left.

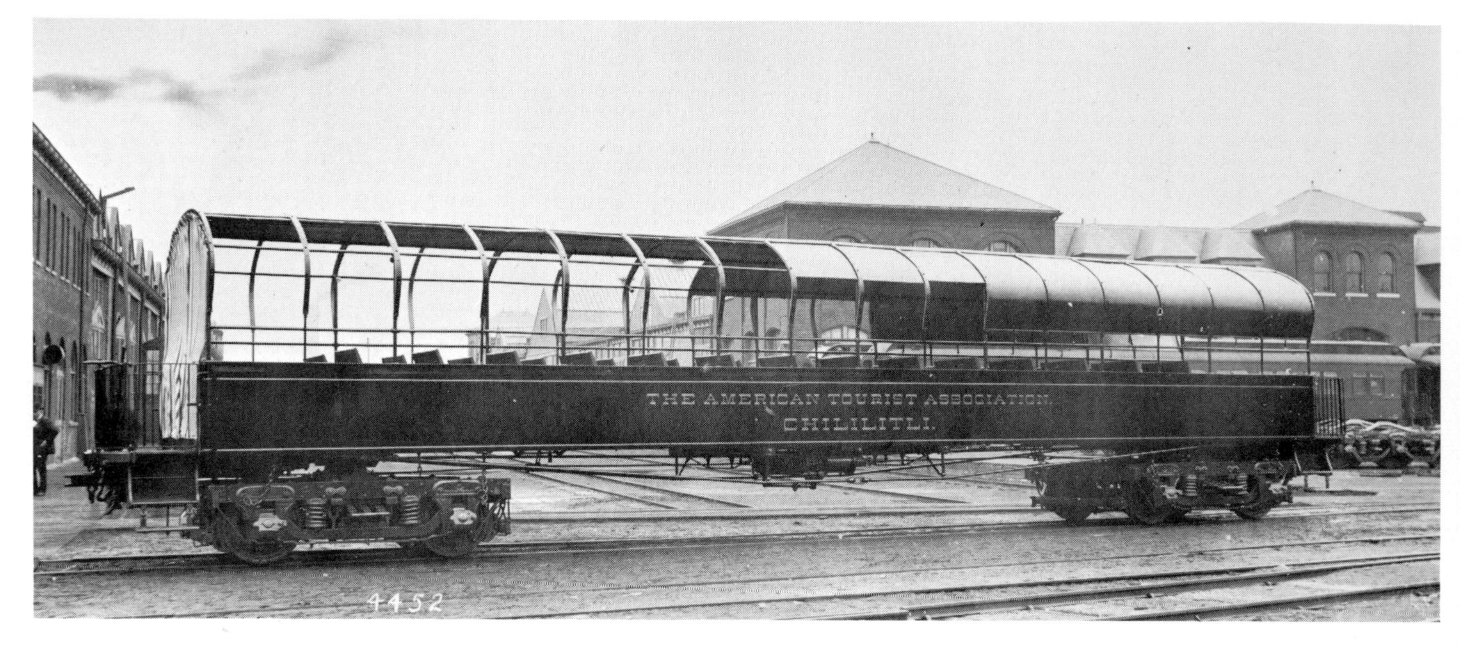

Narrow gauge Mexican tours originating in Laredo used the *Chililitli* on narrow gauge rails when Pullman built it in 1897. It was rebuilt for standard gauge in 1903. *(Arthur Dubin collection)*

Odd-Ball No. 243, built by Alco-Cooke, the only one in its class, is shown ready to leave Puebla on the Atencingo daily mixed. *(Top and below; L. T. Haug)*

the uncompleted branches, turning the concession from Colima to Guadalajara over to the Mexican Central, which later built the line through to Manzanillo. Diaz also requested that Raoul complete the branch from the port of Matamoros to Monterrey as soon as possible. Only 75 miles had been completed in 1888 and nothing had been done since then to close the 131 mile gap which had rendered the finished portion practically useless.

The situation was resolved by banking interests in New York and London. Through Kuhn, Loeb & Co. of New York and Speyer Brothers, Ltd. of London, arrangements were made to float a new bond issue sufficient to pay for standard gauging the main line, to build a cutoff to eliminate the heavy grades of the Toluca-Mexico City section and to buy new standard gauge rolling stock. On March 14, 1902, the National Railroad of Mexico was incorporated in Salt Lake City to build a standard gauge railroad from Laredo to Mexico City, using as much of the narrow gauge roadbed as possible, and to take over the isolated sections operated by the Mexican National Construction Co. The standard gauge Mexican International Railroad, built by C. P. Huntington and associates between Ciudad Porfirio Diaz (later Piedras Negras), opposite Eagle Pass, Texas, to Durango and which was now for sale due to the recent death of Huntington, was purchased by the new company.

Work was begun immediately on the Texas-Mexican Railroad in order for the engineers to gain experience in a new method of changing the gauge, and this work proceeded so rapidly that the line was standard gauged from Corpus Christi to Laredo by May 10, 1902. Instead of laying a third rail of the same weight as the 3-foot gauge rails, new 70-pound steel rails were laid outside the 45-pound narrow gauge rails, every other crosstie being replaced with a standard gauge tie. Later the remaining narrow gauge ties would be replaced as the maintenance crews could get around to it. Before the Texas-Mexican alteration had been completed, crews began changing the gauge south of the Rio Grande. Eighty new standard gauge locomotives were ordered in the U.S., and a program of widening the gauge of 38 of the narrow gauge locomotives was begun, as they could be used on branch lines and for other light service. One of these was to outlast all of its mates as shop switcher No. 639 at Nonoalco Shops in Mexico City, being reported as partly dismantled in the Huehuetoca graveyard of scrapped locomotives, in August 1967.

While the standard-gauging work was progressing, construction of a new line 166 miles long, between Gonzalez Junction, north of Acambaro, and Huehuetoca, 29 miles north of Mexico City on the El Salto branch was begun. Thousands of men were put to work on this cutoff and another thousand built the unfinished Matamoros-Monterrey branch as a standard gauge railroad, widening the gauge of the orphan narrow gauge near Matamoros. The standard gauge rails reached Saltillo from Laredo on March 20, 1903, reached San Luis Potosi, 225 miles south of Saltillo on April 17th and Gonzalez Junction saw the first standard gauge construction train come in from the north on May 1, 1903. The cutoff was completed and the El Salto branch standard gauged on November 1, 1903 and the first standard gauge train left Colonia Station in Mexico City for Laredo on November 8, 1903. All narrow gauge equipment had been brought south from Laredo to Gonzalez Junction, and was used only on the old line from Mexico City to Acambaro, Uruapan and Gonzalez Junction. The Matamoros branch was finished in November 1904, but much of it was washed out by a hurricane which swept in off the Gulf (just as it did in September 1967) and the entire roadbed had to be repaired and reballasted, delaying the opening of the branch until July 18, 1905.

The short lines previously mentioned, except the Michoacan & Pacific were standard gauged as soon as the main line was completed. Gonzalez Junction soon proved to be a poor selection as a transfer point, so the 54-mile leg from there to Acambaro was standard gauged with 70-pound rail removed from the new main line at points where it had proved too light and had been replaced with 85-pound steel. General Palmer's narrow gauge empire had thus shrunk to a small fraction of its original length. The old line from Mexico City to Acambaro and the branch from there to Uruapan left 323 miles of 3-foot gauge still in use. Had it not been for the revolution a few years later, this section would most certainly have been standard gauged within ten years. Once the bills were all received, the net cost of all this work came

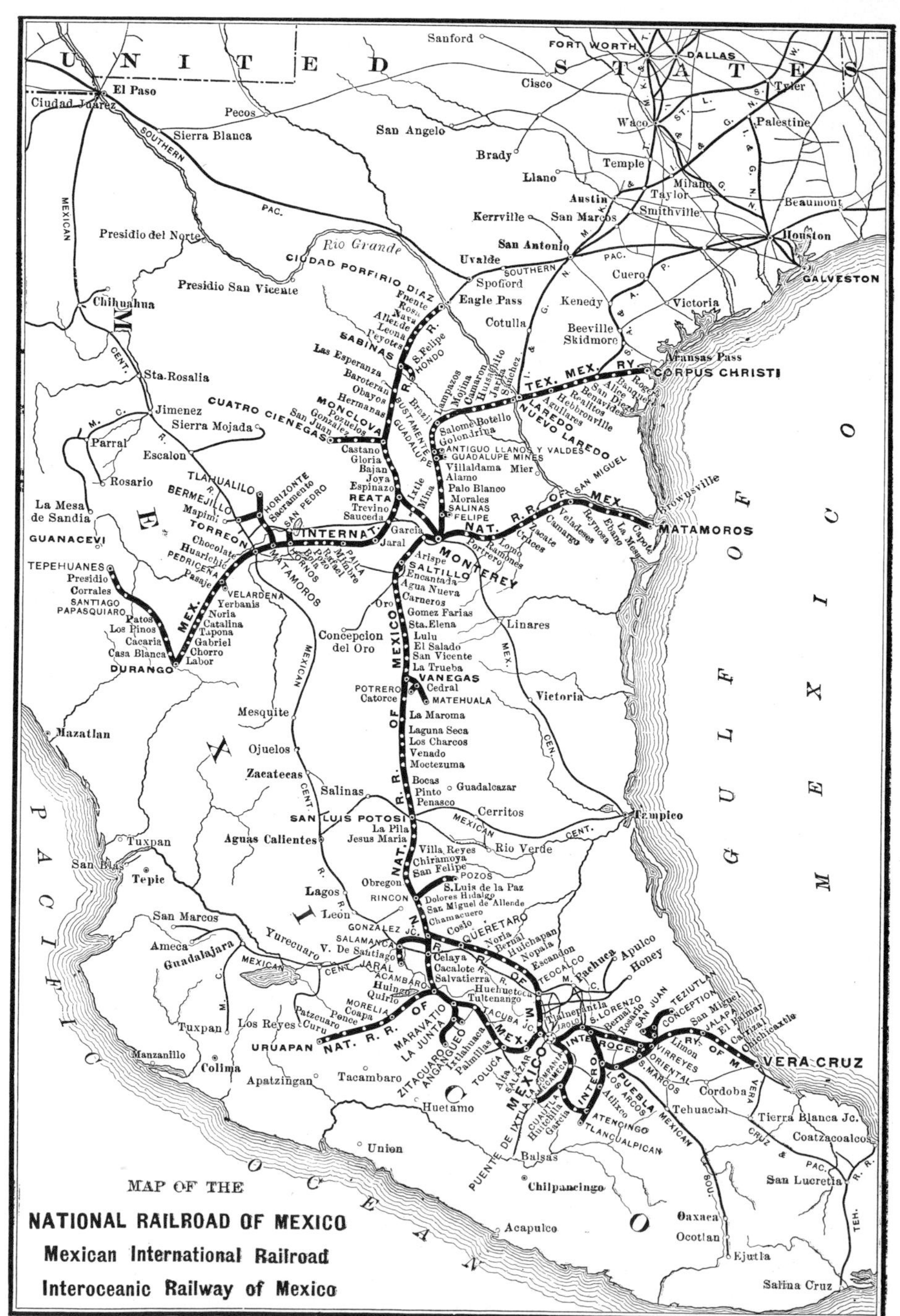

When Pullman built the business car GUADALOUPE for Mexican National in 1883, current taste favored lavish decoration. One may wonder how long the Mexicans permitted the French spelling of the name to remain on the car. *(Lucius Beebe collection)*

Baldwin shipped narrow gauge locomotives by the trainload to the Mexican National in 1888. The high drivers of West Shore No. 12 at Buffalo quite dwarf those of the narrow gauge engines on the flatcars. *(DeGolyer Foundation Library)*

to slightly over ten million dollars, U.S., quite close to the original estimate. Even before the standard gauging had been completed, the Mexican Government, on June 12, 1903 announced that it had obtained a majority interest in the common stock of the National Railroad of Mexico by purchase, and held a very substantial portion of the railroad's bond issues. Since it already owned the Ferrocarril Interoceanico by majority stock control, in effect the government owned a railroad system from Vera Cruz through Mexico City to Laredo. This was but the beginning of the plan to merge all the principal railroads of the country into one government-owned system. On February 28, 1908, the merger terms had been completed and were ratified by Congress in Mexico City, resulting in the formation of Los Ferrocarriles Nacionales de Mexico (National Railways of Mexico). Included in this merger was the Mexican Central, the National Railroad of Mexico, the Mexican International, the narrow gauge Hidalgo & Northeastern and the F. C. Interoceanico. The latter road and its affiliate, the Mexican Southern remained under separate management for many years, with British executives and key supervisory personnel still on the job. Mexico's first large railroad, the F. C. Mexicano was not included in this merger and operated independently.

The idea of the Mexican Government buying up the common stock of the railroads as merged above was conceived by Jose I. Limantour, Finance Minister of the Diaz government and though he was later to be both praised and damned for this action, the first step towards the Mexicanization of the railroads of the country had been taken. Limantour became the chairman of the board for the new company, and half the directorate were Mexican citizens even though some of them were Americans with dual citizenship. The government under the new setup owned 52% of the common stock of the National Railways of Mexico, though the bond holdings were still held by foreigners. British investors owned 37% of all the outstanding bonds of Mexican railroads in 1908, Americans holding 30% and substantial amounts were held by French, Belgian and German groups.

Excluding the F. C. Interoceanico and the Mexican Southern, the narrow gauge mileage at the time of the merger was 533 miles, as follows:

Colonia Station in Mexico City, to Uruapan	323.7
Peralvillo Station in Mexico City to Beristain and other branches of the former Hidalgo & Northeastern	152.2
Michoacan & Pacific R.R. (leased)	57.1
Total	533.0 miles

INTEROCEANIC RAILWAY OF MEXICO (F. C. INTEROCEANICO)

The second largest of the Mexican narrow gauge systems, the Interoceanic has a history full of mergers, failures of the merged roads and attempts to start over again, all too complicated and not of sufficient interest to warrant anything but an outline of the various events.

All of these early railroads had one aim in common; to build a railroad from the vicinity of Mexico City to Acapulco on the Pacific Coast and to Vera Cruz on the Gulf of Mexico, the latter section designed to give the British-owned F. C. Mexicano some much needed competition. The first concession granted by the Diaz government was to the State of Morelos, to build a railroad from Mexico City south through the state to the Amacusac River south of Cuernavaca and thence to the seaport of Acapulco. This concession was transferred on October 5, 1878 to a group headed by Manuel Mendez Cortina, in the name of the Mexico & Morelos Railway Co. Construction work started in the spring of 1879, in the town of Los Reyes, 12 miles from the center of Mexico City and at the terminus of an omnibus line and a stop on the main stage route from Mexico City to Puebla. The track gauge was 3 feet and used 45-pound steel rail imported from England. Some of the locomotives and rolling stock ordered that year came from England, but the majority of the equipment was purchased in the United States. General Palmer's narrow gauge railroads in Colorado had no doubt attracted a great deal of attention in Mexico because of the great economy claimed by proponents of narrow gauge construction as compared with standard gauge.

Mendez Cortina probably selected the narrow gauge as best suited to the terrain, which involved heavy grades for long distances, with many curves if the grade was to be kept at 3% or lower. Starting at Los Reyes at an altitude of 7400 feet, the railroad was built south along the slopes of the extinct volcano Ixtaccihuatl, which towers over the valley of Mexico to a height of 17,343 feet, until a summit was reached in 24 miles near the city of Amecameca, at an elevation of 8050 feet. The remaining 49 miles to Cuautla descended nearly 4000 feet to an elevation of 4265 feet, resulting in a grade with never less than 2% and in the last ten miles to the summit it averaged 3%. The paved highway between Amecameca and Cuautla today is only 27 miles long and does not require any great effort on the part of motorists to ascend it.

With the name shortened to Ferrocarril Morelos, the railroad reached Cuautla late in 1880 and so successful was this first Mexican-built narrow gauge line that a new concession was given by Diaz to the State of Morelos to build a 3-foot line from Los Reyes to a connection with the F. C. Mexicano at Irolo. This concession was promptly transferred to Don Delfin Sanchez, who built the Ferrocarril Irolo along the eastern shore of Lake Texcoco a distance of 53 miles to the town of San Lorenzo, ten miles beyond Irolo. Actually the railroad made no physical connection with the F. C. Mexicano at Irolo, passing south of the village and turning southeast towards Puebla while the Mexicano continued east to Apizaco. Sanchez completed the Irolo Railroad in July 1882. He also built an eleven-mile extension from Los Reyes to Mexico City, building the handsome San Lazaro Station which is still there, 86 years later. A roundhouse and shops were built a half-mile east of the station, together with a freight house and yards. By this time Sanchez had bought the Morelos Railroad from Mendez Cortina and had consolidated it under the name of United Morelos, Irolo & Acapulco Railways on October 19, 1882. This railroad forms half of what is left of the narrow gauge National Railways of Mexico lines in 1968.

While Sanchez was completing his railroads, a concession was granted to Francisco Artega to build a railroad from Puebla north to a connection with the Irolo Railroad at San Lorenzo, under the name of F. C. Puebla a San Martin Texmelucan. Artega received another concession to build a railroad south from the San Martin line, from a junction point called Los Arcos, five miles west of Puebla, to Matamoros-Izucar, under the name of F. C. Puebla a Matamoros-Izucar. A few months after construction work had begun, Artega sold his concession to Delfin Sanchez on February 21, 1882 together with the British-built locomotives and rolling stock he had purchased in 1881. On July 6, 1883, Sanchez opened the southern line from Puebla to San Agustin, 28

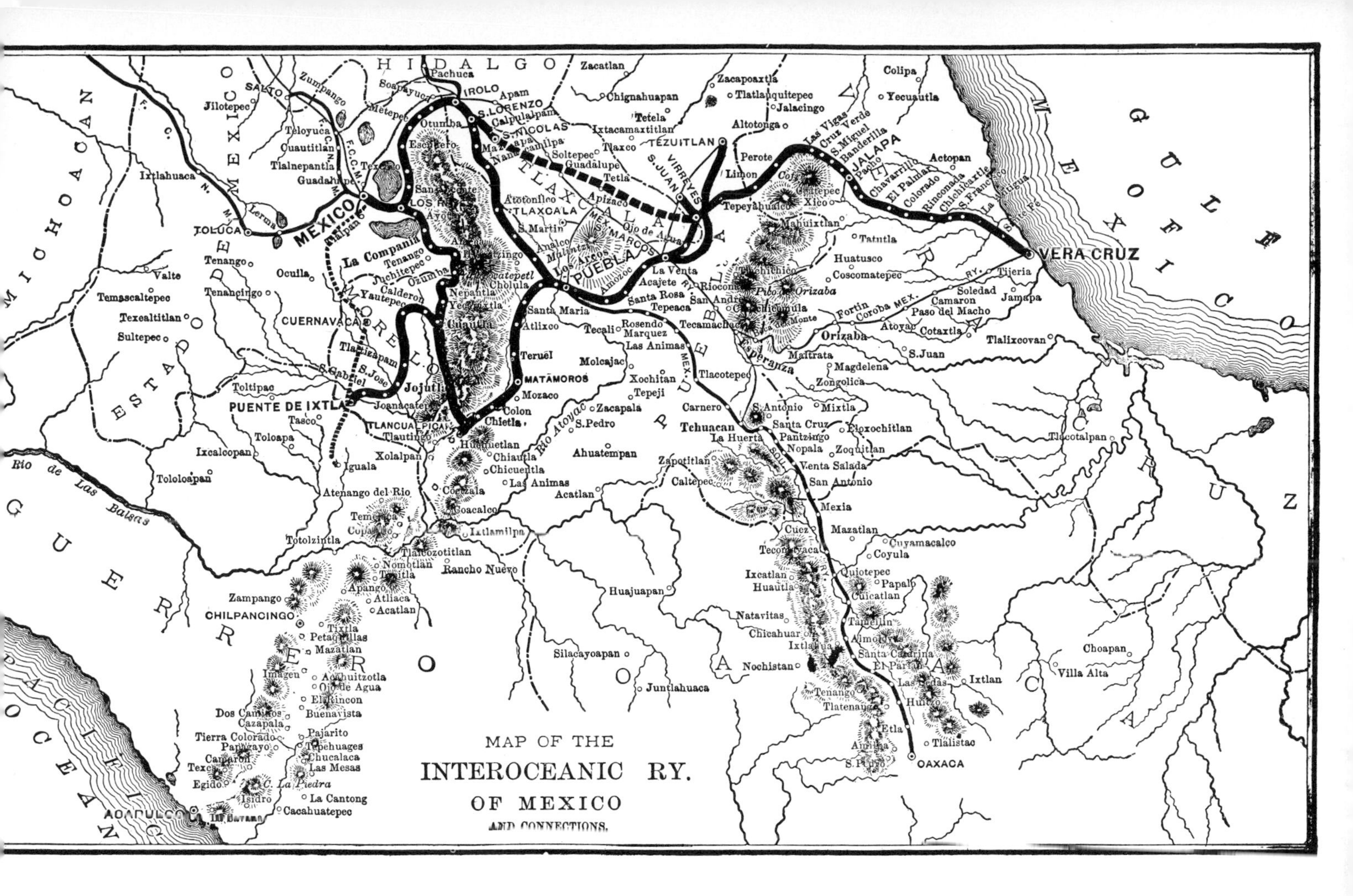

Until the Interoceanic's plan for a line from Puebla to Acapulco was abandoned in 1898, the proposed route was indicated in published maps by a dashed line. In the 1904 map shown above, the line has been deleted, but towns and mountain peaks enroute remained as reminders of an unfulfilled dream. Interoceanic's No. 16 is shown on the Teziutlan branch before it was renumbered No. 25 in 1930. Below, the line's only 0-6-0 No. 1 was the Oaxaca yard switcher in 1930. *(Left: Thomas Norrell collection)*

Every line of the business car *Isabel* reflected the pride of its British owners in 1890. Its carpeted and mirrored interior, with lavishly decorated ceiling, fringed table cover, tooled leather upholstery, fumed oak furniture and brightly polished oil lamps were all calculated to impress visiting dignitaries and to awe ordinary people. The factory photographs of the *Isabel* are proof that the management of the Interoceanic knew all about corporate image decades before such a term had been thought of. For well over sixty years of service, weather, revolution and probably half a dozen remodelings, it continued to serve the narrow gauge, still bearing the maker's name plates and the date. The car appears on page 28, as F.C.I. No. 18, photographed at Puebla station. *(Lucius Beebe collection)*

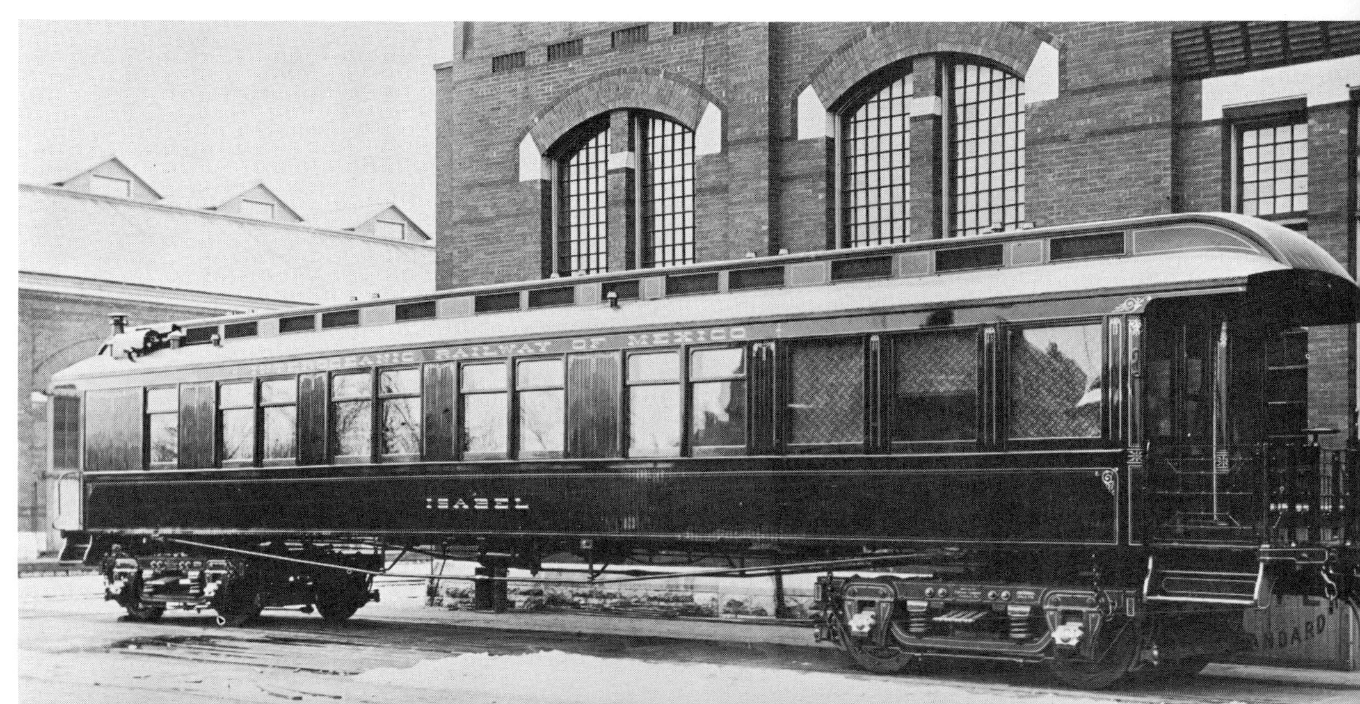

miles; the northern line had reached San Martin, 19 miles north on that date, and he had extended the Irolo Railroad south from San Lorenzo to Calpulalpam.

Still another concession aimed towards completing a railroad from Mexico City to Vera Cruz via Puebla was granted to the State of Puebla on September 14, 1880 to build a 3-foot gauge railroad from Puebla to a connection with the F. C. Mexicano at San Marcos. The concession was transferred to two contractors, Luis Garcia Teruel and Jacobo Borballa, who built the Puebla & San Marcos Railroad, 35 miles long, which opened for traffic April 20, 1883. Most of the equipment was imported from England.

The last group of concessions for the proposed Vera Cruz-Puebla railroad, after passing through several owners were sold by Ramon Zangroniz and Francisco Prida to Delfin Sanchez under the name of the National Interoceanic Railroad, which company they had organized November 21, 1881. Four days after Sanchez had consolidated his other railroads under one title, he added his new concessions and on October 23, 1882, he formed a railroad the name of which was as complicated as the history of the concessions – the United Morelos, Irolo & Vera Cruz Interoceanic Railway, soon dubbed the Interoceanic by the local populace. Except to extend the Morelos line from Cuautla to Yautepec, 14 miles, in the general direction of Acapulco in the spring of 1883, no further construction was undertaken by Sanchez on these projects. Surveys were made from Vera Cruz through Jalapa to San Marcos by an American engineer, Arthur M. Wellington, who furnished cost estimates to Sanchez. Unable to raise the money locally, Sanchez decided to consolidate his railroads and operate them in the hope that the income produced would enable extension of the line from San Marcos towards Vera Cruz. Sanchez operated the following lines at the end of 1883:

Mexico City to Cuautla and Yautepec	99
Los Reyes to Calpulalpam, Irolo railroad	58
Puebla towards Matamoros-Izucar	33
Los Arcos Junction towards Calpulalpam	18
Puebla to San Marcos	35
Total 3-foot gauge	243 miles

Five years passed before Sanchez went to London in 1888 and succeeded in obtaining the backing of a group headed by the Right Honorable A. B. Forwood, M.P. A new company, the Interoceanic Railway of Mexico, Ltd. was chartered April 30, 1888 and Delfin Sanchez turned over all his concessions to the new company in exchange for stock. Ample funds were made available and the British firm of Read & Campbell was given the contract to build the line from Vera Cruz to San Marcos and from San Martin to Calpulalpam. Sanchez retained ownership of the Puebla a Matamoros-Izucar Railroad and extended it to Matamoros-Izucar in 1889 and 1890. In January 1889, Read & Campbell had 2000 men working on the gap north of San Martin and another 2000 working east of San Marcos. In March 1889 the Interoceanic was completed from Mexico City to Perote, 211 miles, and contracts had been let for the balance of the grading between Perote and Vera Cruz. This latter section was the most difficult part of the work, involving many heavy grades, deep cuts through hard rock, with tunnels and fills, requiring at least 6000 more men on the job. To assist Read & Campbell in this work, an American firm, Hampson & Sullivan of El Paso, and Brikman & Turnbull of Mexico City took over half of the contracts and saw the road through to completion. The announced route of the Acapulco line was made in 1891 after the Interoceanic bought the Puebla a Matamoros-Izucar from Delfin Sanchez. It would extend from Puebla through Matamoros-Izucar, Chictla and Chilpancingo to Acapulco, indicating that the route via Cuautla had been given up. To fulfill the requirements of the concession, however, the Cuautla line was extended to Puente de Ixtla on the Amacusac River and was opened for traffic August 1, 1894. No further attempt to extend this branch has been made since that date and the line is still in use after 74 years. South of Matamoros-Izucar, the line reached Chietla in August 1892 and on May 31, 1895 it reached Tlancualpican, 26 miles south of Matamoros-Izucar. This was as far as the company was required to build during that year, under the terms of the concession.

On July 11, 1890 the Interoceanic was completed from Mexico City to Jalapa and on that date, a passenger train with dining car attached, the first to be used in Mexico, was placed in daily service. Starting from Vera Cruz, the contractors built the line on the flatlands bordering the Gulf of Mexico for 28 miles to San Francisco. From there to the summit at Las Vigas, altitude 7938 feet, an ascent of 7486 feet had to be accomplished in 86 miles. The ruling grade was 3% though most of it was 2½%, the minimum radius of curvature was 330 feet and there were 700 bridges and culverts, most of them of iron.

The Jalapa-Vera Cruz section was officially opened on April 1, 1891 only to be closed immediately by washouts caused by a great storm which came in off the Gulf. Nearly six months passed before the damage was repaired, and the line was opened for traffic in October 1891. As the F. C. Mexicano had a long-established through passenger train between its terminals, and was 76 miles shorter than the Interoceanic, the latter did not at first attempt to compete for the through passenger business. Though the F. C. Mexicano had severe grades east of Esperanza, the Interoceanic had equally tough conditions east of Jalapa and other heavy grades between Puebla and San Lorenzo. Its traffic was therefore mostly through freight, with passenger traffic to intermediate points. It required 12 hours and 50 minutes for a passenger to ride from Mexico City to Jalapa, longer than the entire journey from Vera Cruz to Mexico City requires today. Even the ride on the Interoceanic from Mexico City to Puebla was 20 minutes longer than the Mexicano's time, but at least no change of trains was required en route.

In 1895 the Interoceanic suffered two of the worst accidents in the history of Mexican railroads to that date. On March 1, 1895, a passenger train loaded with religious pilgrims was returning to Mexico City from Amecameca, the train being so crowded that the aisles, open platforms and roofs of the cars were filled. While rounding a sharp curve near Tenango, all but two of the coaches were derailed on the outside of a sharp curve and rolled down a steep bank, killing 64 passengers and injuring 50 more, most of them women and children. Had the coaches been of sturdier construction they would have withstood the crash, but due to age and inferior workmanship they crushed like eggshells. No sooner had the hue and cry over this accident died down than another derailment occurred two miles west of the first one, at Temamantla. A mixed train was derailed by a broken rail, 14 passengers were killed together with four crewmen, besides a large number of injured. This resulted in drastic speed restrictions on the old Morelos division, and prison for any engineer exceeding them.

Over fifty miles of the Morelos division had been laid with an English version of the tie, a monstrosity known as the "pot" sleeper, consisting of two cast iron halves, oval in form, the open ends being bolted facing each other, then keyed and bolted to the rails. These were forever coming apart under the pounding of passing trains — engineers would round a curve and see an object standing straight up between the rails in the form of half of a "pot" sleeper, ready to raise havoc with the machinery of the locomotive and the cars behind it. A replacement program was undertaken in 1896, using steel sleepers cast in one piece, six feet long, and weighing 90 pounds. These cost a dollar each while first grade oak sleepers eight feet long and six inches square cost 65 cents each, but the wood sleepers lasted only a few years, so the British owners of the railroad insisted on the metal sleeper and had their way. Some of these sleepers were still in use on the Cuautla line as late as 1955 but a careful examination of miles of the track in 1966 failed to find even one.

While the Interoceanic was more than meeting operating expenses, it was so heavily bonded that it could not meet the interest payments, especially on certain 6% debentures, resulting in a reorganization without receivership in 1896 and replacement of the debentures with new ones bearing lower interest. In 1898 a decision was reached between the Diaz government and the Interoceanic which was to doom a railroad to Acapulco in the foreseeable future. In return for the cancellation of any obligation to build from Puente de Ixtla to Acapulco, the Interoceanic agreed to build a tie line between the Morelos and Matamoros subdivisions, and surveys were made for a 43 mile connection from Cuautla to the town of Atencingo on the Matamoros line. The Mexico, Cuernavaca & Pacific, a standard gauge railroad which began to build a line from

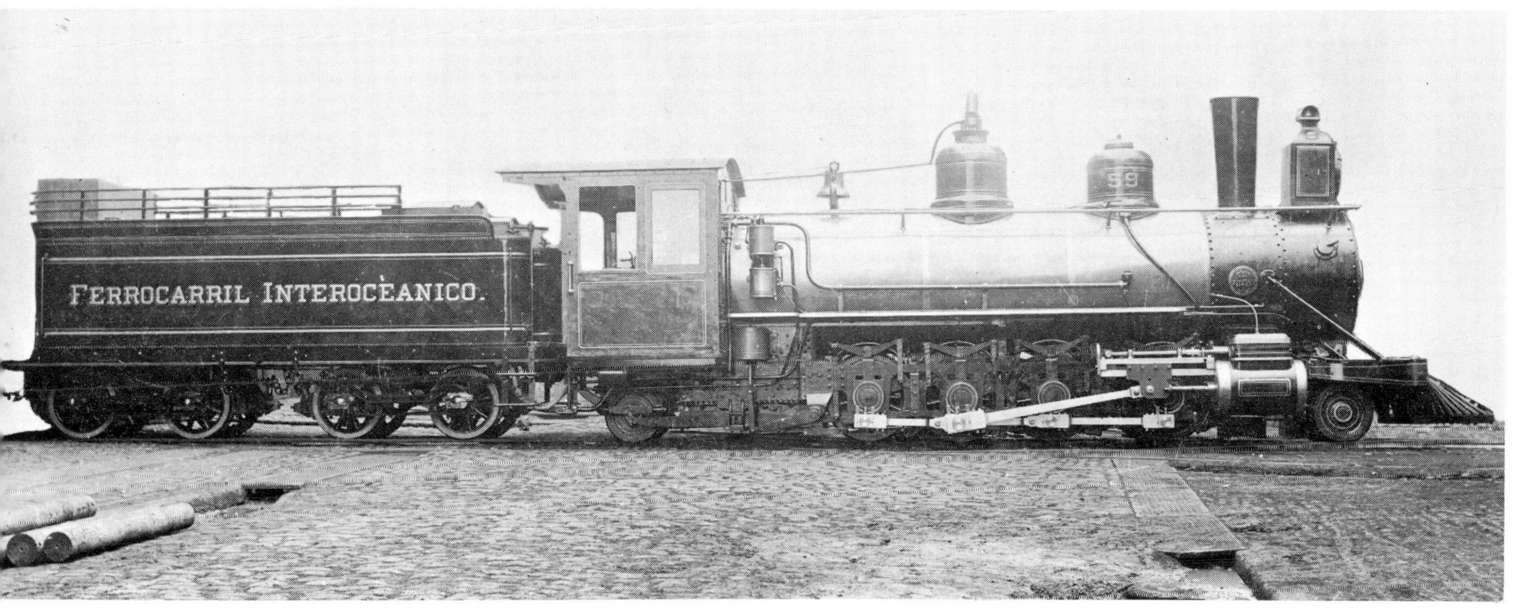

The Morelos Railroad's No. 4, the MORELOS, appears at the top in the only known photograph of original power on what is in 1968 the last narrow gauge main line of the N. deM. A very early 2-8-2 above, dating from 1890, was still going strong —as a 2-8-0—in the 1930s. Cross-compound 4-6-0 No. 28 came from Schenectady. *(Top: Herbert L. Broadbelt collection; bottom: Schenectady History Center)*

Mexico City to Acapulco via Cuernavaca had long since built beyond Puente de Ixtla, and the Interoceanic had no ambition to parallel this more direct route.

To provide rail for this tie line, it was proposed to pull up the last ten miles of both divisions, but as soon as the Interoceanic was told by the government that the company would have to refund the subsidies already paid in for those sections, the idea was abandoned and the rails still remain there at this writing. The Cuautla-Atencingo line was very slow in building, probably because the Interoceanic could see no great traffic advantage from its existence; it required four years to build 43 miles over an easy grade and it was not until October 1, 1903 that President Diaz announced the opening of the new alternative route from Mexico City to Puebla. No attempt was made to provide connecting service at Cuautla for passengers and the two divisions were operated as separate units. There was a through train each way daily from Puente de Ixtla to Mexico City and another from Cuautla to Puebla, but they did not connect with each other. The unwanted Atencingo-Tlancualpican branch received daily service by a mixed train from Puebla, a custom which still prevails.

In 1902 the Interoceanic purchased the San Marcos & Tecolutla Railway, a 79-mile, 3-foot gauge railroad built in 1895 by F. Martel as the San Marcos & Nautla under a government concession. Martel built the railroad to connect the mines at Teziutlan with the F. C. Mexicano at San Marcos, paralleling the Interoceanic from San Marcos until it crossed the former at a point near Virreyes. The Interoceanic management had realized for some time that in order better to compete with the F. C. Mexicano, the route via Puebla would have to be bypassed by a cutoff, and purchase of the San Marcos & Tecolutla was important to this project.

A new company called the Mexican Eastern (Oriental Mexicano) was formed to take over the San Marcos & Tecolutla and to build the cutoff. In October 1902 the Mexican Government acquired stock control of the Interoceanic, and bought a large portion of the outstanding bond issues which were greatly depressed in value at the time. Work had already commenced on the cutoff, which was rushed to completion and opened for traffic on July 1, 1903. The distance between Vera Cruz and Mexico City via the Interoceanic was thus shortened by 48 miles, the ruling grade between Virreyes Junction, now called Oriental, to San Lorenzo was reduced from 2½% to 1½% and thousands of degrees of curvature on the old line were eliminated for through trains. A night train carrying Pullman sleeping cars made the journey between the two terminals in about 13 hours, only an hour and a half slower than the Mexicano.

Having acquired control of the Interoceanic, the government combined it with the National Railroad of Mexico to form the National Lines of Mexico, a temporary name which lasted only a few years until the government bought out the Mexican Central. Thus on February 28, 1908 the Interoceanic became by act of Congress a part of the National Railways of Mexico, though for many years it was to retain its name and separate management. Like the other railroads built with foreign capital, the Interoceanic had British or American managers, roadmasters, office executives and even locomotive engineers, all of which was contributory to a growing resentment on the part of the Mexican employees which would culminate in disaster for all the railroads of Mexico.

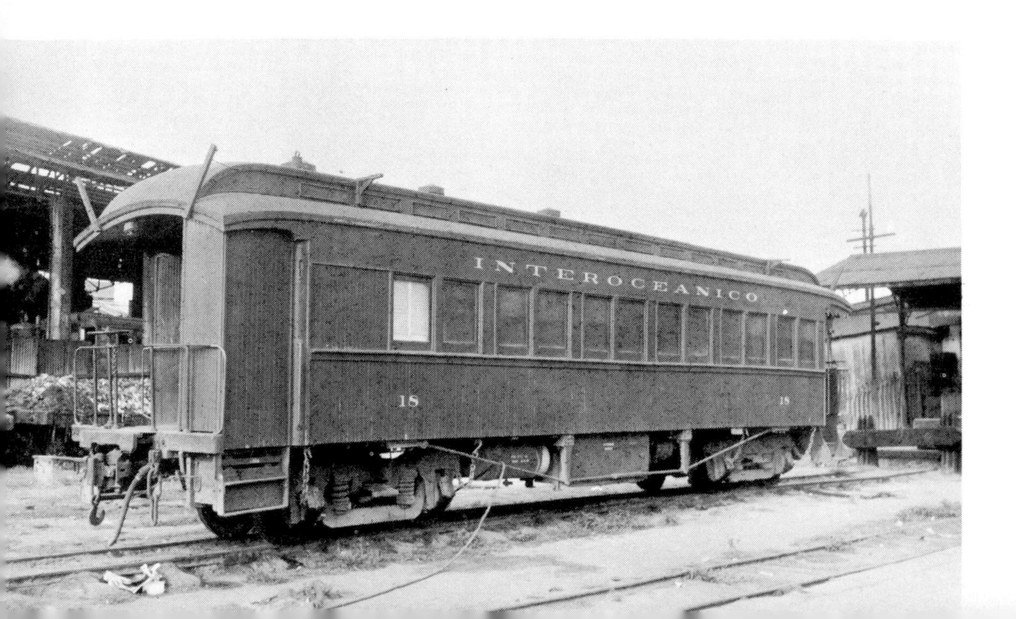

The Interoceanic's last business car, painted a drab green in this 1952 photo taken at Puebla, contrasts sharply with the factory appearance of the ISABEL in the photo on page 24.

Baldwin factory photographs of 2-8-0 No. 20 and 4-6-0 No. 34 show changes in lettering procedure between construction days and the design used during the early years of operation. Later the tender lettering was simplified to F. C. I. *(Both; Herbert L. Broadbelt collection)*

In rugged Tomellin Canyon, 60 miles north of Oaxaca, passenger train No. 7 meets a waiting freight, above. In a companion photo, made in March 1948, from the engine of the same passenger train, one of the many bridges which span the Rio Salada near the summit of the grade can be seen. *(Both; L. T. Haug)*

2

Regional Narrow Gauge Systems

MEXICAN SOUTHERN RAILWAY, LTD. (F. C. MEXICANO DEL SUR)

Though the company which built this railroad was not formed until 1888, the first concession for a railroad within the State of Oaxaca was granted to that state August 25, 1880. A railroad called the Mexican Meridional was organized to build from the Gulf port of Anton Lizardo, south of Vera Cruz, through Tehuacan, Oaxaca and Tehuantepec to Port Angel on the Pacific Ocean. Matias Romero, acting as agent for this company, transferred the concession to the Mexican Southern Railroad, a new company headed by General U. S. Grant. Romero reasoned that an illustrious man such as General Grant serving as the head of the enterprise would lead to an alliance with other projects and produce a great railroad system. Among the directors of the new company were men affiliated with the Santa Fe, the Southern Pacific and the railroads controlled by Jay Gould. Gould had organized the Mexican Oriental, Interoceanic & International Railroad in order to extend his Texas lines to Mexico City, and with the consent of the Mexican Government, the Gould and Grant interests were combined in May 1883. After grading a hundred miles of roadbed for this railroad, the company went into receivership due to the bankruptcy of General Grant and others in New York. General Joaquin de Mier y Teran of Oaxaca then acquired the concession, only to sell it to H. Rudston Read of the contracting firm of Read & Campbell of London in May 1888. Read incorporated the Mexican Southern Railway May 9, 1889 and raised the necessary funds to finance the railroad.

Read's firm was already busy building the Interoceanic, had competent engineers in the country and work began immediately on the grading from Puebla south to Tehuacan, 78 miles, starting on September 6, 1889. Read turned the job of building this section over to the American firm of Hampson & Stanhope, and soon 5000 men were working at various points along the 228 mile line. The most difficult piece of construction was in Tomellin canyon, where the railroad had to share a narrow, rocky gorge with the Rio Salado. This necessitated many bridges, two tunnels and a tremendous amount of blasting work along the rocky shelf above the river. The ruling grade in the direction of Oaxaca from Puebla was 2% to a summit at Tecomavaca, but coming north from Oaxaca, there were several sections of 4% grade which were unavoidable. This required helpers to be permanently stationed at Tomellin, where a turntable and a small roundhouse were erected. A total of 175 iron bridges were installed, the 50-pound steel rail was laid on steel sleepers weighing 110 pounds each, all the material being imported from England. All locomotives and rolling stock were imported, these being largely patterned after similar British colonial railroad equipment in India and South Africa. Passenger service was handled by 4-4-0s, with 4-6-0s on the freight trains and saddle tank engines for yard service and freight helpers.

The road was officially opened by President Diaz on October 7, 1892, during a three-day festival at which many cabinet ministers and other high government officials were present. Daily train service between Puebla and Oaxaca was soon established, with a running time of 13 hours, 35 minutes. Even with four saddle tank engines purchased from the Interoceanic added to the new motive power, the British-built locomotives proved inadequate for the heavier freight trains, so three Baldwin Consolidations arrived two months after the road was opened. A total of 17 locomotives, of

Above, two steam locomotives take their ease in the old Oaxaca engine shed in May 1952, while the new Diesel shed adjacent is under construction. Six weeks later, narrow gauge was gone from Oaxaca. At the right is a view from the cab as a southbound train reaches Las Sedas, 18 miles north of Oaxaca. Below, N. de M. No. 272 picks up speed with the Oaxaca-Puebla daily freight, after crossing the F. C. Mexicano's narrow gauge line near Rosendo Marquez. *(Right: L. T. Haug)*

Mexican Southern's No. 14, one of a class of ten Consolidations, disappeared from the roster during the revolution and was the only one which did not survive to modern times. *(Herbert L. Broadbelt collection)*

The overnight narrow gauge train from Mexico City is shown arriving in Oaxaca yards in May, 1952, a few weeks before conversion to standard gauge.

The wreck of the overnight Mexico City-Oaxaca passenger train in 1936 was the result of excessive speed on the sharp curves of Tomellin Canyon.

which 14 were British made, 23 passenger cars and 292 freight cars served the line until after the turn of the century.

Heavy rains which caused the Rio Salado to flood the canyon near Tomellin in May 1893 closed the line for many months while the right of way through the canyon was relocated on higher ground. Over 2000 men worked three months to repair the flood damage, and the expense of this plus the loss of business resulted in red ink on the ledger at the end of the first year of operation. Read retained full control of the railroad until it was firmly on its feet in 1895. After that time it had very good earnings and was not in any serious financial difficulties such as beset other narrow gauge lines previously built. The railroad had cost over $8,000,000, yet it returned a handsome income after expenses and interest, paying dividends on its common stock for many years.

In 1908 the Tehuacan-Esperanza horse tram, a very old standard gauge railroad built in the mid-1870s to connect Tehuacan with the F. C. Mexicano was purchased by the Mexican Southern. There then occurred what was really a rare event; the narrowing of a standard gauge railroad to three feet and its conversion to steam power, completed December 11, 1908. With mule power the running time between terminals had been 225 minutes for the 31 miles, or about 8 miles per hour, a surprising performance. Using locomotive power, the time was cut to 150 minutes, an improvement over the mules but of no great note.

In 1911 the Mexican Southern built a 20-mile branch to Tlacolula, to open up a large lead mining district and to afford tourists railroad service to the historic ruins of Mitla. Another branch originally planned in 1904 was built for a distance of 35 miles to Taviche, practically running the Oaxaca & Ejutla Railroad out of business. On January 1, 1909 the Mexican Southern Railway was taken over by the National Railways of Mexico, though its British management continued to run the railroad and it retained its corporate title and British directorate for many years.

Three vestibuled sleeping cars are at the rear of the night train, switching in the station yards at Oaxaca in 1948, above. A portrait, guns, cannonballs and bunting in honor of President Porfirio Diaz adorn this Mexican Southern 4-4-0 built by Kitson in England, in an 1899 photo at Puebla. *(Above: L. T. Haug)*

HIDALGO & NORTHEASTERN RAILROAD (F. C. HIDALGO Y NORDESTE)

One of the least known components of the National Railways of Mexico when it was formed in 1908, this line had its beginnings in 1882 when the newest silver discoveries at Pachuca, 45 miles north of San Lorenzo made it imperative that a railroad be built to connect with the Irolo Railroad at the latter point. In 1882 the Hidalgo, Tulancingo & Tuxpam Railway was organized by Gabriel Mancera under a government concession, and began construction of a 3-foot gauge railroad from Pachuca to Irolo. Erroneously reported in trade papers as the Irolo Railroad, this line was completed in record time, on January 12, 1883. It did not go south beyond Irolo to San Lorenzo as originally planned, but connected with the F. C. Mexicano at Irolo station. Animal power was used to haul the construction trains, and the first locomotive, the Hidalgo made a trial run over the entire line on April 6, 1883.

The name was soon changed to Hidalgo Railroad, and Mancera obtained an additional concession to build a connection with the existing railroad and Mexico City. This involved 52 miles of new construction between the suburb of Peralvillo in Mexico City, and the town of Tepa, 16 miles south of Pachuca. Most of this work was done in 1890 and 1891, and Pachuca had direct train service to Mexico City without change of cars as was required for passengers riding the F. C. Mexicano. The latter had built a standard gauge branch from the main line at Ometusco in 1890, which had spurred Mancera to build the Mexico City extension. The name of the Hidalgo Railroad was changed to Hidalgo & Northeastern in 1892, a branch being built from Tizayca on the main line to Zumpango, nine miles, but this branch was later taken up for lack of business. Another branch was built from Tepa Junction to Ventoquipa and Tulancingo, later extended to Tortugas, adding 47 miles to the system. Still another branch, which proved to be a very important one, was built from Ventoquipa to Beristain, 21 miles. Mancera sold the 156-mile railroad to a Belgian syndicate headed by W. L. Pritchard and T. M. Crawford in 1897, and there were various announced plans to widen the railroad to standard gauge and extend it to Tuxpan on the Gulf or even to Tampico, but nothing ever came of these extensions.

The H. & N. E. distinguished itself in 1895 by being the cause of a teen-age boy being executed for train wrecking. It seems that he placed a pile of rocks on the track near Pachuca, derailing a freight train and causing considerable damage as well as severe injuries to the train crew. The boy had previously been imprisoned for the same offense. A federal law having been passed in the meantime making it a capital offense to wreck a train, the boy was summarily shot after a quick trial. This caused the boy's father to become demented, and he committed suicide by throwing himself in front of a train on the same railroad his son had sabotaged.

The Hidalgo & Northeastern continued under its Belgian management through the early years of the present century, with a fleet of 27 locomotives, all Baldwins except one Porter Forney type, until the formation of the National Railways of Mexico. On February 28, 1908, the railroad was consolidated with all the other previously described railroads to form a part of the N. de M. system. Its equipment was taken over in 1908 and relettered with the herald of its new owner, though its terminal continued to be at Peralvillo Station, a mile east of Buena Vista Station in Mexico City, the latter the former terminal of the Mexican Central.

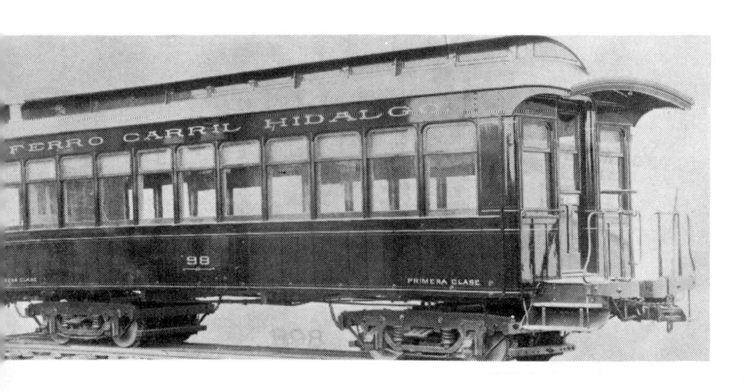

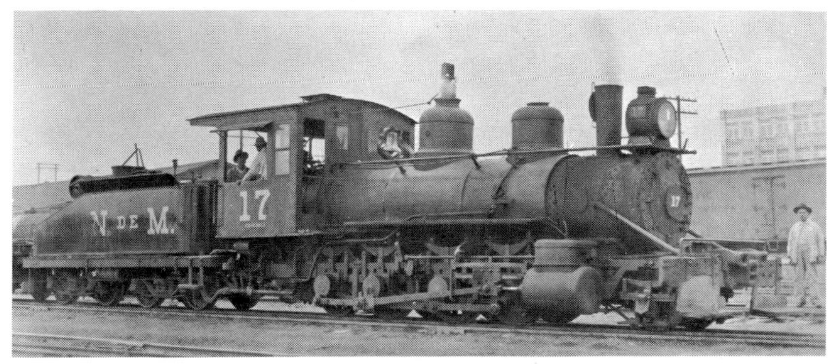

The Hidalgo & Northeastern coach, left, was built by Brill in 1885. N. deM. No. 17 was originally H. & N. E. No. 17, the Huaya, built in 1894. *(Left: Pennsylvania State Historical Society)*

NARROW GAUGE BRANCHES OF THE MEXICAN RAILWAY (F. C. MEXICANO)

The F. C. Mexicano, the first important railroad in Mexico, had no narrow gauge trackage in its early history, being standard gauge throughout the main line and branches. In the years from 1898 to 1903, three short lines were built by various agricultural groups to connect with the main line of the Mexicano, which eventually purchased all of them. These three branches were unique in that they were all of different gauges, ranging from 24 to 36 inches. All of them were in service until 1952 when the 2-foot gauge branch was abandoned, followed closely by the other two. It is fortunate that they lasted as long as they did, for photographs of the three lines made prior to 1947 are practically nonexistent. The history of each branch will be given with the corporate names used before purchase by the F. C. Mexicano.

(i) F. C. TLACOTEPEC A HUAJUAPAN DE LEON, later F. C. SAN MARCOS A HUAJAPAN DE LEON, 3-foot gauge.

Tracing the obscure history of this railroad was a difficult task. It was built almost entirely with capital furnished by its owner, Luis Garcia Teruel of Mexico City, who had gained considerable railroad building experience by completing the Puebla & San Marcos Railroad in 1883. Since there was no public financing, nothing about this railroad can be found in financial publications until 1910 and even then it is inaccurate. As projected by Garcia Teruel, it was to be built from the town of Tlacotepec, on the Mexican Southern 25 miles north of the city of Tehuacan, in a westerly direction to Las Pilas, then south to the town of Huajuapan de Leon in the State of Oaxaca, a total distance of 98 miles. This area was a large producer of the maguey plant from which pulque is made, and being of a semi-arid nature, the region was well adapted to the plant. Garcia Teruel began construction of the 3-foot gauge line from Tlacotepec to Las Pilas in 1897, reaching the latter point, 18.6 miles west on November 25, 1898. Equipment and train crews were furnished by the Mexican Southern. From Las Pilas the line turned due south to Ixcaquixtla, 32 miles from Tlacotepec, and Mucio Martinez, 47 miles. Nineteen miles of track were laid in 1899 and nine more in 1900. Grading was completed from Mucio Martinez to Xayacatlan de Bravo during that year, and track was laid over the grade as far as Ahuatempan in 1901, all work being done by Garcia Teruel without the aid of outside contractors.

Garcia Teruel was not happy with the service he was getting from the Mexican Southern at Tlacotepec, so in 1902 he bought three new 38-ton Baldwin Consolidation type locomotives and a small amount of rolling stock. Since all the traffic was in the direction of Mexico City, Garcia Teruel apparently reasoned that from Las Pilas to Tlacotepec his railroad was going in the wrong direction. Accordingly, he requested and received a concession on November 6, 1903 to build a new railroad north from Las Pilas to a connection with the F. C. Mexicano at San Marcos. This would cross the Mexican Southern at Rosendo Marquez and would shorten the distance from there to Las Pilas by 20 miles. Like all of Garcia Teruel's projects, work was done as labor was available, a few miles a year being built, until in 1907 the line reached Rosendo Marquez and after crossing the Mexican Southern, continued north seven miles to Acatzingo. Garcia Teruel had run out of money, and since he now had a new connection with the Mexican Southern, he removed all rails between Tlacotepec and Las Pilas and transferred his headquarters to Rosendo Marquez, where a small shop and engine shed were installed.

In 1909 Garcia Teruel resumed building north from Atencingo, using the rails from his abandoned Tlacotepec line, and completed the railroad 21 miles from Atencingo to San Marcos in September 1910. This represented the greatest length of this railroad in its history; San Marcos to Ahuatempan, 85 miles. Traffic over the new line barely paid expenses, and soon the disorders which spread all over the area from Puebla to Vera Cruz caused the frequent closing of Garcia Teruel's railroad to any kind of traffic. When things quieted down, he offered the railroad to the F. C. Mexicano for less than half his capital outlay, and it was purchased by the Mexicano on August 13, 1913. The engine repair facilities were removed from Rosendo Marquez to San Marcos where they were

On this and the following page are 1952 photos of the Mexican Railway's 3-foot gauge branch. Baggage-postal car No. 30 at San Marcos was the road's only car of the type. No. 24 arrives with a "mixto" at San Marcos station, in the center picture. Coach No. 10 had first and second class sections. *(Center: C. W. Witbeck)*

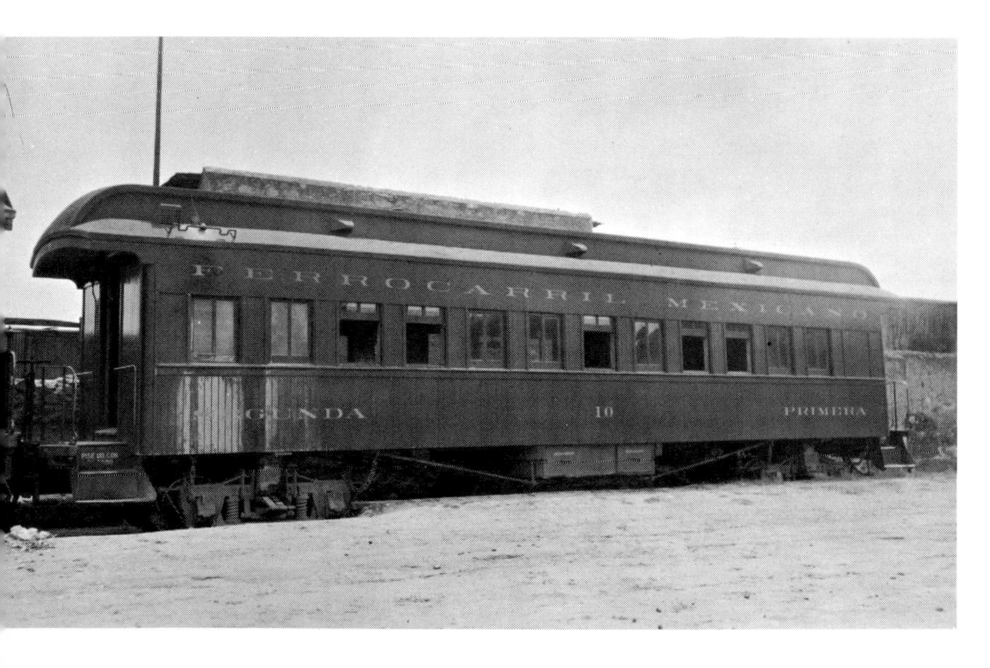

The daily passenger train from Ixcaquixtla arrives in San Marcos on time to the minute, in May 1952. Five years later the branch was abandoned and the equipment scrapped. Only survivor of the F. C. Tlacotepec a Huajuapan de Leon was Mexicano No. 22, former No. 3, the ACATLAN, in the deadline at San Marcos in 1952. *(Above: C. W. Witbeck)*

installed on land south of the main line station. Equipment was relettered "Mexicano" and new passenger cars replaced those destroyed by the revolutionists or which were worn out. New disorders began in the winter of 1913-14, affecting the entire region around Tehuacan and San Marcos by mid-1914. Most of the narrow gauge branch was closed down due to damage to the track and the activities of the contending forces. Some idea of what was happening in this part of Mexico can be gained from reading about the fate of the standard gauge Ferrocarril Esperanza a Xuchil, a lumber railroad which owned one Shay-geared locomotive. This railroad was completely destroyed with all its equipment in 1914, even the crossties being piled up and burned. Ten years later not a trace of the old right of way could be found, so completely had the railroad been erased from view.

From 1914 until 1920 the F. C. Mexicano could operate its 3-foot line only to Rosendo Marquez, but as soon as the country returned to normal in the latter year, the track south of Rosendo Marquez was repaired and service restored as far south as Ixcaquixtla, 57 miles from San Marcos. Any part of the line still existing south of there was abandoned and the rails pulled up. For the next 25 years the branch seems to have returned some degree of profit to its owners. After World War II, traffic decreased to such an extent that almost all maintenance was deferred. Garcia Teruel's Baldwin locomotives were wearing out, and the Mexicano replaced them with secondhand engines rather than buying new ones.

On my first visit to the line in 1952 with Bill Witbeck, we found the track in deplorable condition, with two out of three crossties practically useless due to rot and wear. Yet the train from Ixcaquixtla arrived in San Marcos with its four cars, on time to the minute. At the head end was a former National de Mexico Consolidation weighing 45 tons, testifying to the toughness of narrow gauge track in Mexico even in the face of bad deterioration. The train turned around on a "Y" and backed into the standard gauge station on a stub-end track. The locomotive disappeared and soon came into the enginehouse yard on the other side of a high stone wall which was supposed to block all access to the enginehouse and tiny freight yard, from the station. In this wall was an enormous hole, with a path leading beyond the hole directly to the enginehouse. Many a railfan passed through that hole in the following two or three years for a quick look at what lay beyond, while his train made a five-minute stop at the station.

I was determined to ride at least a portion of this line, but was faced with the fact that there were no hotels in San Marcos or within miles of there. The road from the main highway was almost nonexistent in places, was full of potholes and had put a year's wear in Bill Witbeck's car in an hour's driving. The daily train departed from San Marcos at 6:30 a.m. and since the night train from Mexico City arrived at midnight, a six-hour vigil on a hard bench in the waiting room would be required. I solved the problem in 1955 by staying overnight in Puebla, then setting out in a taxi after breakfast, to catch the train on its return from Ixcaquixtla at some convenient point. I am sure the driver had doubts as to my sanity when I made him turn off the fine paved road near Rosendo Marquez and head south on a secondary dirt road, down which we bumped and jolted for what seemed like hours, to a village called Molcaxac. Luckily we arrived there 15 minutes ahead of the train's schedule, so I paid off the driver, who left shaking his head and muttering about the demented Americano who wanted to ride that terrible train back to Acatzingo, where he was to wait for me.

The sky was heavily overcast and occasional showers kept me inside the tiny waiting room of the station. Fortunately, the train was on time and I was soon riding in the company of dozens of "campesinos" who not only occupied all the seats in both coaches but filled the aisles and baggage racks with their possessions. At the first stop, some of the seats in my coach were emptied by departing passengers and before another swarm filled the seats, I managed to sit next to a window for the rest of the ride, which lasted an hour and a half for the 29 miles I rode the train. The coach rolled from side to side like a small boat in a heavy sea, especially when we reached a curve, for there were no spirals and the track was not banked, so you went into the curve with a jolt which would send some of the standees falling onto those lucky enough to have seats. Everyone seemed good-natured about it, taking the bumps and jerks in stride, this being to them a normal phenomenon of the railroad. We passed Rosendo Marquez, once the headquarters of the railroad, and now served by a dilapidated box car which doubled as a station and freight house. Soon we were in Acatzingo where my driver was waiting, and I returned to Puebla for lunch and a scenic ride on the afternoon standard gauge train to Mexico City.

The F. C. Mexicano, already taken over by the National of Mexico at this time, was being surveyed by a government board of engineers to decide if any branches were unprofitable and should be abandoned. The San Marcos-Ixcaquixtla branch was found not worth either repairing or standard gauging. On September 5, 1957 the line was officially closed, the rails were removed and Luis Garcia Teruel's railroad was shipped away to the steel mills in Monterrey.

(ii) F. C. ATLAMAXAC; 24-inch and 30-inch gauge. Later, the ZACATLAN BRANCH of the F. C. Mexicano.

In April 1904 a concession was granted to Sebastian R. de Mier, Mexican ambassador to France, to build a 2-foot gauge railroad from Munoz, on the main line of the F. C. Mexicano, six miles west of the junction point of Apizaco, to the Hacienda de Atlamaxac, which covered a vast area north of Munoz. The railroad was built in 1904 and 1905, and for most of its length it ran in a straight line to La Galera, 19 miles from Munoz, on the other side of a range of hills. The last few miles on each side of the summit were built to a grade of 2.5%, requiring a Shay-geared midget weighing 26 tons to help the saddle tank locomotives over the hill. Two mixed trains daily were operated over the road, but no attempt was made to extend it towards the city of Zacatlan. In March 1909 it was sold to the F. C. Mexicano, which announced that it would extend the railroad to Zacatlan. The 24-inch gauge was considered too narrow for the traffic which would develop if the branch was extended north, and in 1910 the line was relaid with new 45-pound rail and the gauge was widened to 2½ feet. Four new Baldwin Consolidation locomotives were purchased, the Shay was transferred to the Mexicano's 2-foot gauge branch at Cordoba and the rest of the equipment was sold to unknown buyers.

During 1910, the line was extended 14 miles towards Zacatlan, to Chignahuapan, nine miles short of its destination. Though the branch was always designated in the timetables as the Zacatlan branch, passengers were required to ride a bus to reach Zacatlan. The former terminal of the line at La Galera was renamed Aserradero. A daily passenger train made a round trip from Munoz to Chignahuapan during the following 47 years, connecting in the morning with the eastbound limited from Mexico City, and in the afternoon with the westbound train from Vera Cruz. Freights were run whenever the business warranted it and the four locomotives served the road throughout its life.

To its last day, this branch was kept in a better state of repair than the other narrow gauge lines. A ride on the daily train was an unforgettable experience for a railfan. Though not as spectacular as some of the other narrow gauge rides in the vicinity of Mexico City, its 30-inch gauge was unique in itself, the only one of its kind in use in modern times. The "daily mixto" on the day I rode it had no freight cars and was a fine looking train of three coaches and a combination baggage-mail car. The last coach was half first class and half second, the other two being second class. The journey of 34 miles required 2 hours, 10 minutes, as there were many stops en route. The narrow gauge track at Munoz was on the south side of the station and hence our train had to cross the standard gauge main line, which was done at an angle of 30 degrees. Once across, we turned on a "Y" and headed north for Chignahuapan, my car riding very comfortably with none of the jolts of the ride on the 3-foot gauge branch, though the car swayed from side to side due to its great overhang. Three miles out we crossed the main line of the Nacional de Mexico, once a narrow gauge cutoff line, passing near the new freight car factory set up in the desert by the National Railways. We continued through an agricultural area which contained a magnificent walled hacienda, still in use. At San Luis we began a steady climb up the 2.5% grade, and the Baldwin Consolidation with its wide overhang hauled our train with ease. As we approached the summit, we entered a forest of scrub pine and the line curved for the first time since leaving Munoz. At Kilometer 25 we reached

On this and the two following pages are scenes on the Mexican Railway's 30-inch gauge branch, which in the top photo crossed the standard gauge main line at Munoz at an acute angle to reach the station. At the left are shown the locomotive sheds at Munoz. Below, train No. 41 stops at Llano Verde for water, while the passengers present a busy scene.

Flanked by the two brakemen, the conductor stands in dignity in front of the bell of No. 13, while below him are the fireman, left, and the engineer. No. 13 was Baldwin-built in 1910.

A passenger with a white sombrero boards the second class end of the dual class coach. White sombreros seemed to be in the majority in the crowd at Chignahuapan station, as the train prepares to leave for Munoz.

the summit at an elevation of 8360 feet, a climb of nearly 700 feet in less than nine miles. From the summit we descended into the valley of the Rio Lazaxalpan, still on a uniform grade of 2.5% until we reached the town of Atlamaxac, where we passed under a great stone aqueduct which crossed the valley and brought water to the irrigation districts in the area. In a few minutes we were at Chignahuapan, the end of the line.

Here, all was confusion as the passengers bound for Zacatlan left the train to board several waiting busses, elbowing their way through the crowd which was ready to swarm aboard our train for the return to Munoz. In 25 minutes our engine and baggage car had turned around, the water tank was full and we were ready to go. I was invited to ride on the engine at this point, though I had no VIP letter or any special recommendation for the honor. I think it was as much the display of enthusiasm I had for the train, the scenery and the train crew that was responsible for the invitation, which I accepted with pleasure, and boarded the fireman's side of Engine No. 13 for a memorable ride back to Munoz. No. 13's boiler was so large and the cab so small that there was barely room to squeeze into the narrow space and sit in a small auxiliary seat ahead of the fireman. Verily this was no place for a fat man. Though No. 13 was nearly half a century old, it had been beautifully maintained by its owners, and since I had not expected to ride the engine, I was a white collar passenger for sure. Though not dressed for the occasion, I arrived in Munoz a lot cleaner than after some journeys I could recall on trains in the United States. We backed across the main line at Munoz well in advance of the time the westbound train from Vera Cruz was due. Fortunately for me it was late, so I had plenty of time to watch No. 13 being serviced and put away for the night in the shed with its three mates. The branch had less than two years left when I rode it, and due to the construction of a paved highway from Chignahuapan to Apizaco, Mexico's only remaining 30-inch gauge passenger train made its last run on September 16, 1957. Salvage crews removed the rail within two months, but Engine No. 12 was sold to the Edaville Railroad Museum in Massachusetts, where it is probably the last surviving piece of equipment from one of Mexico's rarest short lines.

The train from Munoz rounds a curve near the summit of the grade, before the stop at Llano Verde, in the last year of the 30-inch gauge line's existence.

(iii) F. C. CORDOBA A HUATUSCO, 2-foot gauge

The first effort to connect the town of Huatusco with the F. C. Mexicano was made in 1883 when a concession was granted to build a railroad from Huatusco to the station of Cameron on the Mexicano, a distance of 35 miles. Some construction of roadbed and culverts was done that year, being paid for by local plantation owners, but no track was laid and the project was abandoned. It was revived again in 1898 when a concession was granted to Ignacio Canseco and associates to build a narrow gauge railroad from Cordoba on the Mexicano, to Huatusco. Captain Porfirio Diaz, Jr., son of the President of Mexico and already proven a competent civil engineer, was engaged to survey the line. Work was begun in 1900 and judging by the size and strength of the steel bridges which spanned several deep gorges which the railroad had to cross, standard gauge must have been in the minds of the builders. However, when the time came to lay the track, a gauge of two feet was selected, and 21 miles of it were laid from Cordoba to Coscomatepec. By far the most difficult piece of engineering was the crossing of the Rio Jamapa at Tomatlan, the distance from the top of the rails to the river below being 255 feet at the center of the bridge. The Jamapa has several branches that rise on the slopes of the great extinct volcano Orizaba, Mexico's highest mountain, which towers 18,541 feet above sea level, with the last 3000 feet to the summit eternally covered with snow. Having spanned two branches of the Jamapa at great expense, the builders could not afford another river crossing, so the railhead remained at Coscomatepec.

Completed in 1902, the railroad was laid out on a fairly easy grade of 1.25% from Cordoba to the crossing of the river at Tomatlan, but from there to Coscomatepec, a distance of 4.4 miles, the grade was 3.7% and some of the curves averaged 19 degrees. This section is probably what led the builders to select a very narrow gauge and contributed to the abandonment of any idea of continuing the line past Coscomatepec. Hence the passengers and freight went over the highway the remaining 12 miles to their destination. Passenger equipment consisted of one coach, a combination first and second class, and several locally built second class cars with open sides, ideal for sightseeing. Apparently the late T. Philip Terry, author of the famous guide books to Mexico did not think much of this line as a tourist attraction, for he passed it by with the remark – "uninteresting." Those railfans who were lucky enough to ride it before abandonment would dispute Terry all the way.

Unable to meet its obligations, the builders of the Cordoba & Huatusco sold the railroad to the F. C. Mexicano on November 4, 1909, and in order

Car No. 102 of the Mexicano's 2-foot gauge branch was third class, but the open air features made it the best car on the train for viewing the scenery, as well as avoiding the tropical heat. *(Two pictures: L. T. Haug)*

The spectacular crossing of the Rio Jamapa at Tomatlan by a steel span heavy enough to handle standard gauge trains is shown in this 1948 photo. The rails lie 225 feet above the water at the center.

F. C. Mexicano No. 3 brings train 72 across Tomatlan bridge in 1948. The only baggage car on the 2-foot gauge branch was appropriately numbered 222. *(Three pictures: L. T. Haug)*

to bring the property up to the high standards required by its new owners, the line was extensively rebuilt, in the course of which three new passenger coaches were added to the roster. The F. C. Atlamaxac's 2-foot gauge Shay was brought over from Munoz and for years it was used as a helper on the grade from Tomatlan to Coscomatepec. I was not fortunate enough to ride on this line, but a letter I received from the late Leonard T. Haug in 1947 describes the ride through the dense tropical forest after leaving Cordoba, the spectacular crossings of the branches of the Jamapa, and the final four miles up the steep grade to the open country at Coscomatepec. Here the engine turned around on the "Y", hauling the baggage car with it, and in twenty minutes they were away downhill for the two-hour ride to Cordoba. This train made two round trips a day, both scheduled as a "mixto" but frequently with no freight cars at the head end. The least profitable of the Mexicano's three narrow gauge branches, it was closed down for lack of patronage on December 1, 1951, though the rails were not removed until 1953. A newly paved highway permitted the busses and trucks to rob the railroad of most of its customers, so there was no economic reason to continue its operation. The Shay was scrapped in 1945 and the three little Baldwins remained inside the shop building at Orizaba through 1954, for sale with no takers, and were cut up there for scrap.

In contemplating the story of these three narrow gauge feeders of the Mexicano, not one of them reached the goals of their builders. The 3-foot gauge Tlacotepec a Huajuapan de Leon did not reach Huajuapan; the 2½-foot gauge Zacatlan branch did not reach Zacatlan, and Huatusco never saw a railroad either. The answer of course lies in the fact that railroads built through agricultural districts of the type served by these three lines could not generate enough traffic to pay their way, and they were easy victims to the gasoline age.

The Mexicano's 2-foot gauge engine No. 1, Baldwin-built in 1902, is pictured at Cordoba in 1948, three years before the branch was abandoned.

The horse-drawn cabs waiting their turn at Central Station in Merida, above, are gone now; replaced by prosaic taxis. At right, the windmills against the sky behind the station still provide water as they did a hundred years ago.

3

Narrow Gauge in Yucatan

The early history of the network of narrow and standard gauge railroads in the State of Yucatan is buried in obscurity, due to the fact that most of the railroads were financed by Mexicans, with little help from England or the United States during the first twenty years of construction and operation.* The Yucatan peninsula was separated from the more populated part of the country by a vast jungle area, with no roads or other means of easy transportation except along the Gulf coast by ship. Until the building of the Sureste Railway after World War II, Yucatan was almost a country unto itself, seldom visited by tourists from other parts of the country and only by adventurous foreigners who sought the Mayan ruins with which the state was filled. The peninsula of Yucatan is an ancient coral formation which has been changed into hard limestone rock, with many underground rivers which have formed channels through the limestone, the rivers always flowing towards the Gulf in a northerly direction. Covering this limestone is a thin topsoil of sandy loam, and in building the early railroads, the clearing and grubbing operation through the thick undergrowth of the jungle must have been fantastically difficult. The soil for many miles to the south and west of the capital city of Merida was suitable for growing only one productive crop, a plant called the *Agave sisalense*, or sisal hemp.

From this plant is extracted a fibre which is very tough, and can be woven into hemp rope. As the sisal plantations spread across the great flat countryside, a vast network of narrow gauge railroads was built, to bring the gathered fibrous leaves to the mill where they were processed and baled for shipment out of the country. At the peak, there were 2500 miles of these 24- and 30-inch gauge railroads which used light rail similar to those of sugar plantations. With few exceptions, mules provided the motive power, though at least two of the sisal areas had small Porter locomotives in the early days. After the advent of the small gasoline locomotive, a number of these were introduced and many are still in service.

It was to connect these tramways as they were called, with the seaports from which the baled hemp could be shipped, that the railroads which later made up the system of the United Railroads of Yucatan were built. The first railroad was a standard gauge line from Merida to Progreso on the Gulf of Mexico, under the name of Ferrocarril Progreso a Merida. Authorized under a concession dated April 22, 1874, nothing was done towards building it for six years; the work started late in 1880. Since there were no grades, no bridges, tunnels or other obstructions, the 24-mile railroad was completed in 1881 and service between the two cities was begun. In 1883 this same company obtained a concession to build a standard gauge line east from Merida via Tixkokob to Izamal, 41 miles, thus connecting a large section of the 400 sisal plantations with direct rail service to the ships at Progreso. Completed in 1885, these 65 miles of standard gauge track comprised the total railroad mileage of that gauge for the following seventy years; everything else was built to 3-foot gauge. The name of this railroad was changed to F. C. Merida a Progreso y Izamal in 1885 and was operated under that name until the consolidation of most of the railroads of the state in 1902.

There were three narrow gauge railroad companies formed between 1878 and 1880; the Merida a Valladolid; the Merida a Calkini and the Merida a Peto. All were built to connect the sisal plantations with a transfer platform in Merida. Low cost per mile was the most important factor and since narrow gauge was very much in the

See map page 175

public eye in Mexico at that time due to General Palmer's Colorado and Mexican projects which were either completed or under way, it was logical for the plantation owners to select 3-foot gauge for their railroads. Brief histories of these three railroads follow.

F. C. MERIDA A VALLADOLID, 3-foot gauge

The concession for this railroad was granted to Francisco Canton on December 15, 1880 to build a railroad from Merida to Valladolid, 112 miles, at the eastern end of the sisal belt and not far from the present border of the Territory of Quintana Roo. About twenty miles from the station of Dzitas is the great Mayan ruin of Chichen-Itza, which until the building of the railroad could only be reached after a very long and fatiguing journey by stagecoach, a trip which discouraged all but the most hardy travelers. Construction of the railroad was begun in 1882, proceeding at the rate of only a few miles a year, since the money for this work had to come from the local planters. The line was built northeast out of Merida to Conkal, then southeast to Tixkokob where it touched the standard gauge Merida-Izamal line. It was then built northeast through the city of Motul to Temax which it reached in 1897, roughly 40 miles from Merida. In that year Canton obtained help from the state in the form of a subvention of $6250 per kilometer in 5% bonds, and work continued until in June 1900 the railroad reached Tunkas, 88.5 miles from Merida. A branch had also been built from Conkal to Progreso, 19 miles, to enable shipment of hemp from the plantations direct to the docks at Progreso without transfer to standard gauge at Merida. For many years there were thus two routes from Merida to Progreso, each with daily passenger service.

In February 1901, Canton let the contracts for the remaining section from Tunkas to Valladolid, and a branch from Dzitas (also spelled Tzitas and Citas) to Tizimin, all work having been completed about the time of the formation of the United Railroads of Yucatan in 1902. The finished railroad, known as the Eastern Division of the United Railroads was as follows:

Merida to Valladolid	112
Conkal to Progreso	19
Citas to Tizimin	34
Total	165 miles

All of the railroad's locomotives burned wood, of which there was a plentiful supply. They were all alike, of the 4-4-0 type built by Baldwin, the heaviest of the nine locomotives weighing only 24 tons. Since there were no grades, these engines proved adequate to the job and some of them were in use as late as 1952.

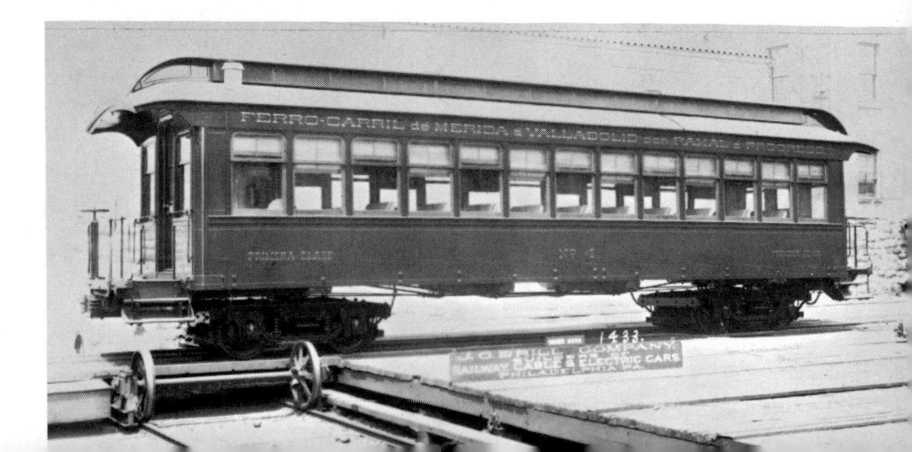

Baldwin built the TUNKAS for the Merida a Valladolid as a Vauclain compound, with backup headlight and pilot for runs where there were no turnaround facilities. Brill built the first class coach No. 4 for this road in 1890. *(Above: H. C. Broadbelt collection; right: Pennsylvania State Historical Society)*

In 1900 the F. C. Merida a Peto issued an elaborate book for the Paris Exposition, showing the progress in construction of the railroad. Pictures on this and the following pages were made by a photographer who was taken by special train over the line. At Ticul, 45 miles from Merida, the station is decorated with flowers and potted plants in honor of the visit. Below, the train has halted at San Antonio's thatched station, 80 miles from Merida. The lantern on the pole at the left of the engine serves as a signal. Local residents in dazzling white garb watch the photographer. *(DeGolyer Foundation Library)*

In the distance, the photographer's train stands at "end of track", while the graders dig a cut through the sandy hill, a few miles from Peto. A round thatched hut, embellished with a thatched canopy at Xoy station, was the chosen design for Yucatan jungle stations. The Baldwin-built engine is No. 6, the MERCEDES. *(DeGolyer Foundation Library)*

Merida's Central Station in 1953, shown with four trains ready for departure, was provided with three-rail tracks for narrow and standard gauge. U. de Y. No. 47, the last wood burner in service, is being turned on the "armstrong" turntable inside Merida's rectangular engine shed.

F. C. MERIDA A CALKINI, later F. C. PENINSULAR DE MERIDA-YUCATAN, 3-foot gauge

This project had as its primary objective a railroad from Merida to the seaport of Campeche in the neighboring state of that name, a distance of 112 miles. The two concessions were granted December 20, 1880 and February 23, 1881, but like the Merida-Valladolid line, construction got under way in 1882 and proceeded at a snail's pace southwest through the sisal plantations, reaching the city of Calkini, 58 miles from Merida in 1889. At this time the company was reorganized and all concessions consolidated under the name of F. C. Peninsular de Merida-Yucatan on October 5, 1889. Construction resumed towards Campeche in 1890 and reached Pomuch, 33 miles from Campeche in April, 1892. The available money from the planters dried up at this time, so it was decided to close the gap between the two sections by building two miles a year from each end, using the track maintenance crews and such labor as could be hired cheaply from the plantations.

Surprisingly enough this system worked very well and in 1898 the entire 112 miles from Merida to Campeche was opened for traffic. A branch was also built from Uman to Hunucma by 1898. Under a concession granted February 21, 1900 another branch of 48 miles was built from Merida to Muna and Ticul, in competition with another narrow gauge railroad, the F. C. Merida a Peto. One of the reasons for building this branch was to provide a direct tourist route to the Mayan ruins at Uxmal, which was within easy driving distance of Muna. At the time of the 1902 consolidation, the F. C. Peninsular was comprised of the following lines, known as the western division of the new company:

Merida to Campeche	112
Merida to Ticul	48
Uman to Hunucma	13
Total	173 miles

F. C. DE MERIDA A PETO, 3-foot gauge

This was the first of the three narrow gauge railroads to be chartered and the last to be completed. Organized March 27, 1878, work which began in the fall of 1881 was sporadic, whenever funds and labor were available, and it did not reach the town of Acanceh, 16 miles from Merida until 1884. Under the supervision of Rogerio G. Canton, the line extended south from Acanceh, reaching Ticoh in 1888 and Ticul in 1892, a total of 47 miles from Merida. Here the terminal remained until 1898 at which time Canton obtained additional funds and resumed building towards Peto, reaching Tzucacab, 86 miles from Merida in December 1898. The remaining ten miles to Peto were completed in January 1902, while a branch from Acanceh to Sotuta, begun in 1899 was also opened in 1902, tapping another network of plantation railroads.

This line boasted of having a parlor car for the tourist business, and twelve locomotives comprised the largest stud of power of any of the narrow gauge lines. The company did not earn a profit after the road was completed, and some of the track built 25 years earlier deteriorated under the traffic so badly that on January 26, 1909 it was forced to accept an offer from the United Railroads of Yucatan to become a partner, known as the Southern Division, as follows:

Merida to Peto	96
Acanceh to Sotuta	35
Total	131 miles

Built in 1910, speeder No. 7 for track maintenance crews was still going strong in 1953 when photographed at Merida. Below, one of the graceful Baldwin-built 4-4-0s, No. 66, has the headlight from No. 28. It is arriving at Merida from Peto, on the three-rail track which also served the Izamal standard gauge line. *(Below: L. T. Haug)*

Three generations of Baldwins stand side by side in the Merida engine shed. No. 33, built in 1890, is flanked, left, by No. 81, the last 4-4-0 built by Baldwin in 1946, and at the right, No. 79, built in 1928. Below, the man in white who has just left motor car No. 6 at Merida seems to have dropped his sombrero. *(Below: L. T. Haug)*

Coach No. 12 of the U. de Y. is remarkably well preserved after more than half a century of service in the tropics since Brill built it in 1900 for the F. C. Merida a Peto.

A mixed train leaves Merida on dual gauge track with Baldwin Mogul No. 76, bound for Valladolid. No. 72, below, the last ten-wheel engine turned out from Baldwin for the U. de Y. in 1925, had a Rushton or "cabbage" stack. *(Above: E. L. DeGolyer, Jr.; below: H. G. Boutell collection)*

UNITED RAILROADS OF YUCATAN
F. C. UNIDOS DE YUCATAN
3-foot and standard gauges

Incorporated in Mexico on November 1, 1902, the Merida a Progreso y Izamal, standard gauge, and the Merida a Valladolid and the F. C. Peninsular were combined to form a new company. Its capital stock was distributed among the owners of the three railroads, and to pay for some badly needed renovation on all of them, a $4,000,000 issue of 5% gold bonds were floated in London, most of the bonds being sold in Europe through the offices of J. Henry Schroeder & Co. The trustees handling this bond issue were Baron Bruno Schroeder, Sir Walpole Greenwell and Ernst Thalmann, and the management of the new company was placed in the hands of Nicolas Escalante Peon. As soon as the bonds were sold, the entire standard gauge line from Merida to Progreso was rebuilt with heavy steel rail, additional locomotives were purchased in both gauges, and much needed replacements in crossties and rails on the oldest sections of the narrow gauge divisions followed the rebuilding of the Progreso line. One of the new standard gauge locomotives purchased from Baldwin in 1904 was of the 4-4-2 or Atlantic type, the only such type in service in Mexico except for a few on the Southern Pacific of Mexico. Built as a coal burner, it was soon converted to burn wood. Through most of its years it sported a giant bonnet stack which was still on the engine when it was scrapped in 1957.

The new company did surprisingly well during its first ten years, paid the bond interest on time and retired a percentage of the bonds when they were due. The disruption of all transportation in Mexico which began in 1911 was felt to a lesser degree in Yucatan than in the states to the north, due to its isolation from the rest of the country. In 1914 when the Constitutionalist party under Carranza occupied Mexico City, all railroads including the U. de Y. were seized and placed under one head. An exception was made in the case of Yucatan and the state was made responsible, the name of the railroad being changed to Ferrocarriles Constitutionalistas en Yucatan. After the election of President Obregon in November 1920, the State of Yucatan returned to a fair degree of normalcy and returned the railroads to the owners.

During this period the state showed a great deal more responsibility towards meeting the financial obligations of the railroad than did the other railroads of the country, and though there were delays in bond coupon payments for as much as a year, they were all paid through the 1911-1921 period. However good the intentions of the stockholders were, the economy of the state was such that expenses of the Yucatan network exceeded the receipts, and in 1927 the railroad was paying bond coupons due in 1924. The 1927 payment was the last ever made on these bonds, and whatever was left from each year's operating revenue was used to buy replacement rolling stock and to keep the track in repair.

The railroad drifted along through the 1930s and the World War II years, the only new equipment being the purchase of two Baldwin 4-4-0s in 1946, the last of this type ever built by that company and the last new steam locomotives to arrive in Mexico. A few narrow gauge Diesel-electric locomotives arrived in 1952, and these enabled the retirement of most of the locomotives built prior to 1900. The last wood burner, No. 46 was converted to burn oil in 1954, as wood was becoming increasingly difficult to obtain.

Under the terms of the agreement with the Mexican government made in 1902, the property was to be turned over to the government in 1970, it being assumed that the bond issue would have been paid off by 1950. The building of the Sureste Railway changed all these plans, for the standard gauge line of 457 miles was built between 1941 and 1949 between Allende, across the Coatzacoalcos River at the end of the Nacional de Tehuantepec, to Campeche where it connected with the United Railroads of Yucatan. The Merida-Campeche line was standard gauged between 1953 and 1957, and through sleeping cars and coaches were run from Allende to Merida, being prevented from running through to Mexico City by lack of a bridge at Coatzacoalcos. This bridge was completed recently and sleeping cars are run without change from Mexico City to Merida.

Now owned by the State of Yucatan, the United Railroads are being converted to Diesel operation, though steam is still used on some of

The Campeche-Merida passenger is shown at Becal, with 4-4-0 No. 80, Baldwin, 1946, at the head end. First class coach No. 81 came from the Catskill Mountain Railway in New York state. All U. de Y. engines had crosshead pumps, similar to those on No. 73 standing in the Merida station. *(Top: L. T. Haug)*

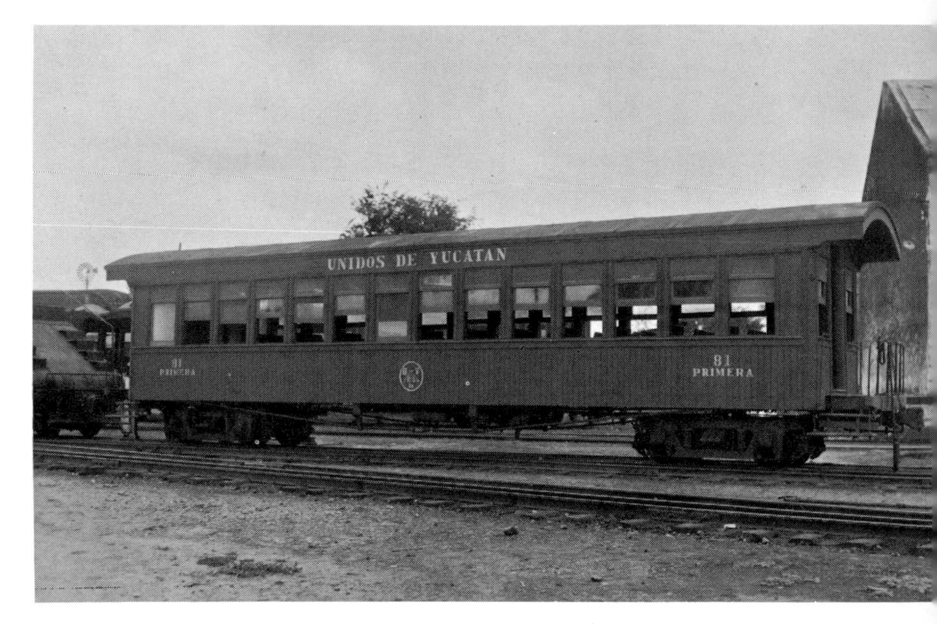

The first parlor car on the Merida a Peto was named for Armando Canton.

the narrow gauge lines and in the yards. A third rail was laid between Merida and Progreso between 1958 and 1960 and the narrow gauge track from Conkal to Progreso was taken up. A large portion of the old Valladolid line was abandoned and the distance greatly reduced by narrowing the gauge of the Izamal-Merida line and building a new 3-foot gauge line directly across country from Izamal to Tunkas. This shortened the distance from Merida to Tunkas from 88.5 to 59 miles and enabled the abandonment of the old line from Tixkokob to Tunkas, this being in very bad condition. New rails were laid between Tunkas and Valladolid and between Dzitas and Tizimin. The narrow gauge branch of the old F. C. Peninsular between Merida and Ticul via Muna was also abandoned, leaving the former F. C. Merida a Peto to serve Ticul and Peto. The narrow gauge lines, not counting the third rail on the Merida-Progreso section now total 264 miles as compared with 468 miles at the peak.

Great changes are taking place in the facilities at Merida, as a direct result of the completion of the Sureste Railway. General Manager Gelasio Luna y Luna has worked miracles by replacing the original La Plancha roundhouse and shop building with a completely new facility having the most modern machinery and service equipment. The first time I saw the old engine terminal building a few blocks from the Merida station, I thought I was stepping back into the last century. Inside the massive walls of the long, rectangular building, into which the locomotives came and went through a tunnel-shaped door, was a turntable with radial tracks of varying lengths according to their direction, the turntable open to the sky to allow for light and ventilation. On these radial tracks were the active steam engines of both gauges, a few of them being under light repairs. Several long tracks extended back into the vast recesses of the ancient structure, to the section filled with machinery for heavy repairs. On one of these tracks were half a dozen partly dismantled engines, among them No. 16, the high-wheeled Atlantic, with boiler jacket missing, no rods, no pilot, but that great bonnet stack still reaching almost to the rafters. It showed few traces of its one-time splendor when it was the hot-shot passenger engine on the Merida-Progreso line. Standing idle was one of the largest Corliss engines I have ever seen, in perfect condition and able to start at a moment's notice. The old overhead shafting and belts were still in place, though all of the machinery in daily use had been converted to electric drive with individual motors. It was a veritable museum of early-day Mexican railroading, and worth going miles to see. Among the engines stored on the radial tracks were two wood-burning 4-4-0s from the early days, with one of the postwar 4-4-0s in between.

With the reduction in narrow gauge mileage, a considerable number of the old passenger cars have been sold to U.S. railfans or have been scrapped, although those still in use have been refurbished and sport bright new paint jobs today. Several new open-platform narrow-gauge coaches have been built within the past year in the new shops, and though all the trains are mixed passenger and freight, there is sufficient demand for passenger equipment to require replacements for wornout cars. Rumor has it that Senor Luna y Luna is soon to become the general manager for both the Sureste and the Yucatan network, which are to be combined into one operating unit. This would be a logical step and should speed the modernization of all the railroads of southeastern Mexico.

ZACATECAS S.A.G
10
SEGUNDA

4

The Principal Narrow Gauge Shortlines

In Mexico's history there have been over a hundred narrow gauge shortlines or industrial railways, most of them in the latter category and operated in connection with mines, sugar plantations or the lumber industry. Some are so obscure that it has been impossible to locate any information on them, so only those for which a reasonably accurate record exists will be listed. A few of them not only served an industry but were common carriers of sufficient importance to rate inclusion in the Official Guide of Railways of North America. Some of them survived into modern times and are still narrow gauge, but the majority of them are gone from the scene, the victims of progress.

F. C. AGUASCALIENTES, 3-foot gauge

This railroad straddled the industrial and common carrier classification, for although it was designed to carry ore, it provided passenger service to non-employees and operated as a common carrier. It was built in 1902 from San Gil to Asientos, 10 miles, and carried ore from the mines at Asientos to a standard gauge loading point at San Gil, a station on the Mexican Central's branch from Aguascalientes to San Luis Potosi. Passenger trains were hauled by one of the Porter saddle tank locomotives, and at the smelter there was a network of 30-inch gauge tracks. The company owned only three locomotives, and was an early victim of the general closure of the mines in Mexico during the revolution and did not reopen for many years. During the 1930s it was replaced by a highway and its equipment was scrapped.

F. C. CAZADERO LA TORRE Y TEPETONGO, 2-foot gauge

Organized under a concession granted in 1895 to build a railroad from the town of Cazadero la Torre, 100 miles north of Mexico City on the Mexican Central, this road was to tap large stands of undeveloped timber to the south and west of Cazadero. Tepetongo is a village on the main line of the Mexican National and like Cazadero is in the State of Michoacan. Construction began in 1896 and the line was built south into the State of Mexico through the upper reaches of the valley of the river San Juan del Rio to Nado, where it turned west for a steep climb up the mountain slopes to the main lumbering center of San Pablo, 36½ miles from Cazadero. Approximately twenty miles of branches were built out of San Pablo as the logging operations expanded. Passenger service was begun between Cazadero and Nado in 1897; soon the little outside-frame Baldwins were familiar sights to the residents of the valley and the traffic in finished lumber continued over the railroad for many years. In 1906 the road was sold to a group who changed the name to F. C. Cazadero y Solis, the latter being the name of a town on the Rio Lerma, twenty miles over the mountains from San Pablo and on the line of the original survey to Tepetongo.

The civil war which swept Mexico between 1911 and 1916 halted all lumbering operations in this area and the railroad was closed down for many years. On December 31, 1921, Jose Rivera Rio was granted a new concession to rehabilitate the railroad and restore it to operation, new spurs into virgin timber lands being built near San Pablo. The name of the road was again changed, this time to Cazadero & San Pablo under which name the line continued in operation until the supply of timber was exhausted. Abandonment followed after World War II, though the track remained in place for ten years. Three of the little side-tank engines which had survived the civil war were still serviceable and ended their days on sugar plantations in other parts of the

Coahuila y Zacatecas No. 12, at left, works up the hill between Avalos and Carneros with an eastbound passenger train in 1961. *(John Pickett)*

Coahuila y Zacatecas Nos. 279 and 11 double-head a short freight across the desert near Concepcion de Oro. Liberal Mexican slogans adorn the side of the C. y Z. business car. *(Above: Stan Kistler; right: Edwin W. Lohr)*

The C. y Z.'s first engine, No. 1, the Saltillo yard switcher, is being turned at the end of a shift. Today it is stored in Pomona, California, saved from the torch by a railfan's dream. F. C. Cazadero la Torre y Tepetongo No. 7 came from the Baldwin works in 1897, the same year C. y Z. No. 1 was built.

Even the Diesels were given patriotic names after they replaced steam power on the C. y Z. *(Top: C. W. Witbeck; bottom: Edwin W. Lohr)*

country. This was the longest of the 2-foot gauge common carriers and probably the least known outside Mexico.

F. C. COAHUILA Y ZACATECAS, 3-foot gauge

Without doubt this railroad is the best known narrow gauge short line in Mexico, visited and admired by many railfans from other countries. It was built by the Mazapil Copper Co., a British corporation, from the city of Saltillo to the mines at Concepcion del Oro, 78 miles southwest of Saltillo. It was natural for the builders to adopt 3-foot gauge, for when it was built, the only railroad passing through Saltillo was the 3-foot gauge Mexican National, which had just announced that it had no plans to standard gauge their line for years to come. The C. y Z. as built, paralleled the Mexican National for the first 25 miles, over a ruling grade of 4% to a summit at Carneros, 6889 feet altitude and 1640 feet above Saltillo. This duplication of track was done because there was ample space for yard and repair facilities at Saltillo, plenty of housing for employees, whereas at Carneros none of these were available. By January 1898 the grading for the railroad had been completed and the rails laid with 45-pound steel to Martinez, 36 miles from Saltillo. So rapidly did tracklaying proceed that the last spike was driven at Concepcion del Oro on April 8, 1898. The three locomotives purchased at the time the railroad was under construction were Baldwin Consolidations. These proved so satisfactory to the British owners that nine more Baldwins, including the only narrow gauge Pacific type ever to run in Mexico were added to the roster. In 1903 a branch was built from Avalos, not far from Concepcion del Oro, to San Pedro Ocampo, 17 miles, to new mines opened at the latter place. Other small branches were built by the C. y Z. in later years.

In its entire history the road owned only three passenger cars, two baggage cars and two business cars, all of wooden construction. In their later years they became classic examples of what happens to wooden cars when the truss rods are

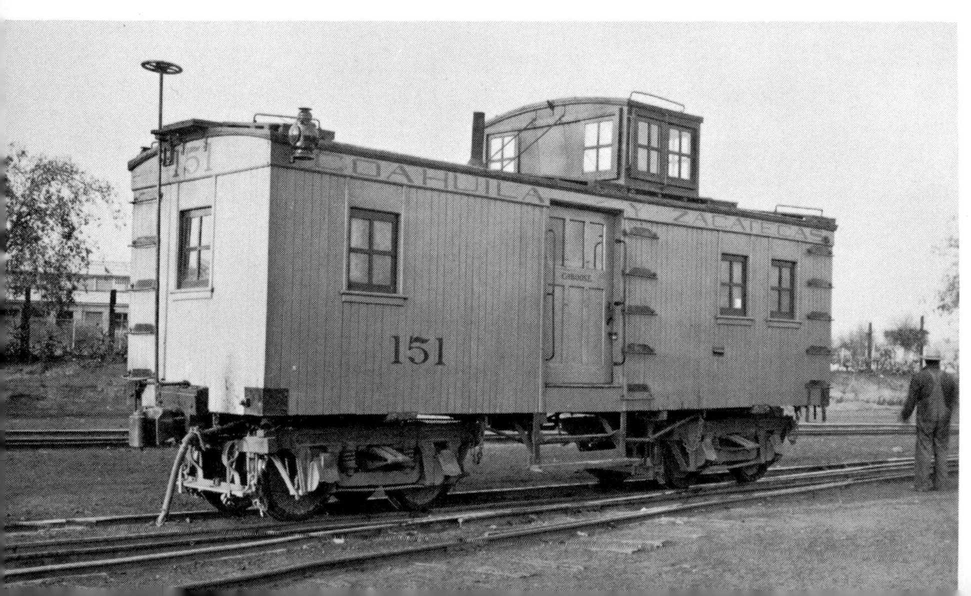

The C. y Z. side-door cabooses were homemade but handsome. Second class coach No. 12, swaybacked and faded after sixty years of service, is shown in its last days on the C. y Z. *(Right: C. W. Witbeck; below: Edwin W. Lohr)*

pulled too tight — the car sits too high in the middle and is sway-backed on each side of the center. However, the locomotives were maintained by Master Mechanic Appleton in true British style, with polished brass capped stacks, smokebox doors held in place by "dogs" placed inside the smokebox and released by a wheel in the center of the door, and above all, immaculate maintenance of the machinery of each locomotive.

The railroad suffered heavily in 1914 during the hostilities between the forces of President Madero and the Constitutionalist armies of General Carranza which were led by Pancho Villa. Railroad property was ruthlessly destroyed, locomotives were blown up by placing dynamite charges in the fireboxes and many of the facilities at the copper smelter including the railroad terminal at Concepcion del Oro were destroyed. It was several years before service was fully restored and conditions were not back to normal until 1917, though the station at Concepcion del Oro was not replaced until 1927. The Mazapil Copper Co. maintained switching locomotives at the smelter in Concepcion del Oro and a standard gauge switcher at Saltillo, these being operated separately from the C. y Z.

The railroad remained as a steam operation until 1963 at which time it was Dieselized and continues to provide passenger service on a mixed-train basis. In 1959 the Mazapil Copper Co. was sold to Mexican interests and operation of the railroad was placed under an administrator, the name being changed to F. C. Coahuila-Zacatecas, A. G. Some of the older locomotives were scrapped by the new management and surplus locomotives from the National Railways of Mexico were purchased or leased until Dieselization. Three of the locomotives and a considerable amount of rolling stock were purchased in 1963 by an American group for use on a railroad to be built at Puddingstone Dam Park near Pomona, California, but the line was never built and the equipment is now stored at Pomona. The Coahuila-Zacatecas is the last survivor of the group of narrow gauge short lines which once connected with the F. C. Nacional Mexicano but as long as the mines remain productive, it will no doubt continue in its present form.

F. C. DESAGUE DEL VALLE DE MEXICO, 3-foot gauge

A literal translation of this name would be "Drainage of the Valley of Mexico Railroad," for this line was built to parallel the Grand Canal, the great drainage project which was begun by the Spanish administrators in 1607 but was not to fulfill its purpose until Porfirio Diaz began a new canal in 1879 and completed it in 1900. The purpose of the canal was to lower the waters of Lake Texcoco and other lakes in the valley to prevent flooding of Mexico City during heavy rains and since there were no rivers serving as outlets to this group of salt lakes, one had to be built. Included in the Diaz project was a tunnel through the Xalpan Mountains near the town of Tequizquiac, from whence the waters flowed into the Rio Tula and Rio Moctezuma to the Gulf of Mexico.

After the original work was completed, it was found that a great deal of additional construction had to be done along the Rio Tula beyond the tunnel, as well as changes in the original canal. A railroad paralleling the canal would therefore make it easier to bring supplies to the various points involved. In 1902 the Department of Public Works (S.C.O.P.) of the Mexican Government built a 3-foot gauge railroad starting from Gran Canal station on the Hidalgo y Nordeste, 12 miles north of Mexico City to Zumpango, a short distance from the southern end of the great tunnel, a distance of 23 miles. Passenger service was provided using locomotives and cars purchased from the Mexican National, which at that time was standard gauging and had a surplus of narrow gauge equipment.

In 1919 the S.C.O.P. began work on the north end of the drainage tunnel, requiring an extension of the railroad. Deciding to become independent of the Hidalgo y Nordeste, the S.C.O.P. built its own line paralleling the canal from its start near the old San Lazaro gate adjacent to the Penitentiary (a short walk from the San Lazaro Station of the Interoceanic), in Mexico City, to Gran Canal Station to connect with the existing line. Passenger trains thereafter ran from Penitenciaria Station in Mexico City direct to Zumpango. In 1921 the railroad was extended north from Zum-

The F. C. Desague del Valle de Mexico was pictured in a report by the Government Department of Public Works in 1920. Engine No. 102, one of the secondhand Baldwins from the N. de M., appears in all three photos on this page. In the top picture, the trestle is supported by finely made stone buttresses, a craft in which Mexican workmen excel. At Gran Canal station, the special photographer's train attracts the usual collection of idlers; the dogs look at each other, and the engine is the centerpiece. Tlaxcoapan had a station with raised platform, for quick handling of large numbers of passengers. *(DeGolyer Foundation Library)*

The MACHALA was built at Pittsburgh Locomotive Works, the El Oro Mining & Railway's first locomotive. *(Schenectady History Center)*

pango through Apaxco to El Progreso and the Rio Tula, the latter place being reached on October 24, 1924.

This 66-mile railroad continued in operation with several passenger trains daily each way until the end of World War II. A program of paving secondary roads and improving all highways in the vicinity of Mexico City was undertaken at that time, the railroad was abandoned and some of the right of way used for the highway north of Zumpango. Of all the railroads which ran into Mexico City, this and the F. C. de Monte Alto were the least known, ignored by the guidebooks and rating only a few lines in the Official Guide. Fortunately the S.C.O.P., proud of its labors on the Gran Canal and the railroad, published a full account of the D. del V. de M. in its 1925 report to the nation.

EL ORO MINING & RAILWAY CO., 3-foot gauge

Under a concession granted May 11, 1897 the American Railroad & Lumber Co. of New Jersey built a narrow gauge railroad from Tultenango, on the Mexican National main line 102 miles north of Mexico City, to the gold and silver mines of the American Mining Co. in the vicinity of Yondese, 30 miles from Tultenango. Construction began January 15, 1898, reaching Yondese early in 1899. All material and equipment was purchased in the U. S., and the line was laid with 40-pound steel rail. The companies then sold out to a British group who formed the El Oro Mining & Railway Co. Ltd. In 1909 a large stand of timber on the slopes of the mountains south of Yondese was exploited and soon the lumber operations were a major source of income. The main line was extended nine miles from Yondese to Palizada, and 26 miles of track radiated out of Palizada into the forests. Motive power for this section were Shay-geared Limas, two of them being purchased by the Suchi Timber Co., a subsidiary of El Oro. Like the Coahuila y Zacatecas, the railroad had a business car as well as five passenger and two baggage-mail cars. It was a first class railroad in every respect and gave the residents of the region daily connection with the main line Mexican National trains. Its obvious prosperity made it an easy target for the revolutionaries in 1911-1914, forcing the mines to close down February 27, 1915. In September 1916 the temporary government directed by Carranza issued a decree ordering all mines anywhere in the country to reopen by November 14th or be confiscated by the government. To avoid this fate, the El Oro mines were reopened in October 1916 and resumed production. The branches into the forests were also reopened, this section of the country remaining in relative peace for the remainder of the unsettled period.

Timbering operations came to an end in the late 1930s and the railroad was abandoned south of Yondese. Within a year the mines other than those in the immediate vicinity of the town of El Oro were closed down for lack of productive ore, resulting in the abandonment of all of the track except a seven-mile section from El Oro to the junction at Tultenango. This short line was taken over by the National Railways of Mexico in 1942. In 1949 when the Mexico City-Acambaro narrow gauge line was standard gauged, the El Oro branch was also widened, thus erasing the last vestiges of a once prosperous short line. Several of the locomotives, including one of the first on the railroad, stood derelict in a field in back of Tultenango Station until well into the 1960s.

F. C. GUANAJUATO A SAN LUIS DE LA PAZ Y POZOS, 3-foot gauge

This railroad made up for its lack of size by having the longest name of any railroad in Mexico at the time it was built in 1890. Its concession was for a railroad between the above three towns, but the builders began work at Rincon, on the Mexican National, 49 miles north of the point which later became Gonzales Junction. The railroad was completed to San Luis de la Paz, 32 miles, in 1902 and was operated primarily in connection with mines at the latter place. It never reached Guanajuato, and remained as an industrial line, the property of a New Jersey group, until 1899 when passenger service was introduced. The railroad was purchased by the Mexican National on April 10, 1902 and arrangements were made immediately to extend it to the mining town of Pozos, six miles south. Here a strange event occurred; the Mexican National, in its haste to extend the railroad to Pozos laid the six miles of track in 3-foot gauge, on standard gauge ties, reaching Pozos early in 1903. As soon as the Mexican National main line had been completely standard gauged, the Rincon-Pozos branch was also widened, this work being completed July 18, 1905. Today a mixed train operates over this branch daily, from Rio Laja, the modern name for Rincon, to Pozos. Even Gonzales Junction has had a name change in modern times, to Empalme Escobedo.

F. C. DE HORNOS, 2-foot gauge

Though owned outright by the Hacienda de Hornos, a large cattle and grain raising property in the State of Coahuila near the city of Torreon, it was a common carrier and had the distinction of owning the only 2-foot gauge Mikado type locomotive ever used in the country. A concession was granted to E. B. Mayo of the Hacienda de Hornos to build the railroad from Hornos to Alamito, 32 miles, with a short branch to Viesca. Construction was begun in August 1902 from Hornos, on the line of the Mexican International, and reached Hacienda Hornos in 1903 where it crossed the main line of the Coahuila & Pacific, continuing south and east from there to Alamito. The branch from Juan Guerra to Viesca of 2.5 miles was built as a short cut from Alamito to the Coahuila & Pacific, at a later date.

The railroad was opened for traffic as a common carrier in 1904 and two trains daily each way from Hornos to Viesca handled both passenger and freight traffic. Ownership of this road was purely local and like its wider companion to the west, the Coahuila y Zacatecas, it suffered from the ravages of the contending armies in 1914. Its last public timetable appeared in 1930 and by then the line from Juan Guerra to Alamito had been abandoned. Passenger service at that time was limited to a mixed train daily, and the railroad disappears from the records of the Mexican Government at the end of World War II.

F. C. IXTLAHUACA, 3-foot gauge

Owned by the Cia. Madrera Mexicana (Mexican Lumber Co.), the first section from Ixtlahuaca to La Garita, 35 miles, was built in 1896 and 1897. Ixtlahuaca is in the State of Mexico, 69 miles northwest of Mexico City on the main line of the old Mexican National's Acambaro division. Though intended to tap the rich timberlands of the district as an industrial railroad, it provided passenger

The only 2-foot gauge Mikado type engine ever built for service in North America, the JUANA, was shipped from Baldwin in 1903 for service at the Hacienda de Hornos. *(Herbert L. Broadbelt collection)*

service and was rated as a common carrier. The name of the road as first built was the Ixtlahuaca y Mani, changed to Ixtlahuaca, Mani y Nijini when a branch was built to the latter town. Locally it was known as the F. C. Ixtlahuaca and was so listed in the Official Guide and in government publications. Its peak mileage was 105, reached just at the start of the revolutionary disturbances, which closed down the line from 1912 until 1919. It then continued as a common carrier until 1946, when the timber reserves had been worked out and the line was abandoned.

F. C. JALAPA y CORDOBA, 3-foot gauge

The Jalapa Railway & Power Co. of New Jersey built this railroad under a concession granted July 16, 1897. First proposed as an electric railroad, using power generated by harnessing a waterfall near Jalapa, the Chicago firm of Albion Construction Co. got the contract for building the railroad. It soon became apparent that the cost of the dam and power plant greatly exceeded the available funds, so the line was built as a steam railroad. Using 56-pound steel rail, the contractors were forced to use expensive construction through the mountains over a section of five miles, with a ruling grade of 5% northbound and nearly 4% southbound. Starting at an elevation of 3256 feet at Jalapa, an altitude of 4289 feet was reached at Teocelo, 18.6 miles from Jalapa, which it reached on July 1, 1898. At this time the owners petitioned the government for release from any obligation to build beyond Teocelo and this was granted. Two five-mile branches were built, with a gauge of 2 feet, to haciendas on both sides of Teocelo, motive power being furnished by mules.

Daily passenger trains ran over the completed line from the summer of 1898, and at its peak the road owned four locomotives, seven passenger cars and two baggage-mail cars. In 1914 the name of the railroad was changed to Jalapa & Teocelo though the management remained the same. A Shay-geared engine was purchased secondhand from the defunct F. C. de Pachuca in 1914 and continued in service until the end of operations in 1945, a new paved highway parallel to the railroad having killed all incentive for the owners to continue.

FERROCARRIL MAPIMI, 30-inch gauge

Though this railroad was classified by the government as an industrial line, it had passenger service, was listed in the Official Guide and by Rand McNally as a common carrier. This very unusual railroad was built by the Cia. Minera de Penoles (Penoles Mining Co.) in 1896 and 1897 to provide access to valuable silver deposits. The railroad started at Bermejillo, in the State of Durango, 23 miles north of Gomez Palacio on the Mexican Central's main line from El Paso to Mexico City. The track from Bermejillo to Mapimi was laid with 35-pound steel rail over relatively moderate grades a distance of 15½ miles. From Mapimi there were two branches, one of three miles to the principal mine shafts and another of six miles to Ojuela. The first branch had the heavier traffic, the grade varying from 9 to 13.5%, requiring the use of the Abt system of rack rail throughout its length. Motive power for this section consisted of four Baldwin rack locomotives similar in design to those used on the Pikes Peak

The workers' houses of the Penoles Mining Co. at Campo Sur, across the gorge from the mine, are reminiscent of the Inca cities of Peru. *(Three pictures: DeGolyer Foundation Library)*

Railway in Colorado. They could push two empty and one loaded gondola up this grade at six miles per hour and control the descent of three loaded cars weighing 36 tons. For switching at the terminals, the adhesion wheels could be locked to the axles and the engine operated as an ordinary locomotive. At the smelter a group of small Baldwins of the 0-4-2T type were used, the Bermejillo- Mapimi traffic being handled by Baldwin 2-6-2s with side tanks.

This very profitable mining operation was controlled by German stockholders through American Metals Co. of New York, but after World War I, control rested in American and Mexican owners. Closure of the mines and railroad occurred in 1914 and work was resumed under the government edict in late 1916. The working out of the bonanza lodes in the vicinity of Mapimi caused the gradual closing down of the operation, and some time in the late 1940s the railroad was abandoned.

F.C. MATEHUALA, 3-foot gauge

Chartered September 26, 1891 as the F. C. Porvenir de Matehuala, it was built from La Paz, in the State of San Luis Potosi, site of extensive gold and silver mines, 13 miles to a connection with the Vanegas, Cedral & Rio Verde at Matehuala. Four branches to various mines were added ten years after the main line was completed in 1892, and passenger service between the towns which grew up around the mines, to the city of Matehuala was provided by beautiful little capped stacked 0-6-0s, with their names in gold leaf on the cab panels. The road was foreclosed by the bond holders in 1902 and the name was changed to F. C. Matehuala.

Though operations were curtailed between 1912 and 1916 during the general shutdown of mines, it continued to operate as a common carrier until World War II. One of the locomotives spent its last days switching for the Mazapil Copper Co. at Concepcion del Oro, terminal of the Coahuila y Zacatecas. Though listed as "Out of Business" by Poor's after 1929, the late Dave Welch visited it in 1938 and found it still operating as a "freight only" carrier.

F. C. MICHOACAN Y PACIFICO, 3-foot gauge

A charter was issued to C. Sebastian Camacho by the government on August 18, 1888 to build a narrow gauge railroad from Maravatio on the Mexican National, through Zitacuaro to Ario, 150 miles. Its purpose was to furnish access to a number of silver mines in the Zitacuaro area. On January 29, 1889 the Michoacan Railway & Mining Co. was

The suspension bridge at Campo Sur carried 2-foot gauge ore cars from the mine to the stamp mill and the yards of the Mapimi Railroad on the opposite side of the gorge. A cable hauled the empties back to the mine. Below, the rack locomotive SOCAVON pushes three empty concentrate cars up the 12% grade along the rock wall of the mountain below the Penoles mill.

The F. C. de Monte Alto used steam car No. 6 for local passenger service between Mexico City and Tlalnepantla. A trailer was usually attached, in the style of the steam dummies of the late 19th century. The Potosi & Rio Verde's Shay No. 3 heads a long train, probably posed for the photographer on commission from the Lima Locomotive Works, as the picture was retouched and used in their catalogue. *(Above: Herbert L. Broadbelt collection; below: Allen County Historical Society, Lima, Ohio)*

registered as a British company, to acquire Camacho's concession and mining properties.

The railroad was completed from Maravatio to Ocampo, 33 miles, with a branch to Angangueo mines in 1891. In 1893 the government permitted a change in the concession to permit extension of the railroad only as far as Zitacuaro. The extension from Ocampo was begun in 1896 and reached Tuxpan that year, and Zitacuaro in May 1897. Motive power was exclusively Baldwin-built and daily passenger service was furnished. This road was sufficiently prosperous to attract the attention of the Mexican National and on August 1, 1900 it was leased for 25 years on a percentage basis. It remained narrow gauge for almost half a century and some of its rolling stock lasted into the 1950s. Today it is the Zitacuaro branch of the National Railways of Mexico, standard gauged in 1949. The last steam locomotive to run over the line was N. de M. No. 2250, formerly Denver & Rio Grande Western No. 458, a narrow gauge Mikado which was sold to the N. de M. narrow gauge during the war emergency twenty years ago, and widened to standard gauge.

F. C. MONTE ALTO Y TLALNEPANTLA, 3-foot gauge

Like the Mapimi Railroad, this was an industrial line originally, built by the Cia. de San Ildefonso, S.A. of Mexico City and designed to carry the output of the cement plant at Progreso Industrial to market. As originally built in 1898 and 1899, it extended from Tlalnepantla, eight miles from downtown Mexico City, to Progreso Industrial, a distance of 15 miles. Transfer of freight to the Mexican Central at Tlalnepantla proved to be an expensive operation and in 1903 the company was granted permission to extend its line from Tlalnepantla into Mexico City. Built on what was mostly abandoned causeways across the great lake which was now almost dry, the line ran a few blocks east of Calzada Vallejo until it crossed Avenida Insurgentes Norte and terminated at the Peralvillo station of the Hidalgo y Nordeste. Actually the passenger service was more of a tramcar operation than a conventional train on a private right of way. The bulk of the passenger service was handled by nine gasoline motorcars and two Baldwin steam cars which hauled trailers.

This was little known by tourists and was not listed in any Official Guide since it was purely a local operation. At the end of World War II the highway to Progreso Industrial had been sufficiently improved to warrant abandonment of the railroad, and the expansion of bus lines within the limits of suburban Mexico City quickly doomed this short line.

MONTERREY MINERAL & TERMINAL RAILWAY, 3-foot gauge

Built in 1894 and 1895 between Monterrey and San Pedro, in the State of Nuevo Leon, this connected the mines at San Pedro with the smelters in Monterrey. It was owned by the Mexican Lead Co. and in 1899 was bought by the Mexican Metallurgical Co., at which time the name was changed to Mexican Mineral Railway. Though primarily an industrial belt line, it provided two passenger trains each way daily between Smelter No. 3 in Monterrey, through the city to San Pedro, 12.4 miles. In January 1903 it was announced that standard gauging of the line would take place at once, for the Mexican National with which it connected had already been standard gauged past Monterrey. By March 1903 it had been standard gauged and soon disappeared from view as an industrial line with no public interest.

F. C. OAXACA A EJUTLA, 3-foot gauge

This was the third and last railroad built by Luis Garcia Teruel. At the time he received a concession in November 1898 there was no railroad south of Oaxaca. By building a railroad south to Ejutla a great deal of agricultural produce could be transported to Oaxaca and turned over to the Mexican Southern, which had refused to take any interest in extending its line south of Oaxaca at that time. Work began on the grading in 1899, Garcia Teruel supplying all the labor and materials as was his custom and in January 1901 the track had been laid 24 miles to Ocotlan, reaching Ejutla, 43 miles from Oaxaca in June 1902. A branch from the station of Teruel to Zimatlan, two miles, was also built at that time. Besides the single locomotive Garcia Teruel had bought from the Mexican Southern in 1899, he received two new Baldwin Consolidations in 1902 and these three locomotives served the road for the rest of its life.

Soon the feud between Garcia Teruel and the Mexican Southern which had caused him to reroute his Tlacotepec a Huajuapan de Leon in 1903 spread south of Oaxaca, and in 1904 the Mexican Southern began construction of a branch which roughly paralled the Oaxaca a Ejutla for most of its length, crossing the latter at Ocotlan and ending at Taviche, 35 miles from Oaxaca. Garcia Teruel held his ground in spite of the competition, but was forced to close down when the contending armies made a battlefield out of the area south of Oaxaca in 1914. Service was restored after the revolution, but in 1931 the railroad gave up the struggle and was abandoned. Today the main highway from Oaxaca south to Puerto Angel follows the line of the Oaxaca a Ejutla all the way between the last two cities.

PANUCO MOUNTAIN & MONCLOVA RAILROAD, 3-foot gauge

Located in the State of Coahuila, it extended from the city of Monclova, on the main line of the Mexican International a distance of 37 miles. Chartered in Texas December 5, 1907 by the Continental Mining Co., it was completed in 1908. Due to the heavy grades west of Monclova, sometimes exceeding 6%, the line was reminiscent of the Uintah Railway in Colorado and likewise used Shay geared locomotives, a rarity on any common carrier which provided passenger service. The Panuco Mining Co. took over the operation in 1910, and the 1914 disorders caused all operations to cease. The American Smelting & Refining Co. took over operation of the railroad and mines in 1917 but returned them to the owners after World War I. The railroad was closed down and stood unmaintained during the 1920s, its equipment stored and its rails rusting away. In 1931 the track was pulled up and the company went out of existence.

F. C. PARRAL Y DURANGO, 3-foot gauge

The Hidalgo Mining Co. of Pittsburgh, Pennsylvania acquired silver and gold claims in the States of Durango and Chihuahua in 1898 and obtained a concession to build a railroad to connect these claims with the city of Parral, Chihuahua and the Mexican Central Railroad. Headed by Samuel E. Gill of Pittsburgh, the work was begun in the summer of 1899, a standard gauge railroad seven miles long being completed between Parral and Minas Nuevas, where the largest of the claims were being worked. From Minas Nuevas to Rincon on this standard gauge track, a third rail was laid. From Rincon south to La Mesa de Sandia, a 42-mile, 3-foot gauge line was built. Completed in January 1902, the narrow gauge section was operated by six locomotives and provided daily passenger service. A locomotive was leased from the Mexican Central to work the standard gauge line.

In 1908 an additional 16 miles was built south of La Mesa de Sandia to new silver mines at Paraje Seco with a later extension for a short distance south to another mining claim. The line was prosperous for many years, with a short period between 1914 and 1916 when no mining could be carried on in the Parral district. In 1916 when General Pershing and a force of the U. S. Army pursued Pancho Villa after his raid on Douglas, Arizona, they went as far south as Parral but failed to locate the elusive Mexican general.

Mining activities decreased during the period in the 1930s when the price of silver became very low, and in 1944 the railroad was abandoned. Its equipment was in such good condition that all of it was sold to various sugar plantations in the State of Vera Cruz, some of it remaining in service in 1968.

POTOSI CENTRAL RAILROAD, 30-inch gauge

Built from Los Charcos, state of San Luis Potosi, on the Mexican National, to Tiro General, 11 miles. Laid with 30-pound steel rail, it opened May 22, 1904. Besides carrying gold- and silver-bearing quartz from the mines to the stamp mills and smelter, it brought charcoal to the smelters and carried passengers as a common carrier. Since the grades were not heavy, Porter Forney type saddle tankers handled the trains. Closed in 1914 by the revolution, mining was resumed in 1917 and the line was standard gauged.

F. C. POTOSI Y RIO VERDE, 3-foot gauge

Like the Parral & Durango, this was primarily a mining railroad, but was a common carrier and furnished passenger service of sorts during its existence. It was built in 1899 and 1900 by the Cia. Metalurgica Mexicana, a U. S. corporation controlled by the American Smelting & Refining Co.

The 3-burro-power streetcar at Tequila, Jalisco, was almost at the end of its career when photographed in 1947; it was soon abandoned as unserviceable and not worth repairing, but the track was used for occasional flatcars loaded with barrels of Tequila headed for the S. P. of Mexico station. *(L. T. Haug)*

Mexico City pleasure seekers of the late 1890s rode the 2-foot gauge F. C. Tacubaya to Tacubaya Park. The line had the smallest 4-4-0 ever built by Baldwin for commercial use. The "maquinista" of the locomotive below is tiny even for such a diminutive engine. *(Everett L. DeGolyer, Jr., collection)*

Popocatepetl dominates the skyline over the village of Chalma past which a San Rafael Paper Co. train, still under steam in 1965, is heading for the mill on rails of the old San Rafael & Atlixco. Potosi & Rio Verde No. 4 approaches the summit of the 3% grade en route from San Luis Potosi to Ahuacatal. *(Above: H. F. Stewart; below: L. T. Haug)*

The mines were located at San Pedro, 14 miles southeast of the city of San Luis Potosi. To supply the smelter, which was built in San Luis Potosi, a branch was constructed from San Pedro Junction, nine miles from the smelter, to Alvarez, 25 miles and to Ahuacatal, four miles beyond Alvarez. This branch tapped a large forested area which was rich in timber, for the mines and for the charcoal pits, and lime rock, for the smelter. Mixed train service was provided several days a week as far as Alvarez and Canon Verde, the latter 36 miles from San Luis Potosi. In this distance the railroad climbed from 6166 feet at San Luis Potosi to 8550 feet at Ahuacatal, with many grades of from 2 to 3 percent and a switchback at milepost 27. A Shay-geared engine was used on the Alvarez branch for many years, all locomotives using wood as fuel until 1924 when they were converted to burn oil.

A ride over this line from San Luis Potosi to Alvarez and return was one of the best and most scenic in Mexico, especially when riding in the ancient passenger coach which had been bought secondhand from the Mexican National in 1900. In its last years the passengers had to ride in the caboose, as the coach became unsafe to use. In 1952 the railroad was abandoned and its two serviceable locomotives were sold to the Chihuahua Mineral Railway.

F. C. SAN GREGORIO, 3-foot gauge

Built in 1901 from the junction point of Marfil, on the Mexican Central's Salao-Guanajuato branch, to mines at El Chorro and El Mineral de San Gregorio, a total of 19 miles. Passenger service was furnished and the railroad was listed as a common carrier until 1904, when the railroad was purchased by the Mexican National with the idea of using the roadbed for part of a new line connecting Gonzalez Junction with Guanajuato. This idea was quickly given up and the railroad was sold to Eusebia Rojas, who operated it until 1914 when the mines closed down, never again to reopen.

F. C. SAN RAFAEL Y ATLIXCO, 3-foot gauge

This ambitious project was built as the Xico y San Rafael, designed to furnish pulpwood to the Fabrica del Papel de San Rafael (San Rafael Paper Co.) in an effort to make Mexico independent of foreign paper suppliers. The first concession was granted on March 23, 1898 to build a 3-foot gauge railroad from Mexico City to Chalco, to buy an animal-powered railroad already in existence from Chalco to Amecameca and to build a new railroad from Amecameca to Atlixco, the latter place being on the other side of the great mountain range of which the volcanoes Ixtaccihuatl and Popocatepetl were the peaks. West of Atlixco, on the Interoceanic 28 miles south of Puebla, were large stands of timber, while other great forests covered the route of the proposed line around the south perimeter of Popocatepetl. Whereas the Interoceanic south of Amecameca descended from an altitude of 8050 feet to 4265 feet at Cuautla, the Xico y San Rafael was surveyed to run at about 8000 feet as it covered a semi-circle around Popocatepetl, gradually dropping down to 5100 feet at Atlixco.

An area of several city blocks south of Calzada de San Antonio Abad, a mile southwest of San Lazaro Station in Mexico City was walled in and equipped with warehouses, a station and facilities for locomotive repair. The line was built south from this station through the Colonia Obrera section of the city, then east across a rolling countryside to Chalco, where it crossed the Interoceanic. Using the roadbed of the old horse railroad from Chalco to Amecameca, the track was laid with 45-pound steel to a summit above Ozumba at an altitude of 8200 feet, then south on a level grade to Apapasco, 69 miles from Mexico City. A one-mile branch was built from Zavetla to the town of San Rafael where the paper mill was erected. On the other side of the mountains, the grade had been built from Atlixco west to Metepec, a distance of six miles, leaving a gap of 35 miles to complete the railroad from Mexico City to Atlixco. This gap involved some heavy grades and expensive construction, with thousands of degrees of curvature required to cross the dozens of small streams which had their sources in the snow-covered upper cone of Popocatepetl. Having already tapped considerable stands of suitable trees south of Ozumba, work on the tieline between the two sections ceased early in 1902. The money had also run out and the company went into receivership.

It was reorganized as the Mexican Great Eastern Railroad on April 11, 1902, the new owners announcing ambitious plans to complete the railroad and even extend it to Coatzacoalcos on the Gulf of Mexico in competition with the Interoceanic. Like its predecessors, the Mexican Great Eastern could not pay the fixed charges and hence a new company, the F. C. San Rafael y Atlixco* emerged on November 19, 1903. Passenger service had been inaugurated between Mexico City and Apapasco as soon as the railroad reached that town, but the new company furnished service only as far as Ozumba, 53 miles from Mexico City. The Interoceanic was ten miles shorter between the two points, but the running time on either railroad was about the same. In 1903 the Interoceanic completed its connecting link between Cuautla and Atencingo, removing some of the incentive to rush completion of the San Rafael y Atlixco. Pulpwood was brought from Atlixco to Amecameca over the Interoceanic, but the paper company was determined to have its own independent operation, and by 1908 had completed twenty miles of railroad from Atlixco to the town of Yancuitlalpan, leaving a gap of less than 15 miles to Apapasco. This section was through a region of deep forests and many canyons; after estimating the cost of completing the railroad and considering it excessive, the paper company cancelled any plans to build the connecting link and for many years the orphan section out of Atlixco supplied additional pulpwood for the mill, with the Interoceanic hauling it nearly 120 miles to Amecameca.

Operation of the railroad from Mexico City to Apapasco was turned over to Jose Moctezum who had a contract with the owners to keep the railroad in repair, provide passenger and freight service and to pay a monthly rental of 10,000 pesos. Moctezum provided passenger service only as far as Amecameca, the line to Apapasco being only for freight trains after 1908. In 1910 a 2-foot gauge railroad was built by the paper company from Apapasco into the forests at higher altitudes, this railroad being powered by a small two-truck Shay, the mill at Apapasco serving only to cut the logs into the short sections required for paper manufacture. Somehow the line struggled through the revolution with occasional shutdowns. Rail motors were used in lieu of steam hauled passenger trains in the 1920s and after World War II the paper company placed the railroad in liquidation, since it had become a liability. The section from the mill at San Rafael to Amecameca, a distance of five miles was taken over by the paper company as an industrial spur and two of the road's locomotives were assigned to this branch. The industrial trackage and warehouses at Mexico City were operated as the Ferrocarril Anahuac, with two more locomotives assigned to this section. This road proved to be one of the most elusive of all narrow gauge lines in the Mexico City area, as the locomotives worked only at night and remained locked up all day behind the bars of the compound.

The section from Atlixco to Metepec, a distance of six miles was sold to the Cia. Industrial de Atlixco in the 1930s, and the rest of that line was abandoned. When visited in 1961 by Harold Stewart, the manager told him the railroad had not been used in thirty years but was being preserved intact in case the Interoceanic was standard gauged from Puebla to Atlixco. In the weeds and in the enginehouse at Metepec were the remains of two steam locomotives, part of the fleet of nine which the San Rafael y Atlixco once owned. The rest of the latter road was pulled up gradually as labor was available, the rolling stock sold or scrapped and the F. C. Anahuac and its walled compound were abandoned in 1963. Today the sole surviving section is the branch from the paper mill to Amecameca, which as of 1968 has two steam locomotives in service, one recently purchased from the Nacional de Mexico.

F. C. DE TACUBAYA, 2-foot gauge

This tiny short line was located entirely within Mexico City and boasted of having the smallest 4-4-0 locomotive ever built by Baldwin for commercial purposes. Weighing only six tons, it was smaller than similar locomotives used today in Disneyland. The railroad was built by Fernando de Teresa in 1896, from a horse-tram line in the Tacubaya district of Mexico City to an amusement park one mile distant. With a German-built locomotive, the 4-4-0 hauled trains in the streets leading to the park until 1910, when the railroad became a part of Mexico Tramways and was converted to standard gauge electric operation. No trace of the locomotives has ever been found on

*See map page 174

Animal power continued in use for local narrow gauge transportation at San Juan del Rio, state of Queretaro, until the mid-1940s. Shown at the right are the passenger and freight trains waiting near the N. de M. station. *(David J. Welch)*

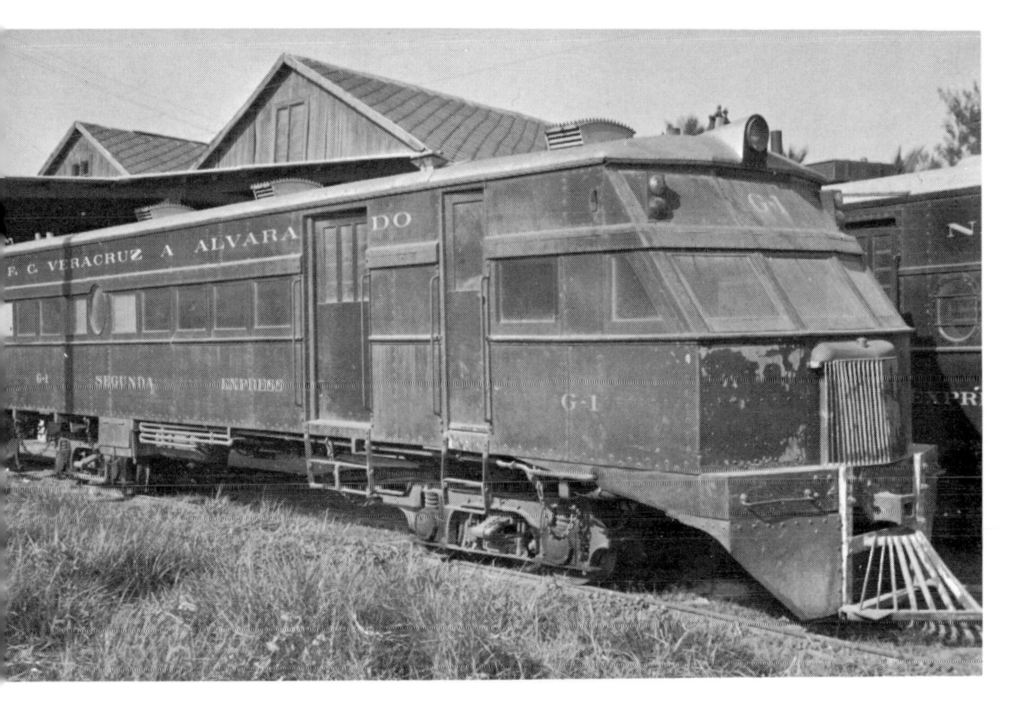

Motor car G-1 of the F.C.V.A. was phased out when the line was standard gauged in 1948, a year after this photo was made at Vera Cruz. The magnificent mountain setting of San Rafael is pictured below as San Rafael Paper Co.'s No. 5 approaches the handsome factory there. *(Two pictures, L. T. Haug)*

other 2-foot lines in Mexico, but they could very well have gone to any one of a dozen sugar plantation railroads of that gauge.

F. C. TOLUCA Y ZITACUARO, 3-foot gauge

Chartered December 10, 1904, this railroad was built from Zitacuaro, in the State of Michoacan and at the terminus of the Michoacan & Pacific, to Xocomusco, a distance of 25 miles. It was designed to exploit a large timber district and operated as an industrial line until closed in 1914 by the revolution. Reopened in 1917, it furnished passenger service as a common carrier from Zitacuaro to Los Cedros, 15 miles, the lines beyond the latter place continuing only as a logging railroad. A very old Shay-geared locomotive purchased secondhand in 1908, and a new Climax acquired in that year were used for the lumbering operation and an old Mexican National Ten Wheeler hauled the trains from Los Cedros to Zitacuaro. The line was abandoned shortly after the Zitacuaro branch of the Nacional de Mexico was standard gauged in 1949, and as recently as 1962, Harold Stewart saw and photographed three of the road's locomotives, including the Shay and the Climax, standing abandoned in a field near where the railroad's terminal once stood.

F. C. TOLUCA A TENANGO Y SAN JUAN, 3-foot gauge

Parts of this railroad were among the oldest in the country, the first one being built in 1883 on what had previously been an animal-powered line. Toluca is the first city of any size west of Mexico City, on the Mexican National's line to Acambaro and is in a beautiful valley at an altitude of 8761 feet, over 900 feet higher than Mexico City. It is a valley of great haciendas, particularly to the south and west of the city. In August 1883 three owners of these haciendas, Arcadio Henkel, Augustin del Rio and Eduardo Vinas began construction of a 3-foot gauge steam railroad west from Toluca towards the town of San Juan, ten miles distant, as an extension of an existing horse railroad. Some opposition having developed to operating steam locomotives in the streets of Toluca, horses and mules were used until 1889 when Henkel bought a steam locomotive from the Porter Manufacturing Co. and demonstrated that it could be used primarily for freight hauling without disrupting the peace and quiet of Toluca. In 1891 Henkel extended the railroad to San Juan and through the years the railroad proved very useful to Senor Henkel, whose Hacienda de Solis covered a vast area south of San Juan. At one time his road had five locomotives in service, with frequent passenger trains between the two terminals.

In 1891 after the death of Arcadio Henkel, his widow and her two sons obtained a concession to build a railroad from Toluca to Tenango, southeast of the city. Before the railroad could be built, Senora Henkel died and her two sons continued the business under the name of Henkel Brothers. In 1895 they began construction of the railroad, reaching Metepec in that year, Tenango, 18.5 miles from Toluca in 1897, and Alta, a mile further in 1900. Motive power for this line was exclusively Baldwin-built. The two roads had operated as separate companies, the Toluca y San Juan and the Toluca y Tenango until 1906 when they were combined under one name. The stations of the two lines were located on opposite sides of Toluca, a mule-operated tram line connecting the two terminals and serving as a means of hauling freight cars, since locomotives were prohibited on the Avenida Independencia.

Like all other narrow gauge railroads of this type in Mexico, the changes in the country during World War II, the development of better roads and the accompanying busses and trucks sounded the death knell of this interesting little railroad and all trace of it vanished in 1946.

F. C. TORRES A PRIETAS (MEXICAN UNION), 3-foot gauge

Built in 1897-99 as the F. C. Torres, Prietas y Represo under a concession granted March 9, 1897, from the station of Torres on the F. C. de Sonora, (later the S.P. of Mexico), to newly opened mines at Minas Prietas, it was ten miles long. As a fairly large town grew around the mines, passenger service was provided, the trains being hauled by Baldwin 4-4-0s bought secondhand from the Denver & Rio Grande. Rabid Rio Grande aficionados have been hunting these locomotives ever since, but after reading this condensed history they will know why their search has been fruitless.

The company dropped the name "Represo" from the end of the title in the early 1900s, and in 1910 a British company bought out the Mexican and American owners, changing the road's name to Mexican Union Railway, Ltd. The new owners extended the railroad 30 miles to Santa Rosalia where additional mines began operation. Efforts were made to keep the mines open during the revolution on a hit-and-run basis; the owners made a brave effort, for when temporary peace was secured in 1916, they reopened the mines to full operation. Six months later the mines were closed down altogether, but the owners left the railroad in charge of J. T. Symonds who had managed it since it was built, with instructions to hold the concession and operate at least one train a week over the line. This must have been extremely difficult, for in 1926 Rodney Long reports that due to washouts at various places along the line, Symonds was able to operate a train only as far as Prietas, and that his only employees besides himself were two boys and the conductor. Symonds soon gave up the struggle, and the entire railroad was abandoned. In 1946 Leonard T. Haug reported that all that was left of the Mexican Union at Torres, on the land where the enginehouse and shops once stood, were a few abandoned mine car trucks and some assorted scrap iron.

F. C. DEL VALLE DE MEXICO – (VALLEY OF MEXICO RAILWAY), 3-foot gauge

This is included in the list of common carrier narrow gauge railways in order to avoid confusion with the Desague del Valle de Mexico Railway. It was a suburban street railway operating for some distance on its own right of way, from the district of Atzcapotzalco north of Buena Vista Station in Mexico City, to the town of Tlalnepantla, about seven miles. The motive power consisted of four Baldwin steam dummies, hauling two trailers each. In 1895 the road was purchased by the Guggenheim Syndicate of New York together with most of the street railways of Mexico City, and became a part of Mexico Tramways Co. Though nearly all Mexico City street lines were electrified by 1910, the Tlalnepantla line remained steam operated until gasoline motor cars gradually replaced steam in the early 1920s. After World War II the railroad was abandoned in favor of busses.

F. C. VANEGAS, CEDRAL Y RIO VERDE, 3-foot gauge

This railroad, one of three narrow gauge short lines which were taken over by the Mexican National shortly before it was standard gauged, has been previously mentioned. It was built to provide access to the rich silver mining claims in the vicinity of the town of Matehuala in San Luis Potosi State, under a concession granted in 1889 at the time the Mexican National was completed. Starting at Vanegas, 120 miles south of Saltillo, the road was built through very rough, mountainous country and over heavy grades to the town of Matehuala, where the largest mines were located, 30 miles from Vanegas. To celebrate the arrival of the first train in Matehuala, which was hauled by a new Brooks 4-4-0 named in honor of the town, the locomotive was first christened by three priests, the crowd was served free champagne and beer and the celebration lasted far into the night. Passenger trains from Matehuala connected with the through trains at Vanegas and the line paid its way from the start. In 1896 a branch from Cedral to the mines at Potrero was built under a subsidy from the Mexican government. The F. C. Porvenir de Matehuala, previously outlined, served as the principal feeder of the road. Branches were added later to various new mines, and in 1901 the road name was changed to Vanegas, Cedral & Matehuala, and under this name it was purchased outright by the Mexican National on October 9, 1902. As soon as the main line of the latter was standard gauged, the track crews turned to the narrow gauge branches, and the Vanegas-Matehuala line change of gauge was completed March 25, 1904.

Today the Matehuala branch of the N. de M. has two mixed trains daily each way, and one can ride the same scenic route over which the engine MATEHUALA passed on its first run in 1891. If champagne and beer are desired at the end of the ride, you will have to pay for it.

F. C. VERA CRUZ A ANTON LIZARDO Y ALVARADO, 3-foot gauge

Organized March 25, 1878, this railroad was a pioneer of narrow gauge in Mexico. It was built over a very level terrain, not more than 15 feet above sea level, reaching Salinas, 32 miles from Vera Cruz, in 1882 and Alvarado, 44 miles in 1883. Nothing is known about the early rolling stock of this railroad; a new Baldwin 4-4-0 was ordered in 1882 as No. 1, and was photographed at Baldwin with the road's name on the tank, but the order was cancelled and the engine sold to the Florida Southern. It owned three locomotives during the 1883-1901 period, probably all British-built. In 1890 the name Anton Lizardo was dropped from the road's name and in 1895 the company acquired a standard gauge short line on the Isthmus of Tehuantepec called the San Juan a Juile, extending 15 miles from Juile on the Nacional de Tehuantepec to the town of San Juan Evangelista.

In 1901 the Vera Cruz Railway, Ltd. was organized by S. Pearson & Son of London who had completed the Nacional de Tehuantepec and its two seaports. It took over the Vera Cruz a Alvarado and the San Juan a Juile, leasing the latter to the N. de T. Operation of the narrow gauge line continued until the 1914 hostilities, at which time most of the rolling stock, buildings, the company records and the equipment were burned or destroyed. The San Juan a Juile fared even worse, as not a building or piece of equipment remained by 1915, although the tracks were still there. Its owners profited greatly by this railroad later, not because of its operating revenue, but due to the discovery of oil on lands belonging to the railroad.

The Vera Cruz a Alvarado was under government operation, when it could operate, between 1914 and 1920, but was returned to its owners at that time, continuing until February 1932 when it was sold to the National Railways of Mexico. It retained its identity as a separate company, however, and its equipment was lettered F.C.V.A. until the last of it was retired in the mid-1950s. One of its passenger cars operated on the Puente de Ixtla branch until 1957. The line was standard gauged in 1948 and today is the Alvarado branch of the National Railways of Mexico.

On a well-ballasted roadbed in austerely beautiful desert scenery, Potosi & Rio Verde No. 4 continues up the heavy grade towards Ahuacatal from San Luis Potosi. *(L. T. Haug)*

5

Principal Narrow Gauge Industrials

The total narrow gauge industrial trackage in Mexico at one time reached a peak of 5000 miles, almost all of it used to transport the products of sugar, mining, lumbering and hemp industries. The majority of the mileage was animal-powered and the gauge of most of these non-steam-powered lines was two feet. It is not possible to list all these railroads, nor all of those which used steam power, for lack of space and for the reason that many of them, long since abandoned have vanished from the records of the Mexican Government. A few of the industrial lines were still in operation after World War II and became familiar to many U.S. railfans who have visited Mexico and they will be described together with such of the others for which accurate data is available. Many of them had free passenger service, for the transport of employees to and from work, but they were not rated as common carriers, their time schedules did not appear in the Official Guide and with few exceptions were ignored by U. S. financial publications.

I was travelling west on the F. C. Mexicano's day train 15 years ago when, after pulling out of the town of Potrero, I became conscious of the sound of the exhaust of a steam locomotive, obviously not on our train for we were hauled by an electric locomotive. There to the right of the observation platform on the end of my train was a narrow gauge train going in our direction, and consisting of a couple of flats and three old flat-roofed passenger cars, all swarming with peons en route to the cane fields. At the head end was a Porter saddle tank locomotive, working hard for the grade was as steep as ours, and for a minute it kept pace with our slow crawl until we gained speed and pulled ahead; the narrow gauge track veered to the north until the little train disappeared into the cane fields. This was the plantation of the Potrero Sugar Co., and the company and the sugar mill were known as Ingenio El Potrero. It was one of many such plantations which were served by narrow gauge railroads, and like the fate of the sugar railroads in Louisiana and Hawaii, most of these railroads have been replaced with giant trucks which now haul the cane over roads to the mill. Gone too are most of the industrials described in this chapter.

F. C. ALAMO A ZAPOTAL, 2-foot gauge

Owned by the Petroleos Mexicanos, S.A., this railroad was built in the early 1930s to transport men and supplies to the oil fields at Alamo in the State of Vera Cruz. Laid with 40-pound rail, it started from Santiago de la Pena, a suburb of the city of Tuxpan, a few miles from the Gulf of Mexico and went due west to Alamo 13.5 miles. Motive power consisted of two Diesel locomotives, with employees and their families carried in five rail motors. After thirty years of operation it was recently abandoned in favor of trucks over newly paved highways.

F. C. BERISTAIN-NECAXA, 3-foot gauge

In 1903, engineers were commissioned by the Mexican Light & Power Co. to harness the Necaxa and Tenango Rivers, which ran parallel to each other a few miles apart, on their way from the central plateau of Mexico to the Gulf in a series of waterfalls and rapids. The Tenango River was diverted through a long tunnel to the Rio Necaxa; below this tunnel at the apex of a waterfall, a great dam was built to create a lake which covered three villages under 125 feet of water. Both the dam and the hydroelectric plant were placed under contract in 1903 and supplies at first were hauled over the wagon road from Santiago, on the Hidalgo y Nordeste, to the site of the dam. This proved to be too slow for the contractors and in 1904, a 3-foot gauge railroad was built from Beris-

Beristain-Necaxa No. 2, one of the two Porter saddle tankers used to switch carloads of supplies at the dam site of the Mexican Light & Power Co. at Necaxa, is still in occasional use there. *(L. T. Haug)*

Typical of many Baldwin industrial narrow gauge engines shipped to Mexico was No. 2 of the Monterrey Steel Co., right. The Shay below is one of the last of its breed in Mexico. TONA LA NEGRA No. 5 of the Beristain-Necaxa, named after a popular Mexican entertainer, was used to haul supply trains up the 6% grades, and is still occasionally used between the dam and Salto Chico. *(Right: Herbert L. Broadbelt collection; below: Harold F. Stewart)*

tain, terminal of the Hidalgo y Nordeste, to the dam site at Necaxa, a distance of 23 miles. The ruling grade exceeded 6% and there were curves of 55-foot radius, requiring locomotives of very short wheel base. Three Shay-geared Limas of 33 tons and two 16-ton Porter saddle tankers filled the bill and in five years hauled all the supplies to the dam site. The railroad was also extended from the dam to the town of Nuevo Necaxa and today, only this four-mile section is still in existence. A Whitcomb gasoline locomotive and rail cars transport employees from the town to the hydroelectric plant and dam; one each of the Shays and saddle tankers have been retained for occasional use when heavy machinery is to be hauled from the highway at Nueva Necaxa to the power plant.

COMPANIA DEL BOLEO—CIA. MINERA DE SANTA ROSALIA, S.A., 3-foot gauge

The isolated and seldom visited narrow gauge railroad is located in the mining town of Santa Rosalia, on the Gulf of California in Baja California South Territory, 400 airline miles south of Tijuana. In 1884, large deposits of copper ore were discovered in the hills back of Santa Rosalia, and a French company called the Compagnie du Boleo was organized to exploit the find. A narrow gauge railroad five miles in length was built from the mine to a smelter located a short distance from the harbor, and docks were built so that ocean-going ships could carry the finished copper ingots across the gulf to the port of Guaymas in Sonora. Though the rolling stock was brought from France, a total of eight Baldwin saddle tankers were purchased between 1886 and 1901, and these 19-ton workhorses hauled the ore and the finished product for nearly fifty years, until a cableway from the mine entrance down the side of the mountain to a dump a mile from the smelter replaced the sharp curves and steep grades of the railroad.

After construction of the cableway, the company name was changed to Ferrocarril y Cablevia Aereo de la Compania del Boleo, S.A., and though rail operations were reduced to about two miles, all told, at least two locomotives were in daily use. The shop building at Santa Rosalia was a veritable museum when the late Richard V. Dodge visited it in the spring of 1958, for inside were two of the Baldwin switchers undergoing repairs, two more were out of service, a third pair were actively working the yards, and the ruins of the other engines showed the result of cannibalizing to keep the active engines running. The locomotives had no air or vacuum brakes, the *maquinista* using a hand brake on the center pair of drivers, while brakemen manned the ore cars and applied hand brakes on whistled instructions from the *maquinista.* Though the engines were equipped with one injector, they also had a crosshead pump which was in regular use. These and the locomotives in Yucatan were the only engines so equipped in Mexico in modern times.

A Mexican company known as Cia. Minera Santa Rosalia, S.A., bought out the French company after World War II, and continues to operate the mines, with an output of nearly 200,000 tons of finished copper a year. The wharf has become too rickety to permit trainloads of blister copper to go from the smelter to the ships, this now being handled by trucks, but one locomotive continues in daily service around the smelter. Manager Ranc assures the writer that with their maintenance force so efficient and with plenty of spare parts on hand, at least one steam locomotive will continue to run at Santa Rosalia for many years to come.

CANANEA CONSOLIDATED COPPER CO., 3-foot gauge

The narrow gauge railroad of this company is located at Cananea, State of Sonora, at the end of a branch of the Ferrocarril del Pacifico which runs from Naco, Arizona to Cananea. The mines were opened in 1901 by the Greene Consolidated Copper Co., later known as the Greene Cananea Copper Co., which was in turn controlled by the Anaconda Copper Co. of New York. The narrow gauge railroad was built in 1900 and consisted of 11.6 miles of main line between the mines and the smelter, with 7.5 miles of branches. Motive power consisted of nine 2-6-2 saddle tank engines built in the U.S., and they were required to negotiate grades up to 5%. A standard gauge railroad was built 39 miles from the smelter to Naco, Arizona in 1902, sold in 1904 to a subsidiary of the Southern Pacific and today, the F. C. del Pacifico.

No. 7 of the Cia. Minera de Santa Rosalia in Baja California, built in 1899, is a fine testimonial to the maker's slogan years ago, that Baldwin locomotives never wear out. It is still in service in 1968. *(Richard V. Dodge)*

The narrow gauge railroad is not a common carrier and only the employees of the company can ride the trains. Steam was replaced by Diesel locomotives in 1962, there being only four steam locomotives left at the time of the changeover.

F. C. CARDENAS A RIO GRIJALVA, 3-foot gauge

This is a very old animal-powered railroad, built by Policarpo Valenzuela under a concession granted January 18, 1883. It connected the town of Cardenas in the southwestern part of the State of Tabasco with Nueva Xelandria, a village on the left bank of the Rio Grijalva, 4½ miles from Cardenas. The river was navigable to light draught steamers and the railroad was built to carry passengers and freight, three mules providing the motive power for each train. The lone passenger car was of the open type, seating fifty passengers; the running time between terminals was forty minutes, barely faster than a walk. The railroad continued in operation until 1960 as a public service, until a new highway from Coatzacoalcos to Villa Hermosa paralleled the railroad and eliminated any reason to continue passenger service, though the line is still used for freight.

F. C. CELAYA A SAN ROQUE Y SANTA CRUZ, 2-foot gauge

This was probably the longest animal-powered narrow gauge railroad in Mexico, for it extended from the Mexican Central Ry. station at Celaya Junction to San Roque, 3.7 miles and another 14.5 miles from there to Santa Cruz. Built in 1893, it never had steam power at any time; the usual line-up at the head end was a trio of mules. The road owned twenty flatcars, which carried a considerable amount of freight during the sixty years of the road's existence, while the dilapidated open passenger car was a familiar sight at Celaya station until abandonment came in 1953.

F. C. MINERAL DE CHIHUAHUA (CHIHUAHUA MINERAL RAILWAY), 3-foot gauge

This very well known industrial narrow gauge railroad has been visited by many U.S. railfans in the past twenty years. Built by E. C. Creel and F. Duclos in 1899, it conveyed ore from the mines in the vicinity of Santa Eulalia, to the smelter outside the city of Chihuahua in the state of that name. Chihuahua is at an altitude of 3500 feet, the 13½ mile railroad climbing to 6000 feet for an average grade of almost 200 feet per mile. Since the loaded cars always came downgrade except for supplies for the mines, it was no problem for a locomotive to bring a heavy consist down to the smelter and haul the empties back to the mine. Passenger service was provided only for employees and the line was at no time considered a common carrier. Though it never had more than four locomotives in service at one time, it owned nine locomotives over a span of 69 years. This railroad was the scene of a terrible mishap in 1906 when a boxcar full of dynamite was being unloaded at Santa Eulalia. A careless handler

Two General Electric 30-inch gauge road engines haul a string of empty ore cars from the smelter in Chihuahua to the mines at Santa Eulalia, in 1962. Half a century earlier, the late Everett DeGolyer photographed the British-built SAN MARCOS of the F. C. Cobos a Furbero in a tropical setting near Tuxpan on the Gulf coast between Tampico and Vera Cruz. *(Above: H. F. Stewart; below: E. L. DeGolyer, Jr., collection)*

dropped a box of the explosive, blew himself to kingdom come and killed forty of his fellow workmen who were within range of the explosion.

In the early 1930s this company came under the control of American Smelting & Refining Co., and today the company is known as Asarco Mexicana, S.A. Steam is still used on the Chihuahua Mineral Railway, one being a Porter Consolidation built for the company in 1926 and the other three are secondhand Baldwin Consolidations. To provide steam for firing up the narrow gauge engines, a standard gauge Consolidation stands outside the enginehouse, a relic of the El Paso & Southwestern, purchased by Asarco in 1916.

F. C. CHORRERAS–TOTECO, 3-foot gauge

This line was built during 1920 and 1921 by International Petroleum Co., between the seaport of Tamiahua at the southern end of the Tamiahua Lagoon in the State of Vera Cruz, to the oil fields at Zacamixtle, a distance of twenty miles. The railroad was originally jointly owned by the Tidemex Oil Co., which sold its interest in the line to International Petroleum Co. in 1922. The original motive power was one Davenport 0-4-0T, later supplemented by seven Milwaukee gasoline powered locomotives. Laid with 40-pound rail, the line ran from sea level to an altitude of 185 feet, a 4½% ruling grade over an intervening hill giving a roller-coaster effect at one point in the journey. Only employees were carried as passengers and the road's rolling stock consisted of fifty freight cars, mostly flats. Mexican highway No. 180, recently completed, has eliminated this railroad.

F. C. COBOS A FURBERO, 2-foot gauge

This railroad was named after Percy Furber, an English oil explorer who pioneered the discovery of oil in Mexico. Built by the Oil Fields of Mexico, S.A. in 1913, it was soon sold to Cia. Mexicana de Petroleo, El Aguila, S.A. (Mexican Eagle Oil Co.). Extending 54 miles from Cobos in a southerly direction, to the oil fields at Palma Sola and Furbero, the grade is practically water-level throughout its length. Cobos is three miles from the city of Tuxpan on the Gulf of Mexico. The early motive power consisted of four British-built tank locomotives with four-wheel tenders, supplemented by two Davenport saddle tankers in later years. Five Kalamazoo gasoline rail cars haul the employees. In 1924 the first Diesel locomotive was introduced and by 1945 all steam had been eliminated. As of 1962, the date of the last visit, it was still in operation.

COLIMA LUMBER CO. RAILWAY, 3-foot gauge

In 1910 the Colima Lumber Co. built a 35-mile railroad from the city of Colima, on the N. de M.'s Guadalajara-Manzanillo line, to timber lands on the lower slopes of Colima volcano, at Sierra Grande. Powered by two Shay-geared locomotives, this line was shut down in 1914 due to the revolution, much of the track being destroyed. For many years only traces of this railroad could be seen due to this destruction, though the equipment remained stored at Colima in good condition. As of 1945 nothing had been done to reactivate the railroad, and it has disappeared from the records of the Mexican government.

CONCHOS RAILWAY (F. C. MINERA DE NAICA), 30-inch gauge

Built between 1900 and 1902 by the Cia. Minera de Conchos, S.A., between the town of Concho, on the Mexican Central seventy miles south of the city of Chihuahua, to the silver mines at Naica, 19 miles distant. Motive power for the main line consisted of three Baldwin Mikado type locomotives weighing less than twenty tons, with two Porter Forney types at the mine yards. Like all other mining railroads, the Conchos Railway was closed down in 1914 by the activities of the revolutionaries, who were particularly destructive in the state of Chihuahua. It reopened in 1920 when it was purchased by the Cia. Minera de Penoles, the Mexican subsidiary of the American Metals Co. It owned a passenger car used for hauling employees and was never listed as a common carrier. Shortly after the end of World War II the mines were abandoned, the railroad removed and not even a passable road exists in the area today.

FERROCARRIL CUSI, 3-foot gauge

Owned by the Cusihuirichic Mining Co., in the town of Cusihuirichic, State of Chihuahua, the railroad was built in 1908. Extending four miles from the mines to a small smelter, it owned one German-built locomotive. Cusihuirichic is on a

The Chihuahua Mineral Railway had not yet removed the initials of the Potosi & Rio Verde from 2-8-0 No. 2 when it was photographed in March 1968, approaching Santa Eulalia with a train of empty ore cars. *(H. F. Stewart)*

Rocking chairs were provided for visiting brass on the inspection car NINA of the F. C. Cobos a Furbero when the late Everett L. DeGolyer photographed it in 1911, above. The steam crane in the distance resembles a rocket launcher. General Electric 30-inch gauge switcher No. 5, when photographed near San Guillermo in 1968, is lettered for its government-owned operator. *(Above: E. L. DeGolyer, Jr., collection; below: H. F. Stewart)*

branch of the Chihuahua y Pacifico, 14 miles south of the town of Cuauhtemoc, which is in turn 83 miles west of Chihuahua. This mine was still in operation in 1949 but the writer has been unable to learn if the railroad exists today.

CIA. INDUSTRIAL Y AZUCARERA, S.A., 3-foot and standard gauge

A modern sugar plantation was established by the above company after World War I, located in the State of Vera Cruz near the town of Acayucan, sixty miles southeast of the city of Alvarado. Narrow gauge steam locomotives are used in the sugar cane hauling operations, and a standard gauge line connects the mill with the Nacional de Mexico. All the locomotives are secondhand except one German-built engine, and the railroad is operated during the cane season in the winter and spring. It is one of the few 100% steam operations left in Mexico in 1968.

F. C. IXTACCIHUATL, 3-foot gauge

This short line connected with the Interoceanic at San Martin Texmelucan on its Puebla-Mexico City line via San Lorenzo. Built in 1898, it extended 11.6 miles to San Juan Tetla at the foot of the mountain for which it was named. Its owners were Alfredo King and Julio Blumenkron of Puebla. The original motive power was a British-built saddle tank locomotive bought secondhand from the Interoceanic. The principal traffic over the line was timber from the forests along the base of the mountain, so it was a certain target for the revolutionaries in 1911. Closed until 1920 and the locomotive having been destroyed, mules were used as motive power, the railroad continuing in service until its abandonment in 1956.

LA DICHA & PACIFIC RAILROAD, 3-foot gauge

This railroad was surveyed over a route which had already been laid out years before by the Interoceanic from the port of San Marques on the Bay of Acapulco to mines and timberlands in Bravo Acapulco, in the vicinity of Chilpancingo in the state of Guerrero. Organized in 1902 by George Mitchell as the La Dicha Mining & Smelting Co., an Arizona corporation, the company had financial troubles from the start and was quickly reorganized as the Mitchell Mining Co. of New York. Construction on the railroad continued from 1904 through 1906, a total of 27 miles of track being laid over rough terrain. Three locomotives and a number of cars were purchased from the Atlantic Equipment Co. and landed from ships at Port San Marques. Another locomotive was purchased from the Southern Pacific's former South Pacific Coast narrow gauge line but was not paid for and stood derelict on Alameda mole for years before it was sold to the Nevada County Narrow Gauge. The mines were profitable for a few years, but the timberlands belonging to the company were not developed, and after paying dividends through 1906, the company ceased construction on the railroad, and mine operations ceased in 1908. The railroad was taken up, and today all that remains of it are a few scars in the hillsides along the modern highway near Acapulco.

MICHOACAN LUMBER & DEVELOPMENT CO., 3-foot gauge

When the Mexican National branch from Acambaro to Uruapan reached the latter place in 1899, an American company of the above name was organized to tap the extensive forests of Michoacan. Read & Campbell, builders of the Patzcuaro-Uruapan branch of the Mexican National built a 3-foot gauge line from Paranguitiro, 32 miles north of Uruapan for a total of 45 miles to the various lumber mills which were set up at strategic locations. Except for one engine, all locomotives were of the geared type. The first Heisler locomotive ever built, used by Read & Campbell on construction projects from 1895, was sold to this lumber railroad which continued in operation until 1914.

At that time, most of the line, the mills and the equipment were destroyed by the revolutionists, and the railroad was never reopened.

MOCTEZUMA COPPER CO. (F. C. DE LA MINA), 3-foot gauge

Located at Moctezuma, near Nacozari, State of Sonora, this railroad serves mines owned by the Phelps Dodge Corporation. Built in 1898, the railroad is six miles long, and connects the mine with the smelter. With a ruling grade of nearly 4.5%, the line was laid with 60- and 80-lb. steel rail, has two tunnels and a long steel viaduct on its main

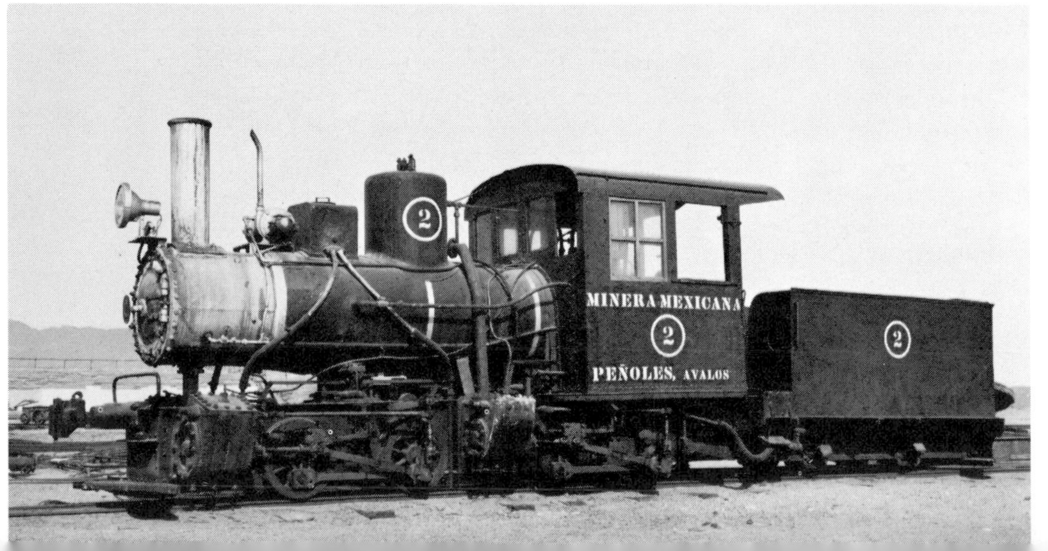

The tiny German-built Mallet compound No. 2 is still an interesting and unique attraction on the nine mile long 2-foot gauge Cia. Minera de Penoles-Avalos. *(Henry Bender)*

Electric road engines lettered “F. C. M. de Chih. S. A.” haul a train of empties up the hill to the Santo Domingo mines. Below, Chihuahua Mineral Railway No. 4 brings its string of empties uphill towards Santa Eulalia mines. *(Left: Donald Duke; below: Stan Kistler)*

line, providing a short but spectacular trip. Powered with Porter saddle tank locomotives in the early days, its later equipment included two heavy Baldwin Consolidations. Although it is only a few miles from the Arizona border this railroad has been little known to U. S. railfans.

FERROCARRIL OGARRIO, 3-foot gauge

This line was built under a concession granted August 22, 1896, for a railroad from Catorce, in the state of San Luis Potosi, to Potrero in the mining district of Matehuala. At first it used animal power, but the grades were so steep that in 1904, two Shay-geared Limas were purchased and these were used until the shutdown of all mines in 1914. When operations were resumed in 1920, the locomotives had apparently been destroyed, as the use of animal power was resumed and continued until closure of the mines during the 1930-35 depression.

F. C. OTUMBA A CUAUHTENGO, 2-foot gauge

Built under a concession granted April 20, 1898, this purely agricultural railroad extended ten miles from the town of Otumba, on the F. C. Mexicano to the hacienda of Concepcion Duarte Vde. de Peon. Cuauhtengo is in a river valley east of Otumba, at the base of Cuauhtengo mountain. Powered by one steam locomotive, this railroad operated sporadically until it was abandoned in 1940.

CIA. MINERA DE PENOLES-AVALOS, 2-foot gauge

This was built under a concession granted in 1902 to Guillermo Purcell of Saltillo to build a connecting line between the Coahuila y Zacatecas station of Avalos, and a mine nine miles distant. This concession was later sold to the Penoles Company and has been operated by them since that time. It was unique in that the principal motive power consisted of two tiny Mallet compound locomotives of the 0-4-4-0 type, built by Orenstein-Koppel. There was no physical connection with the C. y Z. at Avalos and the railroad escaped notice by many railfans who rode the C. y Z., until *Trains* magazine publisher Al Kalmbach spotted one of the Mallets on his first trip to Mexico. Subsequent pictures published in U. S. magazines resulted in Mallet No. 1 and Porter saddle tanker No. 3 being purchased by a Boulder, Colorado group, and the engines are now running on the Cripple Creek & Victor Narrow Gauge tourist railroad east of Cripple Creek, Colorado. The Avalos line is now Dieselized, though the company has retained Mallet No. 2 which is used whenever the Diesel is out of service for repairs.

POTOSI MINING CO. RAILWAY, formerly CHIHUAHUA MINING CO., 30-inch gauge

Still in daily service today, this interesting railroad runs from Hacienda Robinson, a suburb at the south end of the city of Chihuahua, to mines at Santo Domingo, north of Santa Eulalia, a distance of 16 miles. It should not be confused with the Chihuahua Mineral Railway, a 3-foot gauge line. It was build originally in 1884 by the Santa Eulalia Silver Mining Co., the name being changed to Chihuahua Mining Co. in 1889 and to the Potosi Mining Co. in 1921, the latter company being controlled by the Howe Sound Co. of New York. It has no branches and is used exclusively for hauling ore from the mines to the smelter. Under the terms of the government concession it is not allowed to carry passengers, except employees. The railroad roughly parallels the Chihuahua Mineral Railway, ascending from 3500 ft. at Hacienda Robinson to 6000 ft. at Santo Domingo, with grades of from 2½ to 5% intervening.

A total of ten Porter saddle tank locomotives were used from 1884 to 1924, at which time the railroad was electrified and the steam engines were retired. Five new 26-ton, 750 volt D. C. locomotives were purchased from General Electric, and electrification was completed on January 1, 1925. Later two small electric switch engines were added. Lettering on equipment was "F.C.M. de Chih." until after 1945, when it sometimes appeared as "F.C. El Potosi." In recent years the new government-owned Minerales Nacionales de Mexico, S.A. has taken over and in 1968 is in full production, the equipment bearing its initials.

INGENIO EL POTRERO, 3-foot gauge

Owned by the Mexican National Sugar Refining Co., this network of narrow gauge lines was the most accessible of any of the sugar railroads of Mexico to visiting railfans. With headquarters at El Potrero, ten miles east of the city of Cordoba

The very first Heisler, PATZCUARO was used by Read & Campbell, contractors, in building various 3-foot gauge branches of the Mexican National until it was sold to the Michoacan Lumber & Development Co. and finally destroyed by revolutionaries in 1914. Porter built side-tanker No. 4 for the El Potrero sugar refinery in 1910. *(Left: C. W. Witbeck; above: E. L. DeGolyer, Jr.)*

Ingenio San Francisco, another sugar refinery, opened its 30-inch gauge rail network in 1925 and 1926 with an assortment of engines. At the left in the bottom picture is Baldwin No. 2 and next to it, partly dismantled, is the German-built Orenstein & Koppel 2-6-0 No. 3, named LA PONGUETA.

on the F. C. Mexicano, the railroad was built in 1907 and, except for interruptions due to the revolution, has operated continuously since that date. It was a steam operation from the start and for years was powered exclusively by Porter saddle tankers. As the original locomotives wore out, secondhand locomotives were purchased, though a new giant, a 2-8-2 Porter tank engine was purchased as late as 1936. Steam power was eliminated in the early 1960s and such of the cane hauling as is still done by rail is powered by small gasoline locomotives.

CIA. LA PRIMAVERA, 2-foot gauge

Located in the state of Sinaloa, at Navolato, close to the Pacific shore, this was a sugar railroad, with three locomotives which, like those in the Philippines, burned bagasse, compressed cane stalks. Cane was delivered to the F. C. Occidental de Mexico (Mexican Western) and hauled to a mill near Culiacan. Rail operations were abandoned in 1957 and the cane hauled to the mill by trucks. In 1962 all three locomotives sat rusting away in a field near the mill.

QUINTANA ROO RAILWAYS, 2-foot gauge

This most isolated of all Mexican narrow gauge railroads was begun in 1904 by the Mexican Government in an effort to provide the army with quick transportation inland through the marshes from Vigia Chico, on the Bahia de la Ascension, to the interior. There had been frequent uprisings against the government by the Indian tribes of the region, and the first construction was for military purposes. Equipment ordered for this line was lettered F. C. Militar de Quintana Roo.

In 1906 the Laguna Company, incorporated for the purpose of exploiting timber lands west of Vigia Chico acquired the military railroad from the government and extended it west to Santa Cruz de Bravo, a distance of 35.4 miles. The motive power consisted of four tiny, two-truck Shay-geared locomotives and a Davenport Forney type. It operated undisturbed by the revolution, until the Carranza government expropriated it in 1917 and it was thereafter operated by the Secretary of War and Marine. In time the railroad was extended to the town of Felipe Carrillo Puerto, 50 miles from Vigia Chico. Today it is known as the F. C. Forestal de Quintana Roo, is owned by the state, and the motive power is provided by gasoline locomotives. A highway now runs from the city of Peto, on the F. C. Unidos de Yucatan, to Felipe Carrillo Puerto and the products hauled by the railroad are frequently shipped by truck to the U. de Y. railhead.

F. C. SAN BARTOLO Y TENANGO, 3-foot gauge

This road was built in 1912 under a government concession granted to Ignacio de la Torre on May 8th of that year. The railroad was to run 21 miles from San Bartolo to the village of Tenango, but only nine miles were built, to the Hacienda de San Nicolas Peralta. It was purchased by the National Railways of Mexico in 1913 but continued to operate as a 3-foot gauge branch until the early 1930s when it was abandoned.

INGENIO SAN FRANCISCO, 30-inch gauge

This sugar cooperative was opened in 1925 and 1926 at Lerdo de Tejada in Vera Cruz State near Alvarado. The rail lines were used only to bring the cane from the fields to the mill. Powered by five locomotives, some of which were converted from 2-foot gauge to 2½ feet when purchased secondhand, this line was discontinued in 1963 when the plantation was converted to the use of trucks. The five locomotives remain for sale with no customers as of July, 1968.

F. C. SAN JERONIMO A CERRO AZUL, 3-foot gauge

Built by the Petroleos Mexicanos, it extends from San Jeronimo, on Tamiahua Lagoon in the State of Vera Cruz, to Cerro Azul oil fields, thirty miles distant. The first section of the railroad was built in 1911 and little is known of its early operations. Laid with 40-pound steel rail, there were grades as high as 3% at various points, the road was steam operated and had seven rail motors for carrying employees or their families. The shops and roundhouse are located at Cerro Azul, about thirty miles northwest of the city of Tuxpan. In 1962 the steam locomotives were stored, and the railroad was still in use only for the carrying of employees to and from work.

One of the last Shays in Mexico, Teziutlan Copper Co.'s No. 3 is a rare sight as it switches near the smelter in 1968. Santa Barbara Tram & Railroad Co. No. 2 climbs a steep grade en route to Minas Tecolotes y Anexas, in this early day photo. *(Upper: H. F. Stewart; left: El Paso Public Library)*

On one of the few 100% steam operations in Mexico in 1968, Baldwin-built No. 2 of the sugar producing Cia. Industrial Azucarera has just brought a load of sugar cane to the mill at Juan Diaz Covarrubias in Vera Cruz state. Philosophical burros furnished the motive power for the track maintenance crew of the Tatetla sugar plantation in 1952. *(Above: H. F. Stewart)*

One of the smallest Diesels in Mexico is No. 500 of the Penoles-Avalos line, which replaced one of the Mallet compounds in 1966. Teziutlan Copper Co.'s No. 5 was photographed at the Southern Iron & Equipment Co. in Atlanta in 1916. Its history is unknown but it was built by Baldwin. *(Right: Edwin W. Lohr)*

The Baldwin-built Mikado in 30-inch gauge, above, operated on the Conchos Railway, owned by the Cia. Minera de Naica. *(H. L. Broadbelt collection)*

SAN NICOLAS FARM RAILWAY, 3-foot gauge

Under a concession given November 4, 1911, this agricultural line connected the town of Mexicalzingo, in the state of Mexico, on the line of the Toluca y Tenango, with Zapotitlan, seven miles. The railroad was in operation as long as the Toluca y Tenango existed and was abandoned in 1945. Though the railroad was steam powered, no trace of its locomotives can be found in the files of the locomotive builders or the records of the S.C.O.P.

SANTA BARBARA TRAM AND RAILROAD CO. – MINAS TECOLOTES Y ANEXAS, 30-inch gauge

Located at Santa Barbara in the State of Chihuahua, on a branch of the Mexican Central south of Parral, the four-mile railroad was built by the Moctezuma Lead Co. in 1900-01. Due to grades which exceeded 5% in several sections of the line, two Shay-geared locomotives were purchased together with a Porter saddle tanker. In 1910 the network of railroads at the mine and the smelter was electrified and powered by six electric locomotives, though the connecting railroad continued to be operated by steam. In 1911 this company became a part of the "Mine Lines of Mexico," owned by the American Smelting & Refining Co., and though seized by the Carranza government in 1916 when the mines failed to reopen, the government abandoned all operations and the railroad was pulled up.

F. C. CENTRAL TABASQUENA-TABASCO CENTRAL RAILWAY, 3-foot gauge

Policarpo Valenzuela and associates of the city of San Juan Bautista, (now called Villa Hermosa) organized this railroad November 20, 1903 to be built from the city to some point on the Rio Seco from which processed sugar and other farm products could be barged to tidewater on the Gulf of Mexico. The line as built extended ten miles from San Juan Bautista through Jalpa to the cane fields east of Nacajuca, and in the opposite direction from the city for ten miles via Cunduacan to the river. Powered at first by a single Shay-geared locomotive, the company received additional financing from the Tabasco Development Co. of Minneapolis, Minnesota and several Porter saddle tankers were added to the railroad between 1905

Electric motive power brings fuel for the animal power at the mines, ahead of a string of empty ore cars on the railway of the Minerales Nacionales de Mexico, just south of San Guillermo in 1968. *(H. F. Stewart)*

and 1910. The revolution completely disrupted the district and the railroad was abandoned in 1914, never to be restored. San Juan Bautista was the scene of one of the earliest horse tramcar lines in Mexico, known as the Tabasco Tramways. Built in 1881, it extended for eight miles to various villages around the city and was in use until 1918 when it was discontinued, though the tracks and the stored cars remained in existence for nearly thirty years.

F. C. DE TATETLA, 2-foot gauge

A very extensive sugar plantation of this name operated a railroad from the cane fields to the mill at Tatetla, and had steam power over some of its lines until recent years. Tatetla is located on the Nacional de Mexico's narrow gauge line from Cuautla to Puebla, five miles north of Matamoros-Izucar. Though mules were used from 1905 as the principal source of motive power, and are still used today, one steam locomotive was in operation until 1955.

TEZIUTLAN COPPER CO., 3-foot gauge

This mine railroad is located in Teziutlan, State of Puebla at the end of the Nacional de Mexico's orphan 3-foot gauge branch from Oriental. Built in 1901, it owned three Shay-geared Limas, two of which are still in use and two Baldwin Consolidations, both gone since 1945. Ore handling at the smelter is done by Baldwin-built electric locomotives which were among the earliest of their type. The Shays are used to haul the finished product to the N.deM. terminal and for switching within the smelter yards.

INGENIO TILAPA, 2-foot gauge

A sugar railroad built in 1903 which brought cane from the fields to the mill, this interesting little railroad was located at Ayoquezco de Aldama in the State of Oaxaca, on the Mexican Southern. Though closed for a number of years during the revolution, it operated until 1947 when the railroad was abandoned in favor of trucks.

F. C. TOMACOCO A TLALTENANGO, 2-foot gauge

Francisco Noriega and Antonio Escandon built this road in 1910 from the city of Amecameca, State of Mexico, to Tomacoco, 2.5 miles. Tomacoco is southeast of Amecameca and for many years the hillsides were planted in maguey, from which pulque is made. The railroad owned one steam locomotive, a rare Porter cross-compound saddle tanker, which was still stored in a shed near Amecameca as late as 1952 and was seen there by the late Edwin Lohr, who was very frustrated because of his inability to obtain a photo. The shed and the engine were gone when the writer visited it in 1957.

F. C. DE VELARDENA, 3-foot gauge

Part of the "Mine Lines of Mexico" system, owned by American Smelting & Refining Co., this railroad was built in 1903 and extended for 25 miles between Velardena and the two mining towns of Asarco and Cobre. Velardena is on a branch of the former Mexican Central's Durango-Torreon line in the State of Durango. Passengers were carried free and connections were made with trains on the standard gauge line at Velardena. Closed down in 1914 the railroad resumed service in 1917 and was abandoned during the 1930-35 period.

F. C. ZACATECAS A TLALTENANGO, 30-inch gauge

Built under a concession granted to Alfred Slatter on December 17, 1910, this railroad was built 45 miles south from the city of Zacatecas to Tlaltenango. It served several mines in the district through which it ran, survived the revolution and was still in use in 1961, rail motors being run occasionally to hold the franchise.

F. C. ZACATEPEC A JOJUTLA Y TLAQUILTENANGO, 2-foot gauge

A sugar operation located at Jojutla on the Nacional de Mexico's narrow gauge Cuautla-Puente de Ixtla branch, it was built under a concession granted June 19, 1912 to Eugenio J. Canas. There were a total of 12 miles of main line, running from Jojutla to Tlaquiltenango and Higueron, with many branches into the cane fields. This railroad was located relatively close to Mexico City and was visited by Leonard T. Haug in 1947, at which time steam had been eliminated in favor of mules and trucks.

Time is running out for narrow gauge on the Acambaro branch on this bright March day in 1948 when the big Articulated climbs out of the Valley of Mexico en route to Acambaro. Standard gauge ties have already been installed; new rails will soon be laid outside the 3-foot ones and in another 14 months standard gauge trains will work this route. *(L. T. Haug)*

6

Main Line Operation Under Government Ownership

With the formation of the National Railways of Mexico by act of Congress on February 28, 1908, the narrow gauge lines controlled or owned outright consisted of the following divisions:

	MILES
National Division	
Colonia Station to Acambaro, Uruapan and the leased Michoacan & Pacific	380.8
Hidalgo & Northeastern Division	
Peralvillo Station to Beristain and branches	152.2
Interoceanic Division	
San Lazaro Station to Vera Cruz, Puebla, Cuautla and branches	736.0
Mexican Southern Division	
Puebla to Oaxaca and branches	260.0
TOTAL 3-FOOT GAUGE LINES	1529.0

The rolling stock of these roads included 234 locomotives, 253 passenger type cars including eight Pullmans not owned by the railroad, and 3516 freight cars. Those of the National and Hidalgo & Northeastern divisions were combined into one numbering system, the equipment being lettered "Nacional de Mexico" or in the case of the locomotives, the initials "N.deM." The Interoceanic and Mexican Southern divisions and their subsidiaries retained their identity, though the rolling stock was gradually replaced by new equipment lettered with the Nacional de Mexico title. Even so, locomotives with the initials of the Mexican Eastern, Interoceanic and the Mexican Southern survived into the 1960s.

Except for two small branches built by the Mexican Southern, and a tie line built by the Interoceanic between Irolo and San Lorenzo in 1912, no new mileage was added to the narrow gauge system. Some of it was standard gauged in 1911, when the Acambaro-Uruapan line was widened. The grades from Acambaro to Patzucuaro were severe in many places, and the radius of curvature was too small to permit standard gauge locomotives to be used, so most of the grade between these two places was relocated. The real reason for standard gauging this section was the intention of the company to build a connecting line from Penjamo on the Guadalajara line to Aduno on the Uruapan branch. The standard gauge line from Acambaro to Uruapan was opened August 1, 1911 and represented 39 miles of new construction and 100 miles of gauge change. The Penjamo-Aduno cutoff was completed in 1914.

Except for a few locomotives purchased by the Mexican Southern and the Vera Cruz & Alvarado prior to the beginning of the revolution in the spring of 1911, the locomotives and rolling stock of the system remained the same from 1908 until 1921. With a surplus of narrow gauge power on the Acambaro line, many locomotives were transferred to the Interoceanic. The shops for overhaul of all narrow gauge equipment were located at Acambaro and Puebla, although the standard gauge shops of the former Mexican Central at Nonoalco in Mexico City occasionally overhauled narrow gauge locomotives when the other shops were behind schedule or closed down on account of the civil war. Car shops at San Lazaro and Puebla handled the freight and passenger equipment.

From 1908 until the early 1920s there were six railroad stations in Mexico City, of which four were used by narrow gauge lines. The Colonia Station, located on the Paseo de la Reforma had been built in the 1880s to accommodate the trains of the Mexican National. After the 1908 consolidation, the Buena Vista station of the Mexican Central was considered too small and trains from that line were brought into Colonia, leaving only the traffic to Cuernavaca at Buena Vista. Colonia was enlarged, and must have been a busy place, with narrow gauge trains from Acambaro and the through and local traffic from the El Paso and Laredo lines. Just east of Buena Vista was the handsome station of the F. C. Mexicano, standard gauge only. North and east of the Mexicano station, and adjacent to the great shops and roundhouses at Nonoalco was the Peralvillo Station, used by the narrow gauge trains of the former Hidalgo & Northeastern and by the F. C. de Monte Alto. East of the Zocalo was the San Lazaro Station of the Interoceanic, built in 1882 and today the sole survivor of the original group of stations. South and east of San Lazaro Station a few blocks distant was the compound and station of the San Rafael & Atlixco, also exclusively narrow gauge. In 1920 the Penitenciaria Station of the Desague del Valle de Mexico was added for a total of seven railroad stations around the perimeter of the city's center. Connecting all these stations was the Cintura, or belt line, built in 1898 and laid with 3-rail track. All switch engines serving this belt line were equipped with adjustable couplers to enable them to handle either standard or narrow gauge cars.

During the first few years of the National Railways' control over the Interoceanic, overnight sleeping car service between Mexico City and Vera Cruz was provided by an express which covered the 297 miles in 13 hours, this service having begun by the Interoceanic as soon as the cutoff eliminating Puebla from the main line had been completed. No through sleeping car service was provided from Mexico City to Oaxaca, a change of trains being made at Puebla. From time to time the trade publications announced plans to standard gauge the Interoceanic from Vera Cruz to Mexico City, but the unsettled conditions in the country beginning in 1911 prevented any such action for many years.

When Porfirio Diaz was re-elected President and inaugurated in December 1910, the losing candidate, Francisco Madero and the party he represented felt that the so-called benevolent rule of Diaz must come to an end. Madero staged a revolt in the spring of 1911, and there were uprisings all over the country, particularly in the north. In the face of all this active opposition, President Diaz resigned May 25, 1911 after 31 years as head of the nation, exiling himself to Spain and then to Paris where he died in 1915. Emiliano Zapata, a violent opponent of Diaz who had been banished for years in Quintana Roo, had returned and raised an army, to fight for the time being with the Madero forces. Madero and his army entered Mexico City in June 1911 and for a short time there was relative peace. Madero was elected President in November 1911, but when he refused to initiate certain agrarian reforms demanded by Zapata, the latter revolted, taking control of the entire State of Morelos. Generals Reyes and Orozco also revolted against Madero, and these three men created disorders which seriously affected the operation of the railways. Tracks were torn up and the ties piled in heaps and burned; cars and station buildings were burned and locomotives were either blown up or totally disabled. Early in 1912 one of the principal opponents of Madero, General Felix Diaz, captured Vera Cruz, only to be taken prisoner by the Madero army a few days later.

On March 2, 1912 the United States Government warned all Americans to leave Mexico immediately, regardless of why they were there. A hundred thousand U. S. troops had been massed along the Mexican border, and an embargo had been placed on all arms shipments to Mexico. Heeding the warning, all the locomotive engineers and conductors, as well as the station agents, fiscal employees and other key U. S. citizens who worked for the National Railways left their jobs and returned to the U. S. on two special trains, leaving the operation of the locomotives to the native firemen, who were promoted overnight to the right side of the cab. Most of the British employees of the Mexicano and Interoceanic remained, but within two years the majority of them had left for England, never to return. Chaos reigned in Mexico through the rest of the year, Madero obviously being unable to control the country.

A history of the Mexican revolution of 1911-1920 has no place here, but suffice it to say that in 1913 Mexico City was captured and recaptured no less than three times, one battle in the heart of the city lasting ten days. On February 18, 1913 President Madero was overpowered in his office in the National Palace and forced to resign. A temporary President was appointed by the Congress the same day, and 26 minutes later the new President resigned and another was appointed, making three Presidents of Mexico in one day. Any President in office would not be recognized

The new Buena Vista station which opened in 1937 accommodated both standard and narrow gauge trains until 1949. In the last years of the "angosta," as Mexicans refer to 3-foot gauge, its trains for Acambaro were often hauled by Articulateds like No. 366, below on the valley floor, and No. 369, on dual gauge track at Buena Vista. *(Both below: L. T. Haug)*

Standard gauge rails are already in place at the 50 kilometer post near Fresno, where No. 368 brings its train of steel cars across a neat stone bridge. A dozen kilometers closer to Mexico City, where the train passes under a stone aqueduct on the 4% grade near San Martin, the new rails have yet to be laid. *(Both: L. T. Haug)*

by those political parties in opposition to his party, and so the battles raged throughout the country during 1913 to 1915. On one such occasion in March 1915, the Zapata forces occupied Mexico City for a number of weeks, during which all the furniture and records of the National Railways were removed from the office building on Bolivar Street, much of it never to be returned. Apparently it was destroyed when the armies of the Constitutionalist Party retook the city in August, 1915. A frequent entry in the locomotive list of the National Railways issued in 1920, the first year in which such a list had any meaning, read —"Perdida desde 1914"—"Lost since 1914." These were the engines which were destroyed beyond redemption, and could not be located.

All of this turmoil was accompanied by destruction of the railroads of the country for hundreds of miles, completely disrupting train schedules and in many cases forcing an entire main line to close down. Locomotives were destroyed in large numbers according to news accounts of the times, but locomotive records which survived the revolution show quite clearly that not more than a hundred standard gauge and twenty narrow gauge locomotives of the National Railways and affiliated lines had been written off during the whole period of the disturbances. Mexican shop forces displayed a remarkable ability to rebuild locomotives which in normal times would have been scrapped and new ones purchased. Short lines, mining railroads and other industrials were particular targets of the Zapatistas, who specialized in burning wooden bridges and trestles wherever they found them. There were hundreds of these structures on the Interoceanic and Mexican Southern, all built of wood and easily burned by retreating or foraging armies. The Interoceanic was restored to regular service in late 1915 and all narrow gauge lines were in full operation by early 1916. Perhaps the worst destruction of railroad property in the entire civil war occurred in March 1915 when the forces under General Carranza, entered the city of Monterrey, retreating before the forces of Pancho Villa, and had all the available freight cars brought into the yards. There a total of 600 cars were burned at one time, besides the passenger station, shops and offices of the company.

Carranza and the Constitutionalist Party gained almost complete control of the country in 1916 and Carranza was elected President at the end of that year. At this time the government assumed operation of all the railroads in the country just as the U. S. Railroad Administration did in 1917. Attempts were made to replace destroyed standard gauge equipment by the purchase of secondhand locomotives and rolling stock in the United States. The narrow gauge lines had to "make-do" with what they had, and not a single new locomotive or car was purchased during that period, except for such rolling stock as could be built in the railroad shops. The country remained fairly stable from 1917 until 1920, when another brief civil war broke out as Carranza announced that he would not run for re-election in 1920 according to the provisions of the new constitution. Disorders broke out anew in the spring of 1920, and on May 8th, Carranza fled the city, only to be assassinated two weeks later. The country was brought under control by General Obregon, who was elected President in November, 1920. Obregon brought stability which the country had not had for ten years, and except for a few local outbreaks years later, Mexico has since then proceeded on an orderly course.

By the end of 1920 there were 5000 Mexican-owned freight cars and several hundred locomotives laid up for repairs, in addition to those destroyed in the uprisings. Most of the U. S. railroads had placed an embargo against the passage of U. S.-owned freight cars across the border points, as they were never returned. To help in the emergency, various large industries in Mexico purchased locomotives and rolling stock. One enterprising American, Howard T. Oliver, organized the Oliver American Trading Co., and was permitted to operate through freights with his own locomotives and leased rolling stock from certain border points to Mexico City. At one time he had 18 locomotives and 500 freight cars in this service, only to have the locomotives seized by the government a few years later. Oliver was quoted in an interview in 1937 as saying that one of the principal reasons why the railroads suffered so heavily in the civil war was that almost all of them had been built and operated by foreigners, the Mexicans holding only inferior jobs on the railroads,

Narrow gauge still went from Mexico City to Vera Cruz in 1942 when No. 366 was pictured about 25 miles north of Mexico City with train 31. *(C. W. Witbeck collection from official N. de M. negative)*

Not all trains on the Acambaro line went behind Articulateds. Above is 2-8-0 No. 265 bringing the Acambaro-Mexico City passenger train under the aqueduct near San Martin in 1948. Ties by the track suggest that standard gauging will soon be under way.

The yards at Oriental, in the dual gauge era before the Vera Cruz line was completed in standard gauge, presented a bewildering tangle of tracks. *(Both: L. T. Haug)*

and they vented their hate for this situation by cheerfully destroying anything that came in their path.

In 1921 the railroad employees, now 100% Mexican citizens, having formed a labor union called the Confederation of Railway Workers, went on strike in February, completely disrupting railway operations. The management tried to keep going by using strikebreakers, but were eventually forced to settle with the unions, while at the same time retaining over 15,000 strikebreakers. This condition overloaded the railroads with a surplus of employees and paved the way for financial disaster a few years later. Yet when the strike was settled, sufficient credit was available in the U. S. to enable the purchase of a large number of locomotives, including 100 standard gauge and 21 narrow gauge, the latter all of the Consolidation type, built by Baldwin and Alco. In 1924, 18 additional narrow gauge locomotives were purchased from Baldwin, thus providing the Mexico City-Vera Cruz line with the heavy power needed to move the steadily increasing traffic.

Many of the old wooden coaches and sleeping cars of the Interoceanic had been destroyed or worn out. These were replaced by new steel coaches built at the Puebla shops, some of which are still in use. The open platformed bodies of these cars were so large that to the uninformed, they looked like standard gauge cars converted to narrow gauge. Sleeping cars were steel sheathed and the frames reinforced, some of them being provided with vestibules, until the night train from Mexico City to Vera Cruz bore little resemblance to the old style narrow gauge consist. In 1928 when additional locomotives were needed on the Vera Cruz line, the first group of simple Articulated engines was purchased from Alco, followed by more in 1934 and 1937. These handsome machines were able to haul the passenger trains without helpers and could maintain time schedules with ease. A few of the oldest locomotives were then retired, though most of them adorned the scrap tracks for years until the demand for scrap during World War II sent them off to the blast furnaces.

On January 1, 1926 the government returned the railroads to their owners, though with 52% stock ownership of the National Railways, the government was still in the saddle. The physical and financial condition of the railways was in deplorable condition at this time, and for the succeeding five years, commissions from the U. S. visited Mexico and analyzed the railroad situation with little effect. The verdict was always the same: too much bonded debt, too many employees and the equipment and track in poor repair.

Some attempt was made in the early 1930s to improve the service over some of the narrow gauge lines, when part of the old Hildalgo & Northeastern was standard gauged after many complaints had been received about the slow service to Beristain and way points other than Pachuca, which was served by a standard gauge line built during the revolution. In 1933 the overcrowding at Colonia Station caused the decision to build a new station on the site of old Buena Vista Station. In 1935 all traffic which had used Buena Vista and Peralvillo was routed to Colonia, and the former stations were torn down. The new Buena Vista Station, with a third rail on some of the stub-end tracks for the Acambaro narrow gauge trains was opened in 1937, Colonia was torn down and the site converted into parks, the Railway Hospital being the only remaining building in the area which had been the center of railroad activities for so many years. The old Hidalgo & Northeastern as far as San Agustin was pulled up, while the branches to Beristain, San Lorenzo and the other small narrow gauge lines in the vicinity of Pachuca were standard gauged. Except for the F. C. Mexicano, Buena Vista Station handled all standard gauge traffic for the next 25 years, to be replaced by the magnificent new terminal a few blocks north.

In 1937 the Mexican Government expropriated the National Railways of Mexico and the National of Tehuantepec, turning their operation over to the Railway Workers' Union on May 1, 1938 as a political gesture. The results of this act were so disastrous to the railroads that when President Manuel Avila Camacho assumed direction of the country in December 1940, his first act was to issue a decree returning full operation of the railroads to the government. Mexico thus entered World War II with the railroads in very sad condition. The motive power shortage was partly relieved by the purchase in 1941 of over a hundred standard gauge locomotives secondhand in the

Dual gauge track was still in use at Oriental station as late as 1967, 15 years after the top picture was taken. During transition from 3-foot to standard gauge in 1948 there were two engine houses at Oriental, one for each gauge as the track pattern in the middle picture suggests. Below, three engines were needed to haul 26 loads and the caboose up the hill on the Oriental-Jalapa line in 1946. *(Top: C. W. Witbeck; bottom: L. T. Haug)*

Up the steepest grade between Vera Cruz and Mexico City, near Perote, 2-8-0 No. 62 drags the freight over the still-3-foot-gauge rails. *(Lucius Beebe)*

U. S., but all the narrow gauge lines received were two aging Mikados from the Denver & Rio Grande Western.

By war's end the government managers had restored order out of chaos, under the capable hands of engineer Andres Ortiz. The F. C. Mexicano was purchased outright from the British stockholders on June 1, 1946, and plans were already under way at that time to standard gauge the Mexico City-Vera Cruz narrow gauge line. Between San Lorenzo and Vera Cruz the bridges were widened and strengthened, the radii of the sharpest curves were increased and the roadbed prepared for the heavier trains it would support. All crossties placed on the line after 1945 were of standard gauge length and where the ties did not actually need renewal, alternate ties were removed and standard gauge ties substituted. The fundamental plan was to create a new standard gauge line from San Lorenzo to Vera Cruz, and to tie this section to the Mexico City-Pachuca standard gauge line by using the old Hidalgo & Northeastern line from San Agustin through Irolo to San Lorenzo, already standard gauged some years earlier but used only for local traffic. While this was a bit out of the way for through trains, it served to eliminate the old route to Mexico City via Los Reyes into San Lazaro Station.

Once everything was in readiness, crews began laying two 110-pound steel rails outside the 3-foot gauge rails, until by the end of 1947, the work outside the yards was completed. Then began the complicated job of building temporary switches to handle both gauges, for traffic could not be interrupted during the change of gauge. In the yards at Oriental and San Lorenzo the switches were installed on a permanent basis, for the Puebla-Teziutlan and the Mexico City-Oaxaca lines via San Lorenzo and Puebla were still narrow gauge. The Alvarado branch was also widened, and on January 22, 1948 the first standard gauge train operated from Mexico City to Vera Cruz from Buena Vista Station. In the following weeks, all narrow gauge equipment was brought into Oriental from the Vera Cruz end of the main line, and the narrow gauge rails were taken up. Within a year the narrow gauge crossties still in the track had been replaced and the line brought up to the standard of other trunk lines in the National Railways system. All of this work had been paid for by a credit from the Export-Import Bank of New York, which was repaid in installments when due. In 1949 the same bank allocated $17,900,000 for modernization of the Mexican government railroad system, all of which spelled the doom of most of the narrow gauge and steam power.

The elimination of the Interoceanic's main line from the narrow gauge system released a large number of locomotives and cars for use on the remaining narrow gauge divisions, resulting in the transfer of ten Articulated engines to the Acambaro Division, where they handled most of the freight and all of the passenger runs. This line was the next on the standard gauging program, for the advance work had been in progress since 1947. Work was completed in time to open the Mexico City-Acambaro line to standard gauge traffic on May 14, 1949, and Buena Vista Station had seen its last narrow gauge train on the previous day. The roundhouse in back of the station fell into disuse and all standard gauge locomotives were serviced at the two Nonoalco roundhouses.

In 1949 the narrow gauge branch of the Mexican Southern from Tehuacan to Esperanza, built in the 1870s as a standard gauge line and then narrowed to three feet, was widened again. This reduced the 3-foot gauge network to the Mexico City-Puebla-Oaxaca line via San Lorenzo, the Puebla-Teziutlan line via San Marcos and the Puebla-Mexico City line via Cuautla. San Lazaro Station in Mexico City thus became the last surviving narrow gauge station, the San Rafael & Atlixco and Desague del Valle de Mexico railroads having discontinued all passenger service. Through sleeping cars still operated from San Lazaro Station to Oaxaca, and the Articulated locomotives, dispossessed for the second time were moved over to the Los Reyes-Cuautla division, where they accomplished the miracle of running on ancient 45-pound rail, much of it laid in the early 1880s. Between 1949 and 1953 they were a common sight on the big hill north of Cuautla, at Amecameca and in the San Lazaro yards. Their days were numbered, for they were too heavy for the track, and with a surplus of the lighter Consolidations, uneconomical to operate and maintain.

The last standard gauging project of the 1945 plan was begun in 1951, between San Lorenzo and

With a consist that looks its venerable years, No. 71 sets out on its last run from Mexico City to Puebla via San Lorenzo in 1952. The track widening, below, 15 miles north of Oaxaca in 1952, indicates that the twisting Tomellin Canyon line will remain as "sinuosa" as ever.

The turntable at Tomellin was an important facility for the helper engines quartered there for use on the steep segment of the Puebla-Oaxaca line. The lower picture illustrates a meet on the Mexican Southern.

The Oaxaca-Mexico City passenger train has backed into a stub siding at Organal, five miles south of Tomellin, to allow a southbound freight to pass. *(Both: L. T. Haug)*

The passenger train for Puebla, via the northern line, leaves Mexico City past the roundhouse. The switchman with hands behind his back is living dangerously, as he prepares to jump off the moving train, run ahead and throw the switch. The 3-foot gauge terminal at Puebla appears below. Both pictures were taken three months before the line became standard gauge.

The Chipiltepec-Mexico City mixed train with N. de M. No. 262 spews smoke at Azteca. The consist is made up of an express car, caboose and second class coach; this, along with maguey growing by the track, an adobe to the right beyond the engine and the big cactus at the extreme right, combine to give Mexican flavor to this 1964 view. By 1968 this was the last surviving steam operation with passenger accommodations. *(G. G. Allen)*

Puebla, Puebla to Oriental, and Puebla to Oaxaca, including the branches out of the latter terminal. Laying of the additional two rails proceeded all through 1951 until the job was completed June 15, 1952. After all new switches were installed and standard gauge facilities were available at each terminal or helper station, the first standard gauge passenger train was run from Buena Vista Station in Mexico City to Oaxaca on August 20, 1952. This left the narrow gauge line from Oriental to Teziutlan as an orphan, necessitating retention of the complicated three-rail switches and tracks in the yards at Oriental, a condition which still prevails. The traffic over the Teziutlan branch was not considered sufficient to warrant standard gauging at that time, and through the years since 1952, worn-out motive power or rolling stock were replaced by surplus from the remaining narrow gauge lines. Today the Teziutlan branch is fully Diezelized, with one steam locomotive in standby service.

The old narrow gauge line from Los Reyes to San Lorenzo, built as the Irolo Railroad nearly a hundred years ago and over which the trains from Mexico City to Vera Cruz and Oaxaca passed for so many years, was left narrow gauge and operated as a branch, with mixed train service. Gradually the track was standard gauged south out of San Lorenzo to Chipiltepec, leaving the narrow gauge track from there to Los Reyes as a "freight-only" branch, its future clouded by the competition of improved, paralleling highways.

With the elimination of the Puebla-Oaxaca trains in 1952, additional locomotives and rolling stock were released, and pursuing a program established in 1948, ten of the narrow gauge Consolidations and the two former Denver & Rio Grande Western Mikados acquired during World War II were converted to standard gauge, primarily for use on branch lines where the traffic was light and the curves were sharp. The Articulated engines were retired and scrapped, though an attempt was made to interest the International Railways of Central America in their purchase. By 1954 there were only 57 narrow gauge locomotives in service, and these were soon reduced in number by the sale or lease of locomotives to the Unidos de Yucatan and the Coahuila & Zacatecas. In September 1964, ten Diesel-electric locomotives were received from the Electro-Motive Division of General Motors. These were of a new design with a rather unique system of torque drive from motors placed above the frame, inside the locomotive body, rather than mounted on the trucks and geared directly to the axles. This will permit changing to standard gauge any time the narrow gauge is widened. At this writing, Diesels are operating all the passenger trains and all freight trains except the "mixto" on the Chipiltepec branch, with four steam engines in the Mexico City yards, and three undergoing repairs in the Puebla Shops.

Bridges are being reinforced and culverts widened to permit standard gauge tracks; all tie replacements are now standard gauge length, and frequently sections as long as a half-mile are ready for standard gauge track. The question before the management is whether the traffic on this line warrants standard gauging except from Mexico City to the San Rafael Paper Co. plant. As a tourist attraction it still has possibilities with the right kind of promotional work, at least from Mexico City to Cuautla. The highway from Cuautla to Mexico City via the Cuernavaca toll road provides fast and comfortable bus service at frequent intervals, with a running schedule of less than two hours as compared to the four and a half hours on the narrow gauge. The trains on the latter are never on time, except for the Ozumba local, and they usually arrive at their destinations an hour or more late. The through train still consists of four or five flat-roofed coaches with wooden seats for the second class passengers, always filled to overflowing with people going to Mexico City with farm produce or handcraft work to sell in the markets there. At the head end is a baggage-mail car converted from a boxcar, and at the rear is a single steel first class coach, usually about half full. In an article in the June 1965 issue of the magazine "Contenido", a Mexico City writer spoofed the Cuautla train with humorous cartoons, the titles of which are revealing of the benevolent tolerance with which the average city dweller looks on the last relic of bygone days of transportation. In one cartoon he shows the interior of one of the coaches, filled to overflowing with people, bundles and livestock; the caption says, "The only bad feature is that there is no seat for my cow." He cartoons the steam locomotive and says, "The machine runs fine so long as the wrench is applied every five kilometers."

In 1966 I walked the track at various points between Puebla, Cuautla and the San Lazaro yards with my friend, the late Edwin Lohr and out of curiosity we examined every rail in sections we walked over to determine the maker's name and the date the rail was rolled. To our astonishment, the youngest rails we could find were Cockerill and Ougree Steel of Belgium, rolled in 1902; these were between Atencingo and Cuautlixco Junction. Between Los Reyes and Ozumba were hundreds of rails made by Krupp in 1881; West Cumberland Steel of England, 1881; Barrow Steel, 1894 and Angleur of France, 1892. No doubt many of these were relaid rails taken from former narrow gauge main lines, but it is significant that what was once the Morelos Railroad, built in 1881 and 1882, still has many rails rolled in those years, with rails made in 1902 on the Cuautlixco Junction-Atencingo section which was completed in 1903.

There is considerable talk in Mexico City of building a tourist railroad using narrow gauge steam power, from some convenient point within the city to Xochimilco or some other place frequented by visitors, and that the engines being repaired at Puebla are for use on that line. It is the opinion of officials in the mechanical department of the Mexican Government Railway System that when these engines are turned out of the Puebla shop, they will be stored serviceable, and that nothing will be done about a tourist railroad until after the Olympic Games in the fall of 1968.

In the meantime, the Mexico City-Puebla narrow gauge railroad via Cuautla is still going strong, and is worth a detour by rail hobbyists, though the Diesels at the head end will no doubt offend the sensibilities of the steam buffs. It represents one of the most accessible narrow gauge common carrier railroads on the North American continent and is the last survivor of a narrow gauge empire which once extended for over 3000 miles through the heart of Mexico.

The Texcoco-Mexico City mixed train backs the last mile into San Lazaro station in May of 1953. The second coach from the rear was the last surviving Mexican Southern coach built in England.

269

Mexican Album

Mexico City—San Lazaro Station

Of the narrow gauge stations in Mexico City, only San Lazaro survives. It was built in 1882 by Don Delfin Sanchez for the old Irolo Railroad and through more than eight busy decades served the Interoceanic. On these pages and the eight to follow are views of the precincts of San Lazaro during the final days of steam operation. At the left is a view of the yards; the scene below is taken from the engine house through its old-time arches. *(Two pictures: Jim Shaughnessy)*

Earthquakes are not uncommon in Mexico City; the place averages a good shake each year. The one in 1956 was a bit heavier than most of them, but business went on as usual in the San Lazaro shop building.

When the air motor doesn't work, the turntable outside the engine house at San Lazaro has to be operated by the "armstrong" method. *(Below and opposite above: Jim Shaughnessy)*

In the morning sunshine, No. 186 takes water for the first leg of the day's journey. Before backing into San Lazaro station, all passenger trains turned around on the "Y" below.

San Lazaro, Mexico City's second narrow gauge station, is shown on a cold winter morning in 1948. It was a busy place in its day with six first class trains arriving and departing daily for Puebla, Oaxaca and Vera Cruz via the northern route from Los Reyes, and four first class trains, two in each direction, serving the southern route to Cuautla and Puebla. Besides these there were several mixed trains each day. Buffet sleeping cars operated on all trains via the northern route until the Vera Cruz and Oaxaca lines were standard gauged. All inbound passenger trains turned around on a "Y" a half-mile east of the station and backed the rest of the way. This is a hazardous operation these days, as three heavily traveled public streets must be crossed; the rear brakeman blows a crescendo with his air whistle while the conductor gives continuous hand signals to the engineer. *(L. T. Haug)*

Out of date since 1952, this sign still hangs on the rack at San Lazaro Station. Translated, it says: "For arrival and departure of trains to Tehuacan and Teziutlan, Vera Cruz and Suchiate, Puebla and Oaxaca." Suchiate is on the Guatemalan border. *(Below and right: Jim Shaughnessy)*

The last survivor of the Michoacan & Pacific was No. 241. The brakeman in white standing on its pilot almost dwarfs its low boiler, where its number hangs askew. *(C. W. Witbeck)*

The brakeman takes no chances as he boards an extra freight leaving San Lazaro yards for the San Rafael Paper Co. mill. *(C. W. Witbeck)*

One of the last survivors of the old Mexican National, No. 255, drills empties in the San Lazaro yards.
Left and above: Jim Shaughnessy

A day in the life of engine No. 263

On the next four pages are impressions of photographer Jim Shaughnessy as he followed Baldwin Consolidation No. 263 hauling freight between Mexico City and Cuautla. Below, it stands over the service pit in the San Lazaro roundhouse in Mexico City for night maintenance work. Opposite, it appears on two different errands: In the upper picture, after several stops en route, it approaches Chalco where it will pick up a helper engine for the long climb to Amecameca. In the lower picture, it stands on a stub siding, waiting for the double-headed through freight to pass by at Chalco. On this day, No. 263 has freight for way stations, including water cars which will be spotted on various sidings along the way at small communities which lack an adequate local supply of pure water. These tank cars will be filled from Chalco's capacious water tower, after the two engines on the through freight have had their turn at the water spout shown on page 132. Once the through freight is on its way up the hill towards Amecameca, No 263 is ready for its turn at the water tower, where the tedious process of filling the engine's tank and the water cars begins. The engine then continues its scenic journey south to Cuautla.

Chalco station is over
a mile east of the town.

A woman on a freight train? Very important in this case, for the car is the home of the traveling maintenance-of-way crew. Without her, who would prepare the tortillas for breakfast? At the right, above, the train climbs the last hill towards Ozumba, at the base of mighty Popocatepetl.

N. DE M.
263

The Cuautla-Puente de Ixtla Line

This 51-mile branch of the "Via Angosta" links the narrow gauge main line from Mexico City to Puebla at Cuautla with the standard gauge Mexico City-Balsas line at Puente de Ixtla. A "mixto," often with no freight cars, makes a daily round trip, leaving Puente de Ixtla early in the morning and departing from Cuautla after the two through trains from Mexico City and Puebla have passed. In earlier days the "mixto" was a long train, most of the cars filled with sacks of raw sugar from the mill near Jojutla. Only a few freight cars now handle the local business, mostly merchandise for retail stores. On this and the following five pages are scenes of narrow gauge action along this branch.

No. 144 of the Mexican Eastern, with a mixed consist out of Cuautla, will follow the main line to Mexico City 2½ miles to Cuautlixco, where it will branch off toward Puente de Ixtla.

Three miles from Cuautlixco, No. 70 brings a train into Calderon, the second stop, where boxcars stand on the siding waiting to be picked up. *(Both: Jim Shaughnessy)*

The fireman waves to the photographer as No. 70 of the Interoceanic starts the train rolling out of Calderon, above. Below, No. 144 whistles for the main highway crossing approaching San Carlos, 11 miles from Cuautla.

Above, No. 144 gathers speed for the run to Yautepec. In 1967 this engine hauled the last steam powered passenger train on the Nacional de Mexico, on its final run from Puente de Ixtla to Cuautla. No. 256, below, between Atlihuayan and Yautepec, brings the morning train to the summit of the long grade which begins at Jojutla. *(Upper left: Jim Shaughnessy)*

70

The third scheduled stop on the way to Puente de Ixtla is at Tenayo, on a 2% descending grade. There, at the left, No. 70 crosses a siding switch. Two hours after leaving Cuautla, No. 75 reaches Tlaltizapam, above, having averaged 15 miles per hour including stops while descending nearly 2000 feet from the Cuautla plain. Puente de Ixtla is still over an hour's run from this point. *(Left: Jim Shaughnessy; above: H. F. Stewart)*

From Puebla to Cuautla East of the Mountains

The Puebla-Cuautla section of the narrow gauge has less traffic than the busy Cuautla-Mexico City line, due to lower population density. It traverses an historic part of Mexico with many reminders of the early days of the Spanish conquest. On the following seven pages are scenes along this route, from steam to Diesel days. Above, Articulated No. 365 leaves Mexico City with a train of tank cars loaded with gasoline in 1952, its last year of service.

Puebla's station yards were a tangle of narrow gauge tracks with roundhouse and shops on the left. At Cholula, below, a fine old church stands on a mound overlooking rails first laid in 1881. The many standard gauge ties in the 1966 picture foreshadow what took place in 1968, when 14 kilometers of standard gauge track were laid outside the 3-foot gauge rails from Los Arcos Junction to Maria, beginning a program of gradual replacement of the narrow gauge.

At Atlixco, left, the tracks of the orphan San Rafael & Atlixco, now owned by the Cia. Industrial de Atlixco, turn off to the right. Below, the twenty-car excursion train, pictured south of Matamoros-Izucar in 1962, was en route to a carnival at Pastor, 35 miles ahead. *(Left: L. T. Haug; below: H. F. Stewart)*

Train No. 109 with No. 268 at the head end, leaves Puebla at 7:43 in the morning for Cuautla, 108 miles distant, where it should arrive at 1:30 p.m. It will be well after 6 p.m. before it covers the remaining 85 miles to San Lazaro Station in Mexico City. *(Jim Shaughnessy)*

The new engine shed built in 1959 at Puebla services both narrow and standard gauge power, as shown in the night scene above, with standard gauge 2-8-0 No. 1235 towering over narrow gauge Nos. 268 and 288 on the left hand track. On the opposite page are two camera studies of No. 280 being prepared for a train to Cuautla. *(Three pictures: Jim Shaughnessy)*

N DE M
280
280
280

N. DE M.
M.

Puebla station in 1948 was still a busy hub of narrow gauge traffic with trains for Oaxaca, Cuautla, Teziutlan, Vera Cruz and Atencingo departing daily. All second class trains had a caboose-coach as shown on the train at the right above. *(Top and bottom: L. T. Haug)*

Mexican Southern No. 105, the only ten-wheeler of its class, was away from its home road when photographed at the head of the Puebla-Cuautla train at Cholula in 1936. Another 1948 photo at Puebla shows yard engine No. 236 leaving the engine terminal, on the left, No. 112 of the Mexican Southern takes oil, in the center, and F. C. I. No. 8 is ready to leave for Mexico City on the right. *(Middle: John B. Hungerford)*

The daily passenger train from Mexico City to Puebla, a mixture of the old and the modern, leaves Cuautla behind Diesel No. 5404 in this 1965 photo.

En Route From Mexico City to Cuautla

Narrow gauge aficionados visiting Mexico are most likely to see the scenes illustrated on the next 13 pages, for they are on a line still active and easily accessible from Mexico City. In these days, however, those who are partial to steam will note an important difference. As late as 1965, when the picture below was taken, the San Lazaro yards between the round house and the station were filled with smoke. Since then the Diesels have taken over most of the work.

For more than a mile south of Amecameca the narrow gauge line runs between solid rows of old adobe houses.

Baldwin-built Ten-wheeler No. 189 still had its headlight on top of the smokebox in the above 1948 photo at Los Reyes. There is a mad scramble at Ozumba as soon as the train is backed into the station. Baggage goes through the windows and soon each coach is filled. *(Above: L. T. Haug)*

In the striking photograph above by H. F. Stewart, the train seems headed for the base of Ixtaccihuatl as it nears Amecameca. "Primera" coach No. 777, above on the opposite page, has the same headroom as a standard gauge car and, though hardly luxurious, is definitely more comfortable than the "Segunda" which appears below it, with every inch of baggage rack space occupied, and patient people sitting on hard seats.

The classic setting for action photos in steam days, where they were mirrored in the water, was 11 miles from San Lazaro Station. Here, No. 272 picks up speed with a full consist of cars loaded with paper products from San Rafael. Los Reyes is still a refreshment stop for all passenger trains. *(Above: H. F. Stewart)*

Running on the southbound passenger train's time, No. 263 with the morning way freight from Cuautla comes down the siding at Amecameca to clear the main line. Below, the Ozumba local takes water at Chalco.

Through an arch of the centuries-old wagon bridge, long since abandoned, the Ozumba local heads for Mexico City, on its second daily run. At the right, with Popocateptl in the background, No. 262 hauls a consist of water cars a mile south of Ozumba. At Nepantla, above at right, the northbound passenger from Puebla meets a southbound freight. Below, the morning train from Mexico City to Puebla arrives at Ozumba. *(Right and both opposite: Jim Shaughnessy)*

PRIMERA

On the stub-end station tracks at Cuautla, if the first set of wheel barriers doesn't stop the train, the others will.

Railway postal service is still provided on all N. de M. narrow gauge passenger trains. The mail sacks being loaded, above, are bound for way stations between Cuautla and Puebla. With Ixtaccihuatl in the background, left, No. 272 is making time rolling the southbound way freight through the open country near Zoyacingo. A meet at Ozumba is overdue. On Cuautla's shaded platform, passengers keep out of the broiling sun as they await the train for Puente de Ixtla or one of the two main line trains which arrive and depart between 12:30 and 2:30 p.m. *(Left: Harold F. Stewart)*

At Cuautla station, next to the old Spanish church, No. 70 is serviced during its four-hour layover on the Puente de Ixtla run. At the right, No. 74 is greased by hand. *(Right and opposite above: Jim Shaughnessy)*

Bundles of reeds for basket weavers are loaded aboard the express car at Cuautla, left. No. 185, with the Ozumba local, raises dust along the dual gauge track as it parallels the highway out of Mexico City in 1952.

When a main line train arrives at Cuautla in two sections, one is backed into a stub-end siding in what was once the graveyard of the old stone church which adjoins the station. *(Jim Shaughnessy)*

Rosters

F. C. Nacionales Mexicano (Mexican National) 1881-1908

3 foot gauge

- - - - -

G-01 2-8-0 37-16x20-60000-52000-140-13203

No.	Builder	C/N	Date	Disposition
1	Baldwin	#5481	2/1881	To N de M #1 - 1908
2	"	#5489	"	To FCNM 2nd #13 prior 1902
3	"	#5490	"	" 2nd #14 "
4	"	#5491	"	" 2nd #25 "

Uncl. 4-4-0 38-11x16-36000

No.	Builder	C/N	Date	Disposition
5	Baldwin	#3618	7/1874	Ex Mexico, Toluca & Cuautitlan #1 Condemned 1905
6	"	#3621	"	" #2 " "

Uncl. 4-4-0 42 1/2-14x16-42000

No.	Builder	C/N	Date	Disposition
7	Brooks	#367	9/1879	Ex M. T. & C. #4 Sold to Galvey & Casado - 1899

Uncl. 2-8-0 #8 38-14x16-52000 #9 38-15x18-55000

No.	Builder	C/N	Date	Disposition
8	Baldwin	#4282	2/1878	Ex MT&C #3 Sold Michoacan Lbr. & Devel. Co. 1905
9	"	#4788	9/1879	" #5 Sold to H&NE 2nd #5 - 1900

G-01 2-8-0 37-16x20-60000-52000-140-13203

No.	Builder	C/N	Date	Disposition
10	Baldwin	#5614	4/1881	Rebuilt to standard gauge #225
11	"	#5613	"	" #221
12	"	#5617	"	To N de M #12 - 1908
13	"	#5489	2/1881	Ex FCNM #2. Reblt. to standard gauge #212
14	"	#5490	"	" #3. " #213

Uncl. 2-6-0 37-14x20-51000-44000

No.	Builder	C/N	Date	Disposition
13	Baldwin	#5662	6/1881	Sold prior 1902
14	"	#5661	"	"
15	"	#5665	"	"
16	"	#5664	"	"
17	"	#5667	"	Sold prior 1908
18	"	#5663	"	"
19	"	#5668	"	Sold prior 1902

Uncl. 2-10-0 37-18x20

No.	Builder	C/N	Date	Disposition
20	Baldwin	#5697	6/1881	Rebuilt to standard gauge #200
21	"	#5698	"	" #201

Uncl. 0-6-0 37-14x18-43000

No.	Builder	C/N	Date	Disposition
22	Baldwin	#5809	9/1881	Scrapped prior 1908
23	"	#5811	"	Sold to Desague del Valle de Mexico- 1903

Uncl. 2-6-0 37-14x20-51000-44000

No.	Builder	C/N	Date	Disposition
24	Baldwin	#5703	6/1881	Sold prior 1902
25	"	#5739	7/1881	"
26	"	#5741	"	Scrapped prior 1908
27	"	#5684	6/1881	"
28	"	#5688	"	Sold prior 1902
29	"	#5810	9/1881	Order cancelled. Not delivered

G-01 2-8-0 37-16x20-60000-52000-140-13203

No.	Builder	C/N	Date	Disposition
25	Baldwin	#5491	2/1881	Ex FCNM #4 To N de M #25 - 1908
30	"	#5686	6/1881	To N de M 2nd #138 - 1908
31	"	#5687	"	Rebuilt to standard gauge #223
32	"	#5786	7/1881	Scrapped prior 1902
33	"	#5787	"	"
34	"	#5871	10/1881	Rebuilt to standard gauge #218
35	"	#5872	"	To N de M #35 - 1908
40	"	#6994	8/1883	Scrapped prior 1902

Uncl. 2-6-0 32-12x20

No.	Builder	C/N	Date	Disposition
33	Hinkley	#1393	4/1881	Acq. 1901. Previous history unknown. Sold to Desague del Valle de Mexico - 1903

Uncl. 2-6-0 37-14x20-51000-44000

No.	Builder	C/N	Date	Disposition
36	Baldwin	#5869	10/1881	Scrapped prior 1902
37	"	#5870	"	To N de M #37 - 1908
38	"	#5874	"	Scrapped prior 1902
39	"	#5972	12/1881	Scrapped prior 1902
41	"	#5971	11/1881	Scrapped prior 1902

Class B-01 0-6-0 37-14x16-42000

No.	Builder	C/N	Date	Disposition
42	Baldwin	#6794	5/1883	To N de M #42 - 1908
43	"	#6795	"	" #43 - 1908

G-01 2-8-0 37-16x20-60000-52000-140-13203

No.	Builder	C/N	Date	Disposition
44	Baldwin	#6761	5/1883	Scrapped prior 1908
45	"	#6767	"	Rebuilt to standard gauge #216
46	"	#6772	"	To N de M #46 - 1908
47	"	#6779	"	" #47 - 1908
48	"	#6780	"	Rebuilt to standard gauge #210
49	"	#6783	"	To N de M #49 - 1908
50	"	#6785	"	Rebuilt to standard gauge #220
51	"	#6800	6/1883	To N de M #51 - 1908
52	"	#6801	"	" #52 - 1908
53	"	#6813	"	Rebuilt to standard gauge #214
54	"	#6815	"	" #227
56	"	#6823	"	" #226
57	"	#6828	"	" #217
58	"	#6830	"	" #211
59	"	#6856	7/1883	" #222
60	"	#6857	"	To N de M #60 - 1908
61	"	#6871	"	" #61 - 1908
62	"	#6873	"	Rebuilt to standard gauge #224
63	"	#6876	"	" #215
64	"	#6882	"	To N de M #64 - 1908

Uncl. 2-6-0 37-14x20-51000-44000

No.	Builder	C/N	Date	Disposition
55	Baldwin	#5702	6/1881	Scrapped prior 1902
65	"	#6695	4/1883	To N de M #65 - 1908
66	"	#6694	"	" #66 - 1908
67	"	#6760	5/1883	" #67 - 1908

G-01 2-8-0 37-16x20-60000-52000-140-13203

No.	Builder	C/N	Date	Disposition
68	Baldwin	#7003	10/1883	To N de M #68 - 1908
69	"	#7004	"	" #69 - 1908
70	"	#7012	"	" #70 - 1908
71	"	#7014	"	Sold to Dos Estrellas Mining Co. - 1903
72	"	#6819	6/1883	To N de M #72 1908

Uncl. 0-4-2T 36-11x16 Dummy

No.	Builder	C/N	Date	Disposition
73	Baldwin	#7631	6/1885	Operated by FCNM on Zacatecas Street Ry.; to Mazapil Cop. Co. #73. Preserved at Aguas Calientes.
74-80	Vacant			

Uncl. 2-6-0 42-14x18

No.	Builder	C/N	Date	Disposition
81	Baldwin	#10147	7/1889	Ex Michoacan & Pacific #1. Sold in 1904

Uncl. 2-8-0 38-16x20-78000-70000-140-13204

No.	Builder	C/N	Date	Disposition
82	Baldwin	#10957	6/1890	Ex Michoacan & Pacific #2. To N de M #82-1908
83	"	#12875	8/1892	" #3. " #83- "
84	"	#14409	8/1895	" #4. " #84- "

Uncl. 2-8-0 36-17x18-89650-79805-150-18424

No.	Builder	C/N	Date	Disposition
85	Baldwin	#16522	2/1899	Ex Michoacan & Pac. #5. To N de M #85-1908
86	"	#16523	"	" #6. " #86-1908
87	"	#19034	5/1901	To N de M #87 - 1908
88-89	Vacant			

Uncl. 2-6-0 36-14x20

No.	Builder	C/N	Date	Disposition
90	Grant	#1550	9/1882	Ex Guanajuato a San Luis de la Paz y Pozos #1- originally Texas & St. Louis #53 To N de M #90-1908
91	Grant	#1555	10/1882	Ex GaSLde la PyP #2-T&StL#58 To N de M #91-1908

Uncl. 4-4-0 #92 42-13x18 #93 50-15x20

92 Porter #468 12/1881 Ex V.C.& R.V.#1 To N de M #92 - 1908 Note
93 Brooks #1644 4/1890 " #2 " # 93 - 1908
Note; #92 built as Connotton Valley #14. Acq. 1890.

Uncl. 2-8-0 38-16x20-78000-70000-140-13204

94 Baldwin #11783 9/1891 Ex V.C.& R.V.#3 To N de M #94 - 1908
95 " #12969 10/1892 " #4 " #95 - 1908

Uncl. 2-8-0 36-17x18-89650-79805-150-18424

96 Baldwin #15324 5/1897 Ex V.C.& R.V.#6 To N de M #96 - 1908

Uncl. 2-8-0 38-17x20-89000-80000-150-18853

97 Baldwin #15036 9/1896 Ex V.C.& R.V.#7 To N de M #97 - 1908
Built as #5; renumbered #7
98-100 Vacant

F-04 4-6-0 45-14x20-59000-42000-140-8536

101 Baldwin #8630 6/1887 To N de M #101 - 1908 Blt. as D&RG #178
102 " #8631 " " #102 - 1908 " " #179

F-03 4-6-0 48-16x20-70000-52000-139-10374

103 Baldwin #8913 11/1887 To N de M #103 - 1908
104 " #8911 " Rebuilt to standard gauge #276
105 " #8914 " To N de M #105 - 1908
106 " #8982 1/1888 Rebuilt to standard gauge #270
107 " #8983 " " #272
108 " #8984 " " #271
109 " #8985 " " #274
110 " #8994 " To N de M #110 - 1908
111 " #8986 " Rebuilt to standard gauge #278
112 " #8987 " Sold prior 1902

G-02 2-8-0 38-16x20-72000-64000-160-14703

113 Baldwin #8917 11/1887 To N de M #113 - 1908
114 " #9469 9/1888 " #114 - 1908 (Wts. 77400-69760)
115 " #9468 " " #115 - 1908 "
116 " #9471 " " #116 - 1908 "
117 " #9473 " " #117 - 1908 "
118 " #9476 " " #118 - 1908 "

F-03 4-6-0 48-16x20-70000-52000-139-10378

119 Baldwin #9479 9/1888 Rebuilt to standard gauge #273
120 " #9477 " " #283
121 " #9478 " " #287
122 " #9480 " To N de M #122 - 1908
123 " #9484 " " #123 - 1908
124 " #9485 " Rebuilt to standard gauge #275
125 " #9487 " To N de M #125 - 1908
126 " #9486 " " #126 - 1908

127 Baldwin #9492 9/1888 Rebuilt to standard gauge #286
128 " #9488 " " #277
129 " #9930 4/1889 " #285
130 " #9931 " To N de M #130 - 1908
131 " #9932 " " #131 - 1908
132 " #9933 " Rebuilt to standard gauge #281
133 " #9934 " " #282
134 " #9936 " To N de M #134 - 1908
135 " #9935 " " #135 - 1908
136 " #9937 " Rebuilt to standard gauge #284
137 " #9939 " Sold to Coahuila & Zacatecas #5 - 1903
138 " #9940 " Rebuilt to standard gauge #288

G-02 2-8-0 38-16x20-77400-69760-160-14703

139 Baldwin #9963 4/1889 To N de M #139 - 1908
140 " #9969 " " #140 - "
141 " #9962 " " #141 - "
142 " #9992 5/1889 " #142 - "
143 " #9993 " " #143 - "

F-01 4-6-0 46-16x20-70000-52000-140-12422

144 Baldwin #11211 9/1890 To N de M #144 - 1908
145 " #11240 10/1890 " #145 - "
146 " #11220 9/1890 " #146 - "

F-02 4-6-0 46-15x20-64000-47000-160-10956

148 Baldwin #11221 9/1890 To N de M #148 - 1908
149 " #11226 " " #149 - "
150 " #11218 " " #150 - "
151 " #11232 10/1890 " #151 - "

F-014 4-6-0 46-10&17x20-78600-57060-180-10500

147 Baldwin #11247 10/1890 To N de M #147 - 1908 Vauclain Comp.
152 " #12827 7/1892 " #152 - " "
153 " #12828 " " #153 - " "
154 " #12833 " " #154 - " "
155 " #12834 " " #155 - " "
156 " #12839 " " #156 - " "
157 " #12850 " " #157 - " "

H-1 2-8-0 38-10&17x20-83000-75000-175-12193

158 Baldwin #12849 7/1892 To N de M #158 - 1908
159 " #12853 " " #159 - "
160 " #12860 " " #160 - "
161 " #12871 8/1892 " #161 - "

F-014 4-6-0 46-10&17x20-78600-57060-180-10500

162 Baldwin #13363 4/1893 To N de M #162 - 1908 Vauclain Comp.

No. 162 was built as a Baldwin exhibit for the World's Columbian Exposition at Chicago. It was sold to the FCNM 7/1894.

F-02 4-6-0 46- 14 3/4x20-64000-44000-160-10594

163 Baldwin #15749 2/1898 To N de M #163 - 1908
164 " #15750 " " #164 - "

H-2 2-8-0 38-11 1/2&19x20-89000-80000-175-15653

165 Baldwin #15787 3/1898 To N de M #165 - 1908
166 " #15788 " " #166 - "
167 " #15789 " " #167 - "
168 " #15790 " " #168 - "
169 " #16450 1/1899 " #169 - "
170 " #16451 " " #170 - "
171 " #16452 " " #171 - "

F-014 4-6-0 46-10&17x20-82000-61000-175-10101

172 Baldwin #16468 1/1899 To N de M #172 - 1908
173 " #16469 " " #173 - "
174 " #16470 " " #174 - "
175 " #17270 1/1900 " #175 - "
176 " #17271 " " #176 - "
177 " #17319 " " #177 - "
178 " #17320 " " #178 - "
179 " #17361 " " #179 - "
180 " #17362 " " #180 - "

H-2 2-8-0 38-11 1/2&19x20-89000-80000-175-15653

181 Baldwin #17342 1/1900 To N de M #181 - 1908
182 " #17343 " " #182 - "
183 " #17368 " " #183 - "
184 " #17369 " " #184 - "

I 2-8-0 41-18x22-110265-99265-180-21905

185 Baldwin #17986 7/1900 To N de M #185 - 1908
186 " #17987 " " #186 - "

Uncl. 4-6-0 46-14x20-60000-43000-140-8400

2 Baldwin #10065 6/1889 Used on the isolated Zacatecas-Ojo Caliente
3 " #10066 " branch. Sold in 1908

Ferrocarriles Nacionales de Mexico
National Railways of Mexico

3 foot gauge
1908---1930
- - -

For construction numbers and dimensions, see the rosters of the F.C Nacionales Mexicano and the F.C. Hidalgo y Noroeste. From left to right, are the 1908 road numbers, previous numbers, wheel arrangement, class designation of 1908 and disposal information.

1 FCNM 1 2-8-0 G-01 Scr.by 1930
4 H&NE 12 " G-014 Scr.by 1930
5 "2nd 5 " G-011 Scr.by 1930
6 " 6 " G-012 To #223-1930
7 " 7 " " To #224- "
8 " 8 2-6-0 D-02 Scr.by 1930
9 " 9 4-4-0 C-01 "
10 " 10 " " "

11 " 11 2-8-0 G-012 "
12 FCNM 12 " G-01 "
13 H&NE 13 " G-014 "
14 " 14 " G-013 To #231-1930
15 " 15 4-6-0 F-06 Scr. by 1930
16 " 16 " " "
17 " 17 2-8-0 G-015 "
18 " 18 " G-010 "
19 " 19 " G-014 "
20 " 20 " G-012 To #225-1930
21 " 21 " " To #226-1930
22 " 22 " " To #227-1930
23 " 23 " " To #228-1930
24 " 24 " " To #229-1930
25 FCNM 25 " G-01 Scr. by 1930
26 H&NE 26 4-6-0 F-06 Scr. by 1930
27 " 27 2-8-0 G-012 To #230-1930
28 " 25 2-6-0 D-01 Scr. by 1930
35 FCNM 35 0-8-0 J-01 To #163-1930
37 " 37 2-6-0 D Lost 1914-20
42 " 42 0-6-0 B-01b Lost 1914-20
43 " 43 " " To Shop Sw. -1930
46 " 46 2-8-0 G-01 Scr. by 1930
47 " 47 " " "
49 " 49 " " "
51 " 51 " " "
52 " 52 " " "
60 " 60 " " "
61 " 61 " " Lost 1914-20
64 " 64 " " "
65 " 65 2-6-0 D "
66 " 66 " " "
67 " 67 " " "

68 FCNM 68 2-8-0 G-01 Lost 1914-20
69 " 69 0-8-0 J-01 To #164-1930
70 " 70 " " To #165-1930
72 " 72 2-8-0 G-01 Scr. by 1930
82 " 82 " G-03 "
83 " 83 " " To #220-1930
84 " 84 " " To #221-1930
85 " 85 " G-04 To #239-1930
86 " 86 " " To #240-1930
87 " 87 " " To #241-1930
90 " 90 2-6-0 D Lost 1914-20
91 " 91 " " "
92 " 92 4-4-0 C "
93 " 93 " " "
94 " 94 2-8-0 G-03 To #222-1930
95 " 95 " " Scr. by 1930
96 " 96 " G-04 To #242-1930
97 " 97 " " To #244-1930
101 " 101 4-6-0 F-04 Scr. by 1930
102 " 102 " " "
103 " 103 " " "
105 " 105 " F-03 "
110 " 110 " " "
113 " 113 2-8-0 G-02 To #232-1930
114 " 114 " " To FCI 2nd #10
115 " 115 " " To #233-1930
116 " 116 " " To FCI 2nd #11
117 " 117 " " To #234-1930
118 " 118 " " To FCI 2nd #12
122 " 122 4-6-0 F-03 Lost 1914-20
123 " 123 " " Scr. by 1930
125 " 125 " " "
126 " 126 " " Lost 1914-20
130 " 130 " " Scr. by 1930
131 " 131 " " "
134 " 134 " " Lost 1914-20
135 " 135 " " Scr. by 1930
138 " 138 0-8-0 J-01 To #166-1930
139 " 139 2-8-0 G-02 To #235-1930
140 " 140 " " To #236-1930
141 " 141 " " To FCI 2nd #14
142 " 142 " " To #237-1930
143 " 143 " " To #238-1930
144 " 144 4-6-0 F-01 Scr. by 1930
145 " 145 " " Sold to T&Z #3
146 " 146 " " To #125-1930
147 " 147 " " Lost 1914-20
148 " 148 " F-02 Scr. by 1930
149 " 149 " " "
150 " 150 " " "
151 " 151 " " "
152 " 152 " F-01 "

153 FCNM 153 4-6-0 F-01 Lost 1914-20
154 " 154 " " "
155 " 155 " " Scr. by 1930
156 " 156 " " To FCI 2nd #35
157 " 157 " " " " #36
158 " 158 2-8-0 G-06 To #245-1930
159 " 159 " " To #246-1930
160 " 160 " " To #247-1930
161 " 161 " " To #248-1930
162 " 162 4-6-0 F-02 Lost 1914-20
163 " 163 " " To FCI 2nd #37
164 " 164 " " Lost 1914-20
165 " 165 2-8-0 G-07 To #253-1930
166 " 166 " " To #254-1930
167 " 167 " " To #255-1930
168 " 168 " " To #256-1930
169 " 169 " " To #257-1930
170 " 170 " " To #258-1930
171 " 171 " " To #259-1930
172 " 172 4-6-0 F-014 Lost 1914-20
173 " 173 " " "
174 " 174 " " "
175 " 175 " " Scr. by 1930
176 " 176 " " "
177 " 177 " " "
178 " 178 " " "
179 " 179 " " "
180 " 180 " " "
181 " 181 2-8-0 G-08 To #249-1930
182 " 182 " " To #250-1930
183 " 183 " " To #251-1930
184 " 184 " " To #252-1930
185 " 185 " G-09 To #260-1930
186 " 186 " " To #261-1930

Locomotives purchased by the N de M after 1908. For construction numbers and dimensions, see 1930 list.

187 to 206 2-8-0 G-033 To #262-281-1930
207 " G-034 To #243 - 1930
208 2-6-0 D-010 To #167 - 1930
209 to 216 2-8-0 G-033 To #282-289 -1930
217 to 226 4-6-0 F-016 To #181-190 -1930
240 to 245 2-6-6-2 H-01 To #361-366 - "

Note; "Lost 1914-20 indicates records of these engines disappeared during the revo-tion. Some were destroyed; others were dismantled and salvageable parts used to keep others in service.
Class J-01 rebuilt from 2-8-0.
No. 25 originally FCNM #4.

Ferrocarril Interoceanico
Interoceanic Railway

3 foot gauge
1884---1930
- - - -

Uncl. engines taken over from F. C. Morelos

1	2-4-2T	Baldwin	#4625	4/1879	40-8x12	Ex Morelos #1	Sold by 1889
2	"	Dubs & Co.	#1329	/1879		" #2	"
3	"	"	#1330	"		" #3	"
4	4-4-0	Baldwin	#4879	12/1879	41-11x16	" #4	"

Class A-2 2-8-0 38-16x20-76571-66010-145-16606

5	Baldwin #5370	11/1880	Ex Morelos #5.	To FCI #97-1910;	to #50 - 1930
6	" #5438	1/1881	" #6.	" #98- " ;	to #51 - "
7	" #6086	7/1882	Ex Irolo RR #1.	" #99- " ;	to #52 - "
8	" #6537	12/1882	" #5.	" #94- " ;	to #47 - "
9	" #6540	"	" #7.	" #96- " ;	to #49 - "
10	" #6539	"	" #6.	" #95- " ;	to #48 - "

Class A-1 2-8-0 38-16x20-76571-66010-145-16606

20	Baldwin #7516	12/1884	to 2nd #4 - 1889;	to #90 - 1910;	to #33 - 1930
21	" #7517	"	" #1 - " ;	to #91 - " ;	to #34 - "
22	" #7518	"	" #2 - " ;	to #92 - " ;	to #35 - "
23	" #7519	"	" #3 - " ;	to #93 - " ;	to #36 - "

Class G-1 2-6-6-2 38-14 1/2x20-68448

11	Beyer Peacock #3012 - 1889	Fairlie type.	Scrapped by 1914
12	" #3013 - "	"	" "
13	" #3014 - "	"	" 1920
14	" #3015 - "	"	" 1914

Class A-3 2-8-0 38-16x20-87522-75470-145-16606

2nd 10 Baldwin #9469 9/1888 Ex NdeM #114 Acq. 1913. To #21 - 1930
2nd 11 " #9471 " " #116 " " #22 - "
2nd 12 " #9476 " " #118 " " #23 - "
2nd 14 " #9962 4/1889 " #141 " " #24 - "
15 " #9621 11/1888 Scrapped by 1930
16 " #9628 " To #25 - 1930
17 " #9719 1/1889 " #26 - "
18 " #9720 " " #27 - "
19 " #9721 " " #28 - "
2nd 20 " #9729 " " #29 - "
2nd 21 " #9728 " " #30 - "
2nd 22 " #9725 " Scrapped prior 1930
2nd 23 " #9732 " To #31 - 1930
24 " #9730 " " #32 - "

Uncl. 2-6-0 45-14x20-52000-45000

25 Baldwin #6080 3/1882 E. #27;Irolo RR #2. Sold Xico & San Rafael-1898
26 Vacant

Class B-1 4-6-0 47-17&20x27-122431-74665-175-13066

27 Schenectady #5222 9/1899 Cross comp.-Simpled. To #10 - 1930
28 " #4790 8/1898 " " To #11 - 1930
29 " #4791 " " " To #12 - 1930

Class B-2 4-6-0 46-16x20-110162=67200-175-13036

30 Baldwin #10578 1/1890 To #5 - 1930
31 " #10094 7/1889 To #6 - 1930
32 " #10095 " To #7 - 1930
33 " #10096 " To #8 - 1930
34 " #10112 " To #9 - 1930
35 " #12839 7/1892 To #3 - 1930 Ex NdeM #156 Acq. 1909
36 " #12850 " To #4 - 1930 " #157 "
37 " #15749 2/1898 To MdelS #23 " #163 "

Class B-3 4-6-0 47-16x20-91000-55550-175-12900

35 Dubs & Co. #2571 9/1889 Retired prior 1919
36 " #2572 " "
37 " #2573 " "
38 " #2574 " To #2 - 1930
39 " #2575 " Retired prior 1919

Class A-4 2-8-0 38-16x20-76583-66020-145-16606

40 Baldwin #10670 2/1890 To #37 - 1930
41 " #10673 " To #38 - "
42 " #10738 3/1890 To #39 - "
43 " #10739 " To #40 - "
44 " #10747 " To #41 - "
45 " #10750 " To #42 - "
46 " #10836 4/1890 To #43 - "
47 " #10842 " To #44 - "
48 " #10929 5/1890 To #45 - "
49 " #10930 " To #46 - "

Class A-5 2-8-2 38-16x20-75161-66900-145-16828

50 Baldwin #11284 10/1890 Reblt. to 2-8-0 Lost between 1914-20
51 " #11285 " " "
52 " #11324 " " To #53 - 1930
53 " #11325 " " To #54 - "
54 " #11357 " " To #55 - "
55 " #11348 " " Lost between 1914-20
56 " #11371 " " To #56 - 1930
57 " #11372 " " To #57 - "
58 " #11393 " " To #58 - "
59 " #11407 " " To #59 - "

Class A-6 2-8-0 38-16x20-98460-84880-175-16466

60 Schenectady #4792 8/1898 Same number in 1930
61 " #4793 " "
62 " #4796 " "
63 " #4797 " "
64 " #4798 " "
65 " #4799 " "
66 " #5209 7/1899 "
67 " #5210 " "
68 " #5211 " "
69 " #5212 " "
70 " #5213 " "
71 " #5214 " "
72 " #5221 " "

Class A-8 2-8-0 38-16x20-98460-84880-175-20042

73 Kerr, Stuart & Co. #819 5/1904 Same number in 1930
74 " #820 " "
75 " #821 " "

Class A-7 2-8-0 38-11 1/2&19x20-98460-84800-175-16505 Vauc. Comp.

80 Baldwin #17408 1/1900 Simpled in 1926 To #76 - 1930
81 " #17409 " " To #77 - "

90-99 See Nos. 5-10, 20-23 for data

Uncl. 4-4-0 41-12x18-41000-28000

100 Baldwin #6238 6/1882 Ex Irolo R. R. #4. Sold prior 1903

Class C-5 0-6-0 38-14x20-69242-140-10051

101 Schenectady #5169 6/1899 To #1 - 1930

Class C-2 0-6-0 31-12x18-51084

102 Nasmyth-Wilson 1883(approx). Gone by 1920. See note
103 " " " "

Class C-3 and C-4 0-6-0 31-13x18

104 C-3 J. M. Sumner & Co. agents for unknown. bldr. -Gone by 1920 See note
106 C-4 " " " "

Class D-2 2-4-2T 38-10x18-19485

105 Dubs & Co. 1883(approx.) Gone by 1920 See note

Note; Nos. 102-106 were ex Puebla & Matamoros-Izucar Nos. 2-6 incl.

Original roster of the Irolo R. R., taken over by the F. C. I. 1889 3 foot gauge

No.	Name	Type	Builder	Builder No.	Date	Data	Disposition
1	Texcoco	2-8-0	Baldwin	#6086	3/1882	37-16x20	To FCI #7
2	Irolo	2-6-0	"	#6080	"	45-14x20	" #27, #25.
3	Acapulco	4-4-0	"	#6325	8/1882	41-11x16	Sold by 1889
4	Los Reyes	"	"	#6238	6/1882	41-12 1/2x18	To FCI #100
5	Calpulalpan	2-8-0	"	#6537	12/1882	37-16x20	To FCI #8
6	San Lorenzo	"	"	#6539	"	"	" #10
7	Puebla	"	"	#6540	"	"	" #9

Note; No. 4 ordered by Minneapolis, Lyndale & Minnetonka #13; diverted to Irolo R. R.

F. C. Mexicano de Sur
Mexican Southern R. R.

3 foot gauge
1890 - 1930

- - -

The numbers in the left column were adopted in 1909. Previous numbers follow.

Class C-02 4-4-0 45-14x22-61152-39200-140-8582

241 7 Kitson & Co. #3312 2/1891 To #101 - 1930
242 8 " #3313 " Scr. 1920-1930

Class F-09 4-6-0 48-16x22-72800-54880-140-11498

251 1 Kitson & Co. #3257 10/1890 Scr. 1920-1930
252 2 " #3258 " "
253 3 " #3308 12/1890 "
254 4 " #3309 " "
255 5 " #3310 " "
256 6 " #3311 " "

Classes F-010 and F-011 4-6-0 48-16x20-87000-58000-150-11200

261 20 Alco-Cooke #25797 4/1902 F-010 To #103 - 1930
262 21 " #25798 " " To #104 - "
263 22 " #42038 5/1908 F-011 To #105 - "

Class F-012 4-6-0 46-15x20-64000-44000-160-13304

264 23 FCI 37 FCNM 163 Baldwin #15749 2/1898 To #102 - 1930

Classes G-029, G-030, G-031 2-8-0 38-17x20-88000-80135-145-15856

271	15	Baldwin	#13035	11/1892	G-029	To #112 - 1930	
272	16	"	#13036	"	"	To #113 - "	
273	17	"	#13041	"	"	To #114 - "	
274	9	"	#33566	7/1909	"	To #115 - "	
275	10	"	#33567	"	"	To #116 - "	
276	13	"	#27588	2/1906	G-030	To #120 - "	
277	14	"	#27599	"	"	Scr. 1920-1930	
278	11	"	#33598	7/1909	G-031	To #117 - 1930	
279	12	"	#33599	"	"	To #118 - "	
280	20*	"	#33600	"	"	To #119 - "	*In serv. as #280
282	19	"	#32731	3/1908	G-030	To #121 - "	
283		"		/1895	G-030a	Scr. 1920-1930	Note

Note; #283 acquired second hand after 1910. Previous history unknown

Class G-032 2-8-0 37-17x20-88000-80135-145-14761

281	18	Alco-Cooke	#25796	4/1902	To #111 - 1930

During the construction of the Mexican Southern, the contractors brought four 0-6-0T locomotives and two 0-4-0T type from England. After completion of the railroad, the six locomotives were sold to the railroad and occupied the road numbers 9 to 14 incl. Only four have been identified as follows;

11	0-6-0T	Yorkshire Eng. Co.	#435 - 1890	13x20	Named Mariscal	
12	"	"	#436 - "	"	" Dublan	
13	0-4-0T	Manning-Wardle	#1164 - 1890	9x14	Contractors #3	
14	"	"	#1169 - "	"	Named Porfirio Diaz #4	

All of the above locomotives had been sold or scrapped by 1906.

F. C. Oriental Mexicano
Mexican Eastern R. R.

3 foot gauge
1908-1930
- - - -

2-8-0 38-16x20-98460-84880-175-20042

1	Kerr, Stuart & Co.	#822	5/1904	Ex San Marcos & Tecolutla	#76.	To #142-1930
2	"	#823	"	"	#77	To #143- "
3	Baldwin	#20384	4/1902	"	#78	To #144- "
4	"	#20385	"	"	#79	To #145 - "

0-6-0T 36-13x18-51060

5	Hunslet Engine Co.	#309 - 1883	Ex S. M. & T.	#5-	Note	Gone by 1930
6	"	#310 - "	"	#6-	"	"

2-8-0 36-15x20-86275

7 Baldwin Date blt. unknown. Previous history unknown. Gone by 1930

2-8-0 38-15x18, later 15x20

8 Baldwin #16201 9/1898 To #141 - 1930

Note; Built for the Puebla & San Marcos R. R.

F. C. Hidalgo y Noroeste
Hidalgo & Northeastern R. R.

3 foot gauge
1882-1908
- - - -

4-4-0 Class A-1 42-11x16-37000-25800
Class A 48-13x20-60000-40000

1	Hidalgo	Baldwin	#6498	12/1882	Retired prior 1908	A-1
2	Humboldt	"	#6678	3/1883	"	"
3	Terreras	"	#6728	4/1883	"	"
9	Navajas	"	#10699	3/1890	To N de M #9 -1908	A
10	Napateco	"	#10709	"	" #10 - "	"

Uncl. 0-4-4T #4 44-10x16 #5 30-9x14

4	Irolo	Porter	#837	7/1887	Retired prior 1908
5	F. de Trembleque	Baldwin	#8696	8/1887	" 1902

Class E-4 2-8-0 38-15x18-62000-56000

5	FCNM 9 MT&C 5	Baldwin	#4788	9/1879	To N de M #5- 1908
11	Xicotepec	"	#11702	3/1891	" #11- "
12	Tuxpam	"	#11703	"	" #4- "
13	Acayucotlan	"	#12267	10/1891	" #13- "
14	Pachuca	"	#12270	"	" #14- "

Class E-3 2-8-0 38-16x20-78000-70000

6	J. Villagram	Baldwin	# 9867	3/1889	To N de M # 6 - 1908
7	Ocampo	"	# 9876	"	" # 7 - "
19	Tezontepec	"	#14965	7/1896	" #19 - "
20	Zempoala	"	#14964	"	" #20 - "
21	G. Mancera	"	#17456	2/1900	" #21 - "
22	Tulancingo	"	#17457	"	" #22 - "
23	Ti zayuca	"	#17960	7/1900	" #23 - "
24	Honey	"	#17961	"	" #24 - "
27	Zacatlan	"	#25773	"	" #27 - "

Classes H-3 and C-3 2-8-0 H-3 38-9 1/2&16x18
C-3 38-16x18

17	Huaya	Baldwin	#14055	7/1894	H-3	Vauc. Comp.	To N de M #17-1908
18		"		/1880	C-3	2nd hand-1895	" #18- "

Note; #17 rebuilt simple, 16x18; #18, previous history unknown

Class F-06 4-6-0 44-14x20 57000 41000

15	Nor. Georgia 4	Baldwin	#7523	12/1884	Acq. 1894	To N de M #15 - 1908
16	" 5	"	#7869	"	"	" #16 - "

Class F-2 4-6-0 48-16x20-70000-52000

26	Huauchinango	Baldwin	#25839	7/1905	To N de M #26 - 1908

2-6-0 Class B 38-15x20-46500-40000
Class B-1 38-15x18-47000-40500

8	B-1	Baldwin 1883	Acq. 2nd hand 1890	History unkwn.	To NdeM #8-1908
25	B	" 1881	" 1905	"	" #25- "

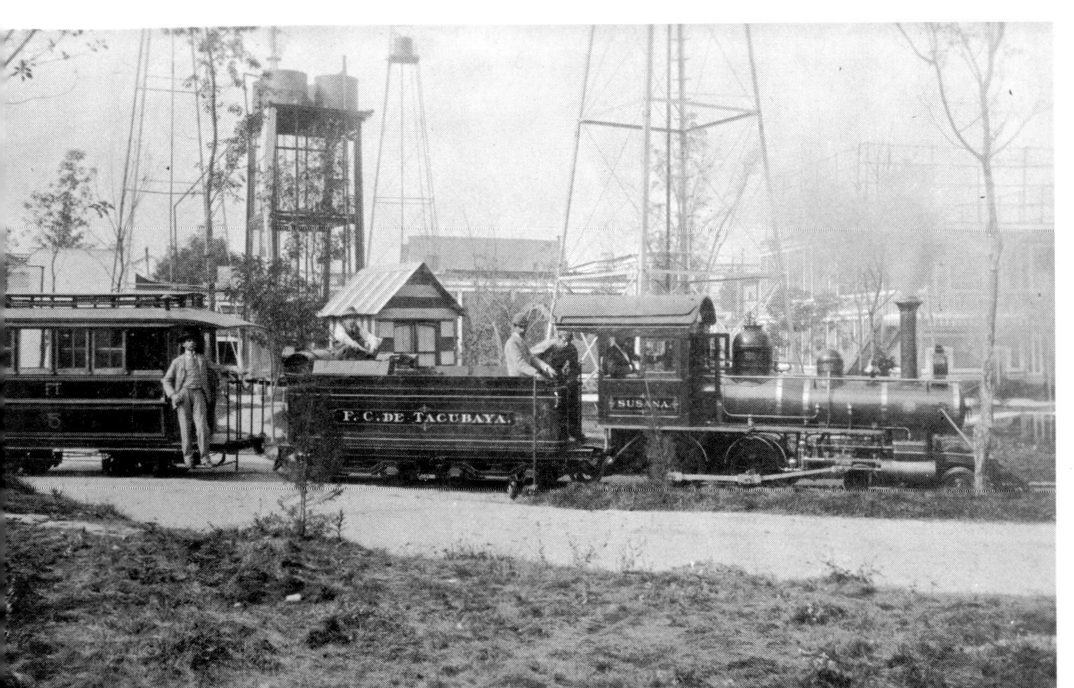

The SUSANA was made for the F. C. de Tacubaya in 1897, the smallest 4-4-0 ever built by Baldwin for commercial purposes. *(E. L. De Golyer Jr. collection)*

F. C. Mexicano
Mexican Railway

Narrow gauge branches

- - -

F. C. Cordova a Huatusco - 2 foot gauge

Class E-1 2-6-0 33-12x18-52820-44847-150-10014

No.	Name	Builder	No.	Date	Note	Disposition
1	Elena	Baldwin	#20092	2/1902	Old Class 1-H	Scrapped 1953
2	Luisa	"	#20140	"	"	"
3	Beatriz	"	#25368	3/1905	"	"

Class S-H 0-4-4-0 Shay 26 1/2-9x9-55927-160-12648

4 Lima #1616 12/1905 Ex F.C. Atlamaxac #3. Acq. 1910. Scr. 1945

Zacatlan branch--Munoz to Chignahuapan - 30 inch gauge

Class E-2 2-8-0 36-15x20-82891-74302-160-17000

No.	Builder	No.	Date			
11	Baldwin	#34312	2/1910	Retired in 1952.	Scrapped 1957	
12	"	#34313	"	"	1957.	Sold Edaville Museum 10/59
13	"	#34314	"	"	" .	
14	"	#34315	"	"	" .	

San Marcos-Ixcaquixtla branch - 3 foot gauge

Class E-3 2-8-0 36-15x18-75123-66891-165-15757

No.		Builder	No.	Date		
20	1	Baldwin	#20370	4/1902	Retired 1951	Note.
21	2	"	#20371	"	" 1952	"
22	3	"	#20372	"	" "	"

Class EE-4 4-6-0 42-17x20-85000-69000-165-19900

23 SR&A 9 Alco-Schenectady #50470 9/1911 Retired 1957

Class G-028 38-17x20-99724-90749-180-23272

No.			Builder	No.	Date		
24	NdeM 259	FCNM 171	Baldwin	#16452	1/1899	Acq. 1950.	Retired 1957
25	257	169	"	#16450	"	"	"
26	258	170	"	#16451	"	"	"

Note; Nos. 20-22 incl. were built for the F. C. Tlacotepec a Huajuapam de Leon. Taken over by the F. C. Mexicano in 1910. No. 1 was named Huajuapam de Leon; No. 2 was named Tepexi; No. 3 was named Acatlan. There was also No. 4, an 0-6-0T acquired from the Mexican Southern, and which was scrapped by the F. C. Mexicano in 1910.

F. C. Unidos de Yucatan
United Railways of Yucatan

3 foot gauge
1902---1968

Nos. 1 to 17 and No. 20 were standard gauge. Dimensions of the narrow gauge engines are given in a list following the roster.

No.	Type	Builder	No.	Date	Disposition
18	2-8-0	Baldwin	#40168	7/1913	Renumbered #280 - 1963
19	"	"	#40169	"	Retired 1960

Engines of the F.C. Merida & Valladolid renumbered in 1902

No.	Name	Type	Builder	No.	Date	Ex		Disposition	
21	Conkal	4-4-0	Baldwin	#6478	11/1882	Ex M&V	#1	Scrapped	1903
22	Merida	"	"	#7129	2/1884	"	#2	"	"
23	Progreso	"	"	#7936	5/1886	"	#3	"	"
24	Valladolid	"	"	#8241	11/1886	"	#4	"	1914
25	Marcus Duarte	"	"	#9873	2/1889	"	#5	"	1923
26	Motul	"	"	#9964	5/1889	"	#6	"	1925
27	Tunkas	"	"	#16022	7/1898	"	#7	"	1947
28	Espita	"	"	#16671	4/1899	"	#8	"	1949
29	Citas	"	"	#18265	10/1900	"	#9	"	1949
30	No locomotive								

Engines of the F.C. Merida & Calkini, later known as the Cia. Peninsular de F.C.. de Merida-Yucatan, renumbered in 1902

No.	Name	Type	Builder	No.	Date	Ex		Disposition	
31	D.O. de Diaz	4-4-0	Baldwin	#6111	3/1882	Ex M&C	#1	Scrapped	1906
32	Uman	"	"	#7144	2/1884	"	#2	"	1946
33	Mexcanu	"	"	#9537	10/1888	"	#3	"	1955
34	Campeche	"	"	#10590	1/1890	"	#4	"	1920
35	Merida	"	"	#13932	1/1894	"	#5	"	1933
36	Hecelchakaru	"	"	#14020	4/1894	"	#6	"	1930
37	Gen. Pedro Baranda	"	"	#16052	8/1898	"	#7	"	1928
38	Halacho	"	"	#17102	10/1899	"	#8	"	1947
49	Loreto	"	"	#18242	10/1900	"	#9	"	1945
50	Muna	"	"	#18735	3/1901	"	#10	"	1947
51		2-6-0	Pittsburgh	#2371	3/1902	"	#11	"	1955
52		"	"	#2372	"	"	#12	Preserved at Merida.	

Engines purchased by the Unidos de Yucatan between 1903 and 1916.

No.	Name	Type	Builder	No.	Date	Disposition
39	Ticul	4-6-0	Baldwin	#23031	10/1903	Scrapped 1949
40	Cansahcab	"	"	#23050	"	Renumb. #270 - 1963
41	Calkini	"	"	#23714	2/1904	Scrapped 1950
42	Becal	"	"	#23723	"	" "
43	Temax	"	"	#23759	"	Scrapped 1955
44	Hecelchaken	"	"	#23758	"	Renumb. #271 - 1963
45	Tenabo	"	"	#23757	"	Scrapped 1949
46	Tinon	0-6-0	Baldwin	#23739	"	Retired 1960
47		4-6-0	Baldwin	#44497	12/1916	Renumb. #272 - 1963
48		"	"	#44498	"	" #273 - "

Engines of the F.C. Merida & Peto, renumbered in 1908

No.	Name	Type	Builder	No.	Date	Ex		Disposition
53	Independencia	0-4-0	Baldwin	#20970	9/1902	Ex M&P	#13	Scr. 1925
54	Ticul	4-4-0	"	#9158	3/1888	"	#4	Scr. 1933
55	Candelaria	"	"	#9684	12/1888	"	#5	Scr.
56	Mercedes	"	"	#10495	12/1889	"	#6	Scr. 1927
57	Estela	"	"	#12420	2/1892	"	#7	Scr. 1955
58	Peto	"	"	#8139	8/1886	"	#3	Scr. 1955
59	F. Ybarra O.	"	"	#15855	4/1898	"	#9	Scr. 1947
60	G. Canton	"	"	#16314	11/1898	"	#10	Scr.
61	R. Romero Ancona	"	"	#17364	1/1900	"	#11	Scr. 1947
62	Catalina A. De Casasus	2-6-0	Baldwin	#21935	4/1903	"	#12	Scr. 1948
63	Acanceh	4-4-0	Baldwin	#5527	3/1881	"	#1	Scr. 1920
64	Tecoh	"	"	#6017	1/1882	"	#2	Scr.
-	Candita ---Steam car		"	#13354	4/1893	M. & P.	#8	Sold 1908

Engines purchased by the Unidos de Yucatan between 1916 and 1958

No.	Type	Builder	No.	Date	Disposition
65	4-4-0	Baldwin	#42914	2/1916	Renumbered #250 - 1963
66	"	"	#42915	"	" #251 - "
67	"	"	#56387	4/1923	Retired 1960
68	"	"	#56388	"	" "
69	4-6-0	"	#45936	7/1917	Renumbered #273 - 1963
70	"	"	#45937	"	Scrapped 1956
71	0-6-0	"	#58442	5/1925	Retired 1960
72	4-6-0	"	#58444	"	Renumbered #274 - 1963
73	"	"	#58445	"	Retired 1960
74	4-4-0	"	#58414	"	"

Former Denver & Rio Grande Western No. 458 is scarcely recognizable after being rebuilt to conform to Mexican narrow gauge standards, as N. de M. 400. *(L. T. Haug)*

75 2-6-0 " #60597 9/1928 " 1962
76 " " #60598 " Renumbered #260 - 1963
77 " " #60599 " " #261 - "
78 " " #60600 " " #262 - "
79 " " #60601 " Retired 1962
80 4-4-0 " #72206 7/1946 " 1960
81 " " #72207 " " "

Engines purchased from the N de M in 1956 and 1958

119 2-8-0 Baldwin #33600 7/1909 Acq. 1956. Retired 1960 Ex MdelS #119
161 " Schen. #4793 8/1898 " " " Ex FCI #61
182 4-6-0 Baldwin #57939 7/1924 " " "
184 " " #57941 " " " "
172 2-8-0 Schen. #5221 7/1899 Acq. 1958. Renumb. #281 - 1963
Ex FCI #72

Dimensions of the F. C. U. de Y. locomotives

18-19 38-16x20-90000-80000-180-20610
21-23 45-12x16-37000-24000
24-26 45-12x16-42416-27000-150-6510
27-29 45-12x18-44480-29610-160-7840 #27 blt. as Vauclain compound, rebuilt simple.
31 45-12x16-42415-27000-130-5660
32-38 45-12x18-44480-29610-130-6370
39-45 44-15x20-72700-56200-180-15660
46 44-16x20-64000-64000-160-15800
47-48 44-15x20-73000-57000-180-13900
49 45-12x18-47565-31410-160-7840
50 45-12x18-44480-29610-130-6370
51-52 42-14x18-59000-52000-160-11700
53 33-12x16-42000-42000-160-9500
54-56 45-12x18-44480-29610-130-6370
57 45-13x18-46300-28100-130-7840
58-61 45-12x18-44480-29610-160-7840
62 40-13x18-51000-42300-160-10350
63 41-10x16-38800-24600-130-4310
64 45-12x16-42415-27000-130-5660
65-66 46-13x18-51000-33000-160-9000
67-68 46-13x18-57000-34000-160-9000
69-70 44-15x20-75400-60400-180-13900
71 44-15x20-72000-72000-180-15800
72-73 44-15x20-74000-60000-180-13900
74 46-13x18-57000-34000-160-9000
75-79 40-13x18-57000-47000-160-10320
80-81 46-13x20-63000-37000-160-9000

For the dimensions of the ex N de M engines, see the N de M list.

Mexico

Narrow gauge shortlines

Aguascalientes R. R. 3 foot gauge

1 0-4-0T Porter #2302 2/1901 30-10x14-29000
2 " " #2459 11/1901 "
3 0-6-2T " #3134 2/1905 36-11x16-44000 30 in. gauge for smelter.

Atlamaxac R. R. 2 foot gauge

1 0-6-0T Builder and date unknown. Sold 1910
2 " " "
3 Shay Lima #1616 12/1905 2 Truck. 26 1/2-9x9-55927 To F. C. Mexicano #4 at Cordova, 1910.

Cazadero La Torre & Tepetongo R. R. 2 foot gauge

1 0-6-0T Builder and date unknown
2 0-4-4T Baldwin. Date unknown
3 2-6-2T " #14992 8/1896 33-11x16-46000-32000
4 " " #14798 4/1896 " Note 1.
5 " " #14799 " " "
6 " " #14976 8/1896 " Note 2.
7 2-6-0 " #15327 5/1897 33-11 3/4x16-39000-34000

Note 1. Sold to Ingenio San Francisco Nos. 4 and 5, gauge widened to 30 in.
Note 2. Sold to Compania La Primavera No. 1.

Coahuila & Zacatecas R. R. 3 foot gauge

1 2-8-0 Baldwin #15435 7/1897 38-16x20-82420 Sold to Early West Rys.
2 " " #15436 " " Scrapped 1946
3 " " #15784 3/1898 " Sold to CIASA #3 - 1945
4 " " #18620 1/1901 38-16x20-82420
3 " " #32665 2/1908 40-16x20-97000 Ex Parral & Dur. #7
5 4-6-0 " # 9939 4/1889 48-16x20-70000 Ex NdeM #137. Scr. 1952
6 " " #24252 5/1904 47-14x20-92160 Sold to Early West Rys.
7 " " #29869 1/1907 "
8 2-8-0 " #30178 2/1907 38-16x20-98630
9 " " #32129 11/1907 38-16x20-108920
10 " " #32647 2/1908 "
11 " " #33554 7/1909 "
12 " " #35990 7/1911 " Sold to Early West Rys.
261 " " #17987 8/1900 41-18x22-110265 Ex NdeM #261. Note.
273 " " #55057 9/1921 " " #273. "
279 " " #55110 " " " #279. "

Note; Nos. 273 and 279 returned to N de M in 1965. Acq. 6/1959. No. 6 was built as a 4-6-2. Weighed 103410. Converted to a 4-6-0 in 1910. Nos. 1, 6 and 12 sold 3/1965 and stored at Pomona, Calif. 1968.

Desague del Valle de Mexico R. R. 3 foot gauge

101 2-6-0 Hinkley #1393 4/1881 Ex FCNM 33 32-12x20
102 4-6-0 Baldwin "
103 " " "
104 2-8-0 " "
105 " " "
106 0-6-0 Baldwin #5811 9/1881 Ex FCNM 23 37-14x18

F. C. del Valle de Mexico(Valley of Mexico R. R.) 3 foot gauge

1 0-4-4T Baldwin #10754 3/1890 37-10x16-48000
2 " " #10873 " "
3 " " #10874 " "
4 2-4-4 " #11889 5/1891 37-12x16-52000

El Oro Mining & Railway Co. 3 foot gauge

1 2-8-0 Brooks #3036 9/1898 44-17x20-104200 Note
2 " " #3037 " "
3 2-6-0 Brooks #3380 12/1899 44-15x20-80000
4 " " #3381 " "

Note. Nos. 1 and 2 were ordered by the America R. R. & Lbr. Co., predecessors to the El Oro Min. & Ry. Co. Nos. 1-4 were used as road engines. The balance of the roster consisted of engines used in the mining and timber operations.

1 0-4-4T Machala Pittsburgh #1842 10/1898 37-10x16
2 " Alco-Pitts. #29536 12/1903 "
1 " Machaca " #46574 6/1909 Note.
3 2-8-0 Alco-Dickson #26595 11/1902
4 Shay Lima # 946 10/1909 Ex #1 26 1/2-7x12
5 " " # 947 " " #2 "
6 " " # 2337 6/1910 Note.
7 " " # 2421 2/1911 "

Note; The Machaca was ordered as a replacement for the Machala. Nos. 6 and 7 were ordered by the Suchi Tbr. Co., a subidiary of El Oro.

F. C. Guanajuato a San Luis de la Paz y Pozos 3 foot gauge. See FCNM 90-91

F. C. de Hornos (Hornos Ry.) 2 foot gauge

1 0-6-0T Porter Date unknown. Furnished by the contractor
2 2-4-0 Baldwin #20871 8/1902 28-8x14-19600 Named Adela
3 2-6-0 " #21823 3/1903 28-9x14-24000 Named Concepcion -Note
4 2-8-2 " #21825 " 28-10x14-40000 Named Juana

Note. No. 3 sold to Godchaux Sugar Co. #7 9/1909 for Elm Hall & Foley R. R.

F. C. Ixtlahuaca, also known as the Ixtlahuaca, Mani y Nijini R. R. 3 foot gauge

1 2-8-0 Baldwin #14920 9/1896 38-16x20-76000
11 " " #24812 11/1904 38-16x20-78000

Note; There were also two unidentified second-hand 2-6-0 locomotives.

F. C. Jalapa & Teocelo, formerly Jalapa & Cordova R. R. 3 foot gauge

1 2-6-0 Brooks #2839 10/1897 48-15x20 Sold to F. C. V. A 2nd 5 - 1914
2 " " #2840 " " Renumb. J & T. 2nd #3 - "
3 2-8-0 Porter #1900 10/1898 40-16x20 " " #1 - "
4 " " #2210 9/1900 " " " #2 - "
4 Shay Lima # 839 10/1903 26 1/2-8x8-75000 Ex F. C. de Pachuca #1 Acq. 1914

Mapimi R. R. 30 inch gauge

Mapimi 0-4-2T Baldwin #15047 9/1896 35-9x16-28000
Penoles " " #15048 " "
Ojuela " " #15049 " "
San Ygnacio " " #15172 2/1897 "
San Judas " " #15682 1/1898 "
Bermejillo 2-6-2T " #18355 11/1900 35-12x16-46000
San Pedro " " #21721 3/1903 "
- - " " #36796 3/1911 "

Rack engines, used only in mining operations.

Socavon #1 0-6-2T Baldwin #15110 12/1896 Vauclain compound
Santa Rita #2 " " #15111 " "
San Vicente #3 2-6-2T " #15653 1/1898 "
Chona #4 " " #17696 4/1900 "

Dimensions; 24 3/4-9 1/2&15x22-59000. Nos. 3-4 weighed 62000.

F. C. Matehuala, originally called F. C. Porvenir de Matehuala 3 foot gauge

1 Esperanza 0-4-2T Baldwin #13025- 10/1892 24-7x12 Note
2 La Paz 0-6-0 " #13205 2/1893 36-16x18-63000
3 La Esmeralda " " #16470 5/1899 "
4 Nueva Paz " " #19152 6/1901 " Note
5 " " #35966 1/1911 36-16x18-66000

Note; No. 1 was 30 in. gauge, operated only in the mine yards. No. 4 Sold to Mazapil Copper Co., Concepcion del Oro.

Mexico, Toluca & Cuautitlan 3 foot gauge See FCNM for data.

The M. T. & C. engines were named as follows; No. 1, Cuautitlan; No. 2, Tlalnepantla; No. 3, Barrientos; No. 4, Tula; No. 5, Nochistongo.

Michoacan & Pacific R. R. 3 foot gauge See FCNM Nos. 81-87 for data

Monte Alto & Tlalnepantla R.R. 3 foot gauge

1 2-4-4T Baldwin #16432 12/1898 40-14x20
2 " " #16433 " "
3 " " #29276 10/1906 "
4 " " #23905 3/1904 " Ordered by the Cia. San
5 " " #23967 " " Ildefonso. (Nos. 1-2)
6 2-2-0 Steam car Baldwin #57606 11/1923
7 " " " #57607 "

Monterrey Mineral & Terminal Ry. 3 foot gauge

20 0-6-0 Rogers #5016 - 1894 36-14x20
21 2-6-0 " #5102 - 1895 36-16x20

Morelos R. R. 3 foot gauge See F.C.I. Nos. 1 to 6 for data

The Morelos engines were named as follows; No. 1, Carlos Pacheco; No. 2, Benito Juarez; No. 3, Porfirio Diaz; No. 4, Morelos; No. 5, Manuel Mendoza Cortina; No. 6, Sacro Monte.

Oaxaca & Ejutla R. R. 3 foot gauge

1 Unknown
4 Oaxaca 2-8-0 Baldwin #20150 3/1902 36-15x18
5 Ocotlan " " #20149 " "

Panuco Mountain & Monclova R.R. 3 foot gauge

1 0-4-2T Baldwin #17762 5/1900 30-9x14-29000 Ex Panuco Sugar Co. #1
2 " " #17833 6/1900 " " #2
3 Shay Lima # 1689 10/1906 26 1/2-8x8
4 " " # 1839 4/1907 "

Parral & Durango R. R. 3 foot gauge

1 2-6-0 Baldwin #16496 7/1899 40-14x20-71400 To CIASA 1st #3
2 " " #17681 4/1900 " " #2
3 2-8-0 Rogers # 5608 /1900 38-14x20 To Ingenio El Potrero #6
4 2-6-0 Baldwin #18644 1/1901 40-14x20-71400 To CIASA #4
5 " " #19041 5/1901 " " #5
6 2-8-0 " #25886 6/1905 50-17x20-108000 To Ing. el Pot. #8
7 " " #32665 2/1908 40-16x20-97000 To C. & Z. 2nd #3-1940

Potosi Central R. R. 30 inch gauge

1 0-4-4T Porter #2992 2/1904 40-13x16-44000 Note; factory records show
2 0-4-4T " #3006 " 33- 9x14-33000 locos. built 3 ft. gauge.

Potosi & Rio Verde R. R. 3 foot gauge

1 2-8-0 Baldwin #16524 12/1899 36-14x18-65000-55000
2 " " #16525 " " Note
3 Shay Lima # 833 9/1903 29 1/2-10x12
4 2-8-0 Baldwin #24306 6/1904 36-15x18-74500-65500 Note
- 0-6-0T Porter # 4641 6/1910 26-9x14-27500 30 in. gauge. Note

Note; Nos. 2 and 4 sold to Chihuahua Mineral Ry. The 30 in. gauge engine was used on a mine branch at San Pedro.

Puebla & Matamoros-Izucar R. R. 3 foot gauge See FCI 102-106 for data.

Puebla & San Marcos R. R. 3 foot gauge

1 2-4-2T Porter Blt. prior 1882 33-10x16-20000 Scr. prior 1904
2 No record
3 0-6-0T Dubs & Co. #1600-1882 36-12x18-42104 Sold prior 1904
4 " " #1601- " " "
5 " Hunslet Eng. Co. #309-1883 36-13x18-51060 To SM&T #5-1902
6 " " #10- " " " #6- "

Note; Engines No. 5 and 6 became Mexican Eastern, same numbers. The following engines bore names; No. 3, Motobinia; No. 4, Jose Mansu; No. 5, Jose Maria LaFragua; No. 6, Esteban Antunano.

San Gregorio R. R. 3 foot gauge

1 2-6-0 Baldwin #18556 1/1901 40-12x18-

San Rafael & Atlixco R. R. 3 foot gauge

1 2-8-0 Baldwin #16391 12/1898 37-16x20-87000 Built as 2-8-2 Note.
2 2-6-0 " # 6080 3/1882 45-14x20-52000 Ex Irolo RR #2 Note.
3 2-8-0 " #16105 8/1898 37-16x20-87000 Built as 2-8-2 Note.
4 " " #16106 " " " "
5 4-6-0 " #17381 1/1900 42-17x20-88000 Note.
6 " " #17382 " " Note.
7 2-8-0 " #27507 2/1906 37-16x20-87000 "
8 " " #27508 " " "
9 4-6-0 A-Schen. #50470 10/1911 42-17x20-85000 To F. C. Mexicano #23

Note. Nos. 1, 3, 4, 7 and 8 were built as 2-8-2 type. Rebuilt to 2-8-0. Nos. 4 and 5 became San Rafael Paper Co., same numbers. Nos. 3 and 8 became F. C. Anahuac, same numbers. No. 2 acquired in 1898.

F. C. de Tacubaya (Tacubaya R. R.) - 2 foot gauge

1 0-4-0T Krauss 1896
2 4-4-0 Baldwin #15241 3/1897 23-6x10-12000 Named Susana

Toluca to Tenango & San Juan R. R. 3 foot gauge

Tenango line
10 4-4-0 Baldwin #15122 12/1896 42-12x18-54000-34000
11 2-8-0 " #24603 8/1904 37-15x20-68000-60000
12 " " #15123 12/1896 42-12x18-54000-34000
13 " " Date unknown 37-15x20-70000

San Juan line
1 0-6-0 Porter #1070 10/1889 30-9x14-22500
2 " " #1590 5/1895 "
3 2-4-2T " #1627 11/1895 33-9x14-31000
4 0-6-0 Baldwin #24707 9/1904 33-10x16-29000
5 " " #30257 2/1907 33-11x16 (used at Hacienda de Solis)

Toluca & Zitacuaro R. R. 3 foot gauge

1 4-6-0 Baldwin #11240 10/1890 40-16x20 Ex NdeM #145
2 0-4-4-0 Climax # 848 /1908
3 " Lima # 212 5/1888 28-10x10 Shay. Ex Wilson, Luther & Wilson.

Torres & Prietas R. R. (Mexican Union R. R.) 3 foot gauge

1 4-4-0 Baldwin #5042 4/1880 45-14x18-40000 Ex D&RG #85
5 " " #5198 7/1880 " " #88
6 2-6-0 " #37811 6/1912 42-14x18

Note; In 1914 there were five locomotives in service. The identity of the two not listed above is unknown. No. 5 went to the Carmen Island Salt Co. from the D&RG, then to the T&P. It became Mexican Union No. 2 in 1920.

Vanegas, Cedral & Rio Verde R. R. 3 foot gauge See NdeM Nos. 92-97

The engines were named as follows; No. 1, Cedral; No. 2, Matehuala; No. 3, Vanegas; No. 4, Rio Verde; No. 5, San Ysidro; No. 6, Potrero.

Vera Cruz & Alvarado R. R. 3 foot gauge. 1921 list.

1 Vacant
2 2-4-2 Baldwin date unknown 40-14x18 Class E
3 0-4-0T " " 30- 9x14 "
4 2-8-0 " #36909 8/1911 38-15x20 " G-035 Note.
5 4-4-0 " #15985 6/1898 46-14x18 " B Note.
5 2-6-0 Brooks # 2839 10/1897 48-15x20 " D To NdeM #151
6 2-8-0 A-Pitts. #30512 1/1905 39-16x20 " G-1 " #152
10 4-4-0 Unkwn. Acq. 1919 48-13 1/2x20 " B-2 Note
15 " Baldwin " 42-12x18 " B Note

Note; No. 4 became NdeM #153 - 1930; No. 5 gone by 1919; Nos. 10 and 15 acquired 2nd hand; origin unknown. All but Nos. 4-6 scrapped 1930.

Mexico

Narrow gauge industrial lines

Beristain-Necaxa R. R. 3 foot gauge

1 0-4-0T Porter #3005 5/1904 33-10x16 Scrapped
2 " " #3009 " " Stored serviceable 1968
3 Shay Lima # 898 6/1904 28-10x10 2-truck Scrapped
4 " " # 981 1/1905 " " Stored 1968
5 " " # 982 " " " Scrapped

Note; No. 2 bears the name "La Burrita;" No. 4 is Tona La Negra.

Compania du Boleo---Cia. Minera de Santa Rosalia, S. A. 3 foot gauge

1 Bufalo 0-6-0T Baldwin #7811 2/1886 36-11x16-37000 Retired 1945
2 Morueco " " #7815 " " In shop 1968
3 Toro " " #7817 " " Retired 1945
4 Pinna " " #8364 2/1887 " In shop 1968
5 Cabria " " #8541 5/1887 " Serviceable
6 " " #12979 10/1892 " Scrapped
7 " " #16484 1/1899 " In serv. 1968
8 0-8-0T " #17391 1/1900 36-15x18-71000 Scrapped

Cananea Consolidated Copper Co. 3 foot gauge

1 2-6-2T Porter # 2348 5/1901 40-12x18-56000 Note
2 " # 2349 " " "
3 " Baldwin #20486 5/1902 34-14x16-86100
4 " #20487 "
5 " Unknown Acq. 2nd hand 14x22-80560
6 " Porter # 2967 2/1904 44-15x20-100000
7 " A-Schen. #30317 1/1905 44-16x20-115200
8 " A-Dickson #29717 7/1906 44-15x20-104000
9 " Baldwin #30528 11/1910 38-17x20-128500

Note; Nos. 1 and 2 were built for the Greene Consol. Copper Co.

Chihuahua Mineral Ry.---Asarco Mexicana S. A. 3 foot gauge

1 No record
2 2-8-0 Porter # 2028 10/1899 33-12x16-73040 Derelict since 1950
3 " " # 4462 12/1909 33-12x16-79746 Scrapped prior "
4 4-6-0 Baldwin Date unknown 45-14x20-93390 Ex NdeM. Acq. 1910
5 2-8-0 " #37566 3/1912 36-12x18 Lost 1914-1920
6 " Porter # 6950 2/1925 36 14x18-64000 In service 1968
7 " Baldwin #58530 7/1925 36-15x20-80550 " "
2 " " #16525 12/1899 36-14x18-65000 " "
4 " " #24306 6/1904 36-15x18-74500 " "

Note; No. 7 ex Thunder Lake R. R. #5; #2 and #4, ex Potosi & Rio Verde, same numbers. Acquired in 1953.

Chorreras-Toteco Ry. 3 foot gauge

1 0-4-0T Davenport #1762 12/1919 30-9x14

Note; In 1925 the company owned seven 0-4-0 Milwaukee gas engines, two of 8 1/2 tons; two of 6 1/2 tons and three of 3 1/2 tons.

Cobos-Furbero R. R. 2 foot gauge

1 Furbero 0-4-0T Hudswell-Clarke 1910 20-6x10 4 wheel tender
2 El Meson " Bagnall Ltd. 1911 19-6 1/2x9 "
3 San Marcos " " " " "
4 " " " " "
5 0-4-0T Davenport #1869 4/1921 7x12
6 " " " "

Compania Industrial Azucarera, S. A. 3 foot gauge

1 2-8-0 Baldwin #18620 1/1901 38-16x20-82420 Ex C. & Z. #4
2 2-6-0 " #17681 4/1900 40-14x20-71400 Ex P. & D. #2
3 2-8-0 " #15784 3/1898 38-16x20-82420 Ex C. & Z. #3
4 2-6-0 " #18644 1/1901 40-14x20-71400 Ex P. & D. #4 Scr.
5 2-6-0 " #19041 5/1901 " Ex P. & D. #5
265 2-8-0 " #55026 9/1921 41-18x22-110265 Ex N. de M. #265
1 " Orenstein & Koppel 1936. Ex Ing. de Mante #1. Derelict.

Colima Lumber Co. 3 foot gauge

1 Shay Lima #2392 12/1910 26-8x12
2 " " #2433 3/1911 "

Conchos Railway----Cia. Minera de Naica 30 inch gauge

1 0-4-4T Porter #2895 8/1903 24-6x10-16500
2 " " #2896 " "
3 2-8-2 Baldwin #24202 5/1904 28-10x14-37500
4 " " #24331 6/1904 "
5 " " #28952 9/1906 30-12x18-44500

Cusi Railway 3 foot gauge

1 2-6-0T A. Borsig, Berlin 1909 44800 total weight.

Ixtaccihuatl Ry. 3 foot gauge

1 0-6-0T Yorkshire Eng. Co. 1890 13x20 Ex M. del S.

Mazapil Copper Co. 3 foot gauge

1 0-4-0T Porter #4068 5/1908 30-9x14-25000
2 " " #4279 8/1909 "
1 0-6-0 Baldwin #19152 6/1901 36-16x18-63000
Ex Matehuala Ry. #4

Michoacan Lumber & Development Co. 3 foot gauge

1 Heisler Stearns Mfg. Co. #1001 /1894 Ordered by Read & Campbell
2 2-8-0 Baldwin #4282 2/1878 38-14x16 Ex FCNM 8
3 Shay Lima #2092 4/1908 29 1/2-10x10
4 " " # 143 1/1886 28-10x10
5 " " #1584 10/1905 29 1/2-10x12

Note. No. 1, the first Heisler, was used by the contractors who built the FCNM Patzcuaro-Uruapan extension. No. 4 was originally J. E. Potts Salt & Lbr. Co. All locomotives except No. 3 acquired in 1905.

Moctezuma Copper Co. (F. C. de la Mina). 3 foot gauge

1 0-4-0T Porter #2667 10/1902 28-7x12-20000
5 0-6-0T " #1851 5/1898 30-11x14
6 2-8-0 Baldwin #49926 9/1918 41-18x22-108000

Ogarrio Railway 3 foot gauge

1 Shay Lima #899 7/1904 26 1/2-7x12
2 " " #966 12/1904 "

Otumba & Cuauhtengo R. R. 2 foot gauge

1 Porfirio Diaz Vulcan #229 8/1899 28-8x12 Ordered by A. Koppel & Co.

Cia. Minera de Penoles-Avalos 2 foot gauge

1 0-4-4-0 Orenstein-Koppel 1902 Mallet compound
2 " " " "
3 0-4-0T Porter #7063 7/1927 30-9x14

El Potosi Mining Co.---Minerales Nacionales de Mexico, S. A. 30 in. gauge

1 0-4-2T Porter # 673 12/1884 24-8x12-17000 Nos. 1 and 2 built for
2 " " # 948 6/1888 " Santa Eulalia Silver
3 " " #1180 6/1890 30-8x14-25000 Mines.
4 " " #1181 " "
5 0-6-4T " #2623 10/1902 33-10x16-40000
6 " " #2740 5/1903 "
7 " " #3309 4/1905 "
8 " " #5109 7/1912 "
9 " " #6558 9/1920 40-13x18-50500
10 " " #6559 " "
Electric - 600 volt D. C. -Replaced all steam power in 1925-1926
11 0-4-4-0 Gen. Elect. #9624 12/1924 In service 1968
12 " " #9625 " "
13 " " #9626 " "
14 " " #9627 " "
15 " " #9628 " "
4 0-4-0 " #10082 7/1926 "
5 " " #10863 4/1929 "

Ingenio El Potrero 3 foot gauge

1 0-6-0T Porter #4023 10/1907 30-10x16-36000
2 " " #4024 " "
3 0-6-2T " #6680 10/1921 36-12x16-48000
4 0-4-2T " #4672 9/1910 44-12x18-48500 Ex Tabasco Cent. #4
5 " " #4019 10/1907 " " #3
6 2-8-0 Rogers #5608 /1900 38-14x20 Ex Parral & Dur. #3 Note.
7 2-8-2T Porter #7234 7/1936 40-16x18-110000
8 2-8-0 Baldwin #25886 6/1905 50-17x20-108000 Ex P. & D. #6

Note; No. 6 built for H. Marquard & Co. #9, then Parral & Durango #3.

Compania La Primavera 2 foot gauge

1 2-6-2T Baldwin #14976 8/1896 33-11x16-46000 Ex C. La T. & T. #6
2 2-6-0 " #21630 2/1903 30- 9x14-28500 Ex Natl. Salt Co. #2
3 " " #21618 " " " #1

Note; No. 1 retired 1947; Nos. 2 and 3 retired 1955.

Quintana Roo Railways (The Laguna Company). 2 foot gauge

1	0-4-4T	Davenport	#521	5/1908	24-8x12	
2	Shay	Lima	#2084	4/1908	22-6x10	2 truck
3	"	"	#2085	"	"	"
4	"	"	#2042	2/1908	"	"
5	"	"	#2102	7/1909	"	"
6	Heisler		#1336	/1916		

Ingenio San Francisco El Naranjal, S. A. 30 inch gauge

1	0-4-2T	Porter	#1591	5/1895	30-8x14-20000	Note 1.
2	0-4-4	Baldwin	#14842	5/1896	30-9x14-34500	Note 2.
3	2-6-0	Orenstein-Koppel	#1140	/1926	24 in. drivers	
4	2-6-2T	Baldwin	#14798	4/1896	33-11x16-46000	Note 3
5	"	"	#14799	"	"	

Note 1; Built for Cia. Industrial Mexicana, Chihuahua. Note 2; Built for Fletcher & Creel, Chihuahua. Note 3; ex Cazadero, LaTorre & Tepetong #4 and #5---Gauge changed from 24 to 30 inches. All retired June 1964.

San Geronimo to Cerro Azul R. R. --Mexican Petroleum Co. 3 foot gauge

1	2-8-0	Orenstein-Koppel		1936		Sold to C. I. A. S. A. 1953.
3	0-4-0T	Baldwin	#57991	9/1924	29-10x16	
5	2-6-0	"	#39193	1/1913	40-14x20	
6	"	"	#39194	"	"	
102	"	"	#54238	1/1921	"	

Note; Except for No. 1, the above locomotives were derelict in 1963. This road operated 48 km. of 3 foot and standard gauge in connection with the refinery known as Ingenio de Mante. The railroad is now powered by diesels.

Santa Barbara Tram & R. R. Co. --Minas Tecolotes y Anexas 30 inch gauge

1	Shay	Lima	# 753	8/1902	26-7x12	2-truck.
2	0-6-0T	Porter	#2279	1/1901	28-10x14-32000	
3	Shay	Lima	# 712	2/1902	26-7x12	2-truck.

Tabasco Central R. R. 3 foot gauge

1	Shay	Lima	#1565	6/1905	22-6x10	2-truck.
2	0-4-2T	Porter	#3350	11/1905	40-12x18	
3	"	"	#4019	10/1907	44-12x18	To Ing. El Potrero #5
4	"	"	#4672	4/1910	"	" #4

Tatetla Railroad 2 foot gauge

1	2-6-0	Baldwin	#34117	12/1909	28-9x14-24000	Out of service in 1959

Teziutlan Copper Co. 3 foot gauge

1	Shay	Lima	# 1847	1/1907	29 1/2-10x12 2-truck	Retired 1954
2	"	"	# 1848	"	" "	In service
3	"		# 2449	5/1911	" "	In service
4	2-8-0	Baldwin	#35723	12/1910	41-18x22-118000	To NdeM #297. Note
5	"	"		Date blt. unknwn.		Note.

Note. No. 4 acquired from the Vera Cruz Terminal Ry. #15. Sold to NdeM in 1944. No. 5 purchased from Southern Iron & Equip. Co. #1033-1916

Electric locomotives.

1	0-4-0	Baldwin	#24142	4/1904	100 HP-12 ton
2	"	"	#24143	"	"
3	"	"	#25730	5/1905	"

Ingenio Tilapa 3 foot gauge

1	2-6-0	Krauss		/1903		
2	0-6-0T	Vulcan	#3207	9/1921	30 1/2-10x16	Named Guipuzcoa.

Note; Both locomotives ordered from Orenstein-Koppel. Derelict in 1945

Tomacoco to Tlaltenango R. R. 2 foot gauge

1	0-6-2T	Porter	#4757	12/1910	12x16x10 compound	Derelict in 1952

Velardena R. R. 3 foot gauge

1	2-6-0	Porter	#2744	5/1903	40-12x18-44000
2	"	"	#2745	"	"
3	0-4-4T	"	#2687	2/1903	40-12x16-46000

The Cia. Industrial Azucarera's No. 3 originally carried the same number for the Coahuila & Zacatecas. It is shown at Juan Diaz Covarrubias, Vera Cruz State, in 1968. *(H. F. Stewart)*

Ferrocarriles Nacionales de Mexico
National Railways of Mexico

3 foot gauge
1930---1968
- - -

Engines 1 to 77 incl. were ex Interoceanic Ry. and retained the initials FCI on the tank. Their old FCI numbers are at the right of the new number.

Class B-01 0-6-0 38-14x20-69242-140-12276

1 101 Schenectady #5169 6/1899 Retired 6/1/1939

Class F-04 4-6-0 47-16x20-91000-55550-175-12900

2 38 Dubs & Co. #2574 9/1889 Retired 1931

Class F-09 4-6-0 46-16x20-81130-60848-160-15137

3 35 Baldwin #12839 7/1892 Orig. NdeM #156 Scrapped 1942
4 36 " #12850 " " #157 Retired 6/1/1930

Class F-011 4-6-0 48-16x20-110162-67200-175-15867

5 30 Baldwin #10578 1/1890 Retired 1948
6 31 " #10094 7/1889 " "
7 32 " #10095 " " 1946
8 33 " #10096 " " 1949
9 34 " #10112 " " 1948

Class F-012 4-6-0 48-16x20-92455-66495-175-16366

10 27 Schenectady #5222 9/1899 Retired 1945
11 28 " #4790 8/1898 Retired 6/22/1954
12 29 " #4791 " Retired 1945

Class G-08 2-8-0 38-16x20-87522-75450-145-16606

21 10 Baldwin #9469 9/1888 Wrecked 12/31/1936. Scrapped
22 11 " #9471 " Retired 1944
23 12 " #9476 " " 1945
24 14 " #9962 4/1889 " "
25 16 " #9628 11/1888 " 11/1949
26 17 " #9719 1/1889 " 1945
27 18 " #9720 " " Awaiting scrap 2/1941
28 19 " #9721 " " 11/15/1949
29 20 " #9729 " " Awaiting scrap 2/1941
30 21 " #9728 " " " " "
31 23 " #9732 " " Retired 12/16/1949
32 24 " #9730 " " Awaiting scrap 2/1941

Class G-09 2-8-0 38-16x20-76571-66010-145-16606

33 90 4 20 Baldwin #7516 12/1884 Retired 6/20/1949
34 91 1 21 " #7517 " Awaiting scrap 2/1941
35 92 2 22 " #7518 " Retired prior 1941
36 93 3 23 " #7519 " Retired 1946

Class G-010 2-8-0 38-16x20-76583-66020-145-16606

37 40 Baldwin #10670 2/1890 Retired 12/26/1938
38 41 " #10673 " " prior 1941
39 42 " #10738 3/1890 " "
40 43 " #10739 " " 3/23/1935
41 44 " #10747 " " 1948
42 45 " #10750 " " 1946
43 46 " #10836 4/1890 " Awaiting scrap 2/1941
44 47 " #10842 " " 1948
45 48 " #10929 5/1890 " Awaiting scrap 2/1941
46 49 " #10930 " " 7/16/1939

Class G-011 2-8-0 38-16x20-76571-66010-145-16606

47 94 8 Baldwin #6537 12/1882 Retired 6/20/1949
48 95 10 " #6539 " " 1946
49 96 9 " #6540 " " prior 1941
50 97 5 " #5370 11/1880 " "
51 98 6 " #5438 1/1881 " 6/20/1949
52 99 7 " #6086 7/1882 " 11/15/1949

Class G-012 2-8-0 37 1/2-16x20-75161-66900-145-16828

53 52 Baldwin #11324 11/1891 Retired prior 1941
54 53 " #11325 " " 1947
55 54 " #11357 " Awaiting scrap 2/1941
56 56 " #11371 " Retired prior 1941
57 57 " #11372 " " 1947
58 58 " #11393 " " 1948
59 59 " #11407 " " 1946

Class G-023 2-8-0 38-16x20-98460-84880-175-20042

60 Schenectady #4792 8/1898 Sold to Edaville Museum - 1963
61 " #4793 " Sold to F.C. Unidos de Yucatan #161 1/1956
62 " #4796 " Retired 7/14/1954
63 " #4797 " Sold to F.C. U. de Y. #163 1/1956
64 " #4798 " Retired 1967
65 " #4799 " Retired 6/19/1954
66 " #5209 7/1899 Out of service 1968
67 " #5210 " In service as of 6/1968
68 " #5211 " Retired 7/14/1964
69 " #5212 " Out of service 1968
70 " #5213 " "
71 " #5214 " "
72 " #5221 " Sold to F.C. U de Y. #172 - 1958

Class G-024 2-8-0 38-16x20-98460-84880-175-20042

73 Kerr, Stuart & Co. #819 5/1904 Laid aside in 1968
74 " #820 " Retired 3/13/1965
75 " #821 " Laid aside in 1968

Class G-025 2-8-0 38-16x20-100380-90380-175-20042

76 80 Baldwin #17408 1/1900 Retired 3/13/1965
77 81 " #17409 " Laid aside in 1968

Engines 101 to 121 incl. were ex Mexican Southern R. R., and retained the initials M del S on the tank. Old numbers appear on the right of the 1930 number.

Class D-01 4-4-0 45-14x22-61152-39200-140-8582

101 241 7 Kitson & Co. #3312 2/1891 Retired in 1931

Class F-04 4-6-0 46-15x20-64000-44000-160-13304

102 263 FCI 37 FCNM 163 Baldwin #15749 2/1898 Retired in 1945

Class F-05 4-6-0 48-16x20-97196-73723-175-15867

103 261 20 Alco-Cooke #25797 4/1902 Scrapped 6/22/1954
104 262 21 " #25798 " " 6/10/1954

Class F-06 4-6-0 48-16x20-87000-58000-175-15867

105 263 22 Alco-Cooke #42038 5/1908 Retired 9/11/1948

Class G-013 2-8-0 37-16x20-88000-80135-145-17055

111 281 18 Alco-Cooke #25796 4/1902 Retired in 1951

Class G-019 2-8-0 38-17x20-88000-80135-145-18747

112 271 15 Baldwin #13035 11/1892 Retired 2/23/1954
113 272 16 " #13036 " Retired 2/14/1954
114 273 17 " #13041 " Retired in 1948
115 274 9 " #33566 7/1909 Retired 2/14/1954
116 275 10 " #33567 " Retired 6/19/1954

Class G-020 2-8-0 37-17x20-88000-80135-145-19254

117 278 11 Baldwin #33598 7/1909 Retired 2/23/1954
118 279 12 " #33599 " Retired 2/23/1954
119 280 " #33600 " Sold to F.C. U. de Y. #119 1/1956

Class G-021 2-8-0 37-17x20-88000-80135-145-19254

120 276 13 Baldwin #27588 2/1906 Retired 9/18/1951
121 282 19 " #32731 3/1908 Retired 2/23/1954

Engines 141-145 incl. were ex Mexican Eastern, with initials O.M. on the tank, and engines 151-153 were ex Vera Cruz & Alvarado R. R., with FCVA on the tank. Previous numbers are to the right of the 1930 number.

Class G-03 2-8-0 38-15x20-69600-60000-140-14092

141 OM8 SM&T8 Baldwin #16201 9/1898 Retired in 1952

Class G-024 2-8-0 38-16x20-98460-84880-175-20042

142 OM 1 SM&T 76 Kerr, Stuart & Co. #822 5/1904 Laid aside in 1968
143 2 77 " #823 " "
144 3 78 Baldwin #20384 4/1902 "
145 4 79 " #20385 " Retired 3/13/1965

Class E-01 2-6-0 42-15x20-68083-59075-135-12009

151 FCVA 5 J&C 1 Brooks #2839 10/1897 Awaiting scrap 2/1941

Class G-02 2-8-0 39-15x20-65815-59582-135-13240

152 FCVA 6 FCVA 100 Alco-Pittsburgh #30512 1/1905 Retired 10/16/49

Class G-04 2-8-0 38-15x20-70604-60582-140-14092

153 FCVA 4 Baldwin #36909 8/1911 Retired 4/29/1948

Engines 163 to 455 incl. were N de M engines renumbered in 1930 or purchased since that date, several of them second-hand. The previous numbers are at the right of the 1930 number.

Class C-02 0-8-0 37-16x20-68000-140-16467

163 35 Baldwin #5872 10/1881 Reblt. to 2-8-0 - 1941 See #200
164 69 " #7004 10/1883 Retired 6/1/1953
165 70 " #7012 " Retired 2/24/1954
166 138 30 " #5686 6/1881 Reblt. to 2-8-0 - 1941 See #201

Class E-02 2-6-0 39-15x20-77491-61993-160-16105

167 208 Alco-Cooke #62094 9/1920 Retired 9/11/1948

Class F-08 4-6-0 46-16x20-80135-58025-160-15137

175 146 Baldwin #11220 9/1890 Retired 10/16/1947

Class F-013 4-6-0 49-17x20-109283-88519-180-18048

181 217 Baldwin #57938 7/1924 Retired 2/23/1954
182 218 " #57939 " Sold to F.C.U. de Y. 1/1956
183 219 " #57940 " Retired 6/19/1954
184 220 " #57941 " Sold to F.C.U. de Y. 1/1956
185 221 " #57942 " Retired 6/15/1965
186 222 " #57943 " " 3/30/1965
187 223 " #57962 8/1924 " 6/19/1954
188 224 " #57963 " " 6/15/1965
189 225 " #57964 " " 2/23/1954
190 226 " #57965 " " 6/15/1965

Class G-05 2-8-0 37-16x20-74000-66200-140-16467

200 163 35 Baldwin #5872 10/1881 Reblt. from 0-8-0 - 1941 Note.
201 166 138 30 " #5686 6/1881 " " " " "

Note; Nos. 200 and 201 were 2-8-0s for two years. In 1943 they were converted back to 0-8-0 type and renumbered 163 and 166. Retired 1948

Class G-07 2-8-0 38-16x20-78000-70000-140-16034

220 83 M&P 3 Baldwin #12875 8/1892 Retired 6/19/36. Scr. 1952
221 84 4 " #14409 8/1895 Retired prior 1941
222 94 VC&RV 3 " #11783 9/1891 "

Class G-014 2-8-0 38-16x20-87010-78760-150-17179

223 6 H&NE 6 Baldwin # 9867 3/1889 Retired 11/15/1949
224 7 7 " # 9876 " " 2/19/1954
225 20 20 " #14964 7/1896 " 2/19/1954
226 21 21 " #17456 2/1900 " prior 1941
227 22 22 " #17457 " " in 1945
228 23 23 " #17960 7/1900 " 2/19/1954
229 24 24 " #17961 " " in 1945
230 27 27 " #25773 5/1905 " 10/2/1953

Class G-015 2-8-0 38-16x20-84700-76230-155-17752

231 14 H&NE 14 Baldwin #12270 10/1891 Retired 2/24/1954

Class G-016 2-8-0 39-16x20-89650-81356-160-17854

232 113 Baldwin #8917 11/1887 Retired 1948
233 115 " #9468 9/1888 " 1947
234 117 " #9473 " " "
235 139 " #9963 4/1889 " 1949
236 140 " #9969 " " 1945
237 142 " #9992 5/1889 " 1948
238 143 " #9993 " " 2/19/1954

Class G-017 2-8-0 36-17x18-89650-79805-150-18424

239 85 M&P 5 Baldwin #16522 2/1899 Retired in 1931
240 86 6 " #16523 " " 2/19/1954
241 87 7 " #19034 5/1901 " 2/19/1954
242 96 VC&RV 4 " #15324 5/1897 " 1947 Note

Note; #242 rebuilt with 17x20 cyls., 19918 TE.

Class G-018 2-8-0 38-16x20-83000-76000-160-18446

243 207 Alco-Cooke #62095 9/1921 Retired 6/3/1951

Class G-022 2-8-0 38-17x20-89000-80000-150-19393

244 97 VC&RV 5 Baldwin #15036 9/1896 Retired 1/1/1950

Class G-026 2-8-0 38-16x20-94092-75276-175-20042

245 158 Baldwin #12849 7/1892 Retired 3/13/1965
246 159 " #12853 " " 9/18/1951
247 160 " #12860 " " 8/12/1953
248 161 " #12871 8/1892 " 2/24/1954

Class G-027 2-8-0 38-17x20-89000-80000-180-23272

249 181 Baldwin #17342 1/1900 Retired 2/19/1954
250 182 " #17343 " " 6/21/1954
251 183 " #17368 " " 10/28/1964
252 184 " #17369 " " 6/21/1954

Class G-028 2-8-0 38-17x20-99724-90749-180-23272

253 165 Baldwin #15787 3/1898 Retired 11/30/48. Scr. 1953
254 166 " #15788 " Laid aside in 1968
255 167 " #15789 " Retired 3/13/1965
256 168 " #15790 " " "
257 169 " #16450 1/1899 Sold to F. C. Mexicano #25 8/21/49
258 170 " #16451 " " " #26 "
259 171 " #16452 " " " #24 11/1/48

Class G-029 2-8-0 41-18x22-110265-99265-180-26600

260 185 Baldwin #17986 7/1900 Retired 6/15/1965
261 186 " #17987 " Leased to Coahuila & Zacatecas 1/10/60

Class G-030 2-8-0 41-18x22-110265-99265-180-26600

262 187 Baldwin #55023 9/1921 In service as of 6/1968
263 188 " #55024 " Laid aside in 1968
264 189 " #55025 " Reblt. to std. ga. #931 12/31/52
265 190 " #55026 " Sold to a sugar refinery - 1968
266 191 " #55027 " Retired 2/19/1954
267 192 " #55051 " Laid aside in 1968
268 193 " #55052 " Retired 8/30/1965
269 194 " #55053 " In service as of 6/1968
270 195 " #55054 " Laid aside in 1968
271 196 " #55055 " Retired 6/15/1965
272 197 " #55056 " In service as of 6/1968
273 198 " #55057 " Laid aside in 1968. Note.
274 199 " #55058 " Reblt. to std. ga. #930 10/16/52
275 200 " #55059 " Undergoing repairs, Puebla 5/1968
276 201 " #55060 " Retired 6/15/1965
277 202 " #55061 " Retired 10/11/1965
278 203 " #55109 " Retired 3/13/1965
279 204 " #55110 " Undergoing repairs, Puebla 5/1968
280 205 " #55111 " Retired 10/11/1965
281 206 " #55112 " Undergoing repairs, Puebla 5/1968
282 209 " #57922 7/1924 Retired 6/15/1965 #282-289 had
283 210 " #57923 " " 2/19/1954 Baker valve
284 211 " #57924 " " 6/15/1965 gear.
285 212 " #57925 " " 2/19/1964
286 213 " #57926 " Sold to San Rafael Paper Co. 6/15/65
287 214 " #57927 " Retired 6/15/1965
288 215 " #57928 " " "
289 216 " #57918 " " 2/19/1954

Note; Engines 273 and 279 were sold to the Coahuila & Zacatecas 6/1959. They were returned in 1963 and restored to service on the N de M.

Class GR-031 2-8-0 41-18x22-118000-110000-180-26600

290 Alco-Schenectady #68740 7/1936 Reblt. to std. ga. #902 10/26/1949
291 " #68741 " " #904 3/27/1952
292 " #68742 " " #900 1/31/1948
293 " #68743 " " #905 6/28/1952
294 " #68744 " " #906 8/ 8/1952
295 Acambaro Shops 5/1944 " #901 9/21/1949
296 " " " #907 8/29/1952
297 Baldwin #35723 12/1910 " #903 8/25/1950

Note; Nos. 295-296 were assembled at Acambaro Shops from spare boilers and parts furnished by Alco. No. 297 acquired from Teziutlan Copper Co. #4, originally Vera Cruz Terminal Ry. #15.

Class HR-01 2-6-6-2 43-15x22-204000-161500-210-41100

361 240 Alco-Schenectady #67706 12/1928 Retired 6/19/1954
362 241 " #67707 " " 2/22/1954
363 242 " #67708 " " "
364 243 " #67709 " " "
365 244 " #67710 " " "
366 245 " #67711 " " "

Class HR-01 2-6-6-2 43-15x22-216000-172500-210-41100

367	Alco-Schenectady	#68644	6/1934	Retired 6/ 1/1951
368	"	#68645	"	" 6/19/1954
369	"	#68773	10/1936	" "
370	"	#68774	"	" "

Classes KR-03 and KR-04 2-8-2 40-17x22-139535-111375-200-27021

400	D&RGW 458	Baldwin	#21910	4/1903	KR-03	Reblt. to std. ga. #2250 7/31/1949
401	" 459	"	#21936	4/1903	KR-04	Reblt. to std. ga. #2251 6/15/1949

Class G-O 2-8-0 36-17x18-88500-79220-150-18424

455	TC Co. 1 MS 4	Baldwin	#19126	6/1901	Acq. 1941	Retired 1945 Scrapped 1959 Note

Note; No. 455 was brought to Mexico by the Tiger Chalk Co. (Yeso El Tigre) in 1925 and operated on an industrial line from the station of El Tigre, four miles south of Los Reyes on the Mexico City-Cuautla line. It was seized by the N de M in 1941 in a debt settlement, retired in 1945 but was held in litigation and stored in the San Lazaro shed from 1945 to 1959.

Explanation of initials in connection with earlier road numbers.

FCI -	Interoceanic Railway	MS-	Morenci Southern R. R.
FCNM-	Mexican National R.R.	MT&C-	Mexico, Toluca & Cuautitlan
FCVA-	Vera Cruz & Alvarado RR	OM-	Mexican Eastern R. R.
H&NE-	Hidalgo & Northeastern RR	SM&T-	San Marcos & Tecolutla RR
J&C-	Jalapa & Cordova R.R.	T&StL-	Texas & St. Louis R. R.
M&P-	Michoacan & Pacific R. R.	VC&RV-	Vanegas, Cedral & Rio Verde

No. 263 heads south near Popo Park, with a bad order boxcar trailing behind the caboose. *(Jim Shaughnessy)*

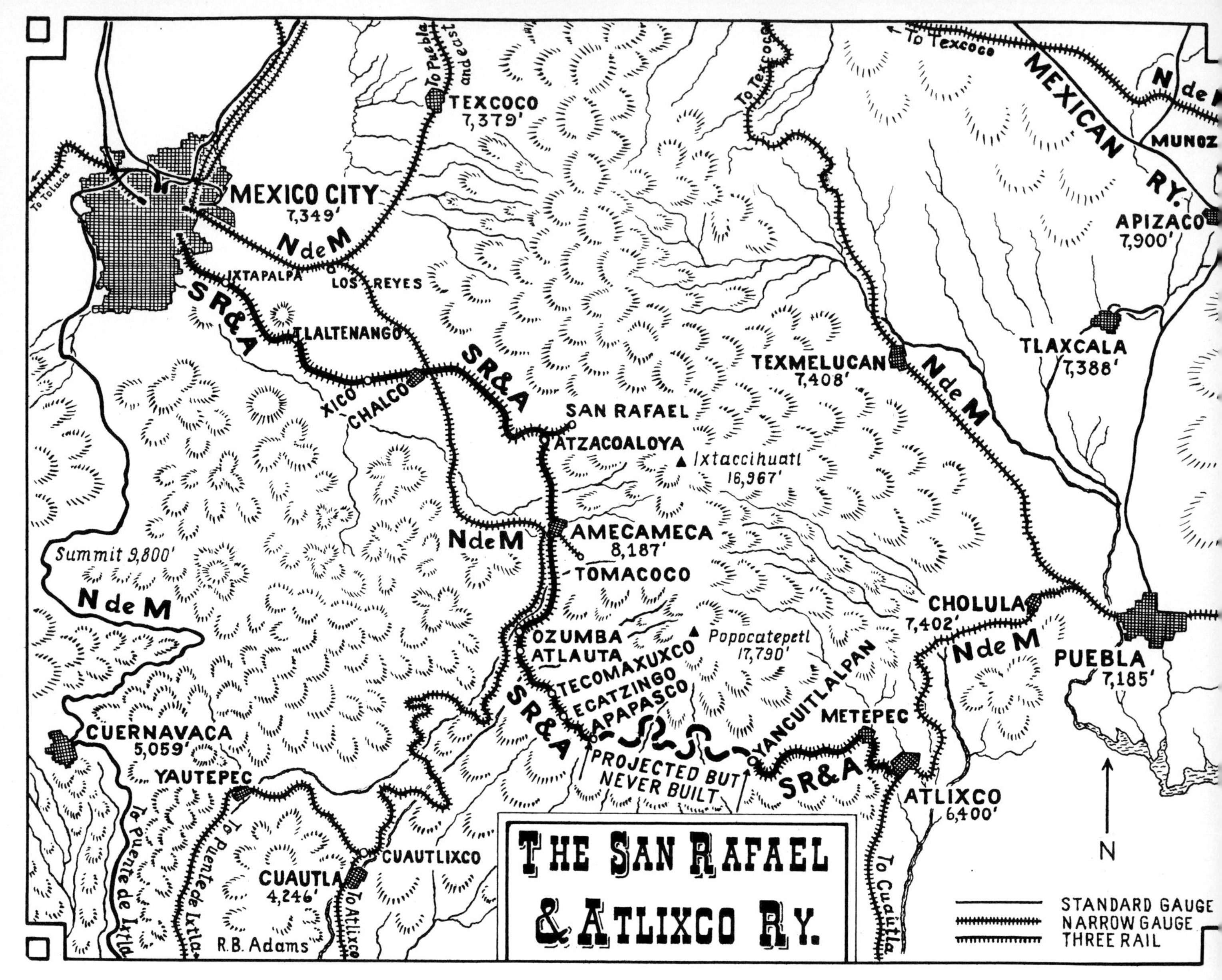

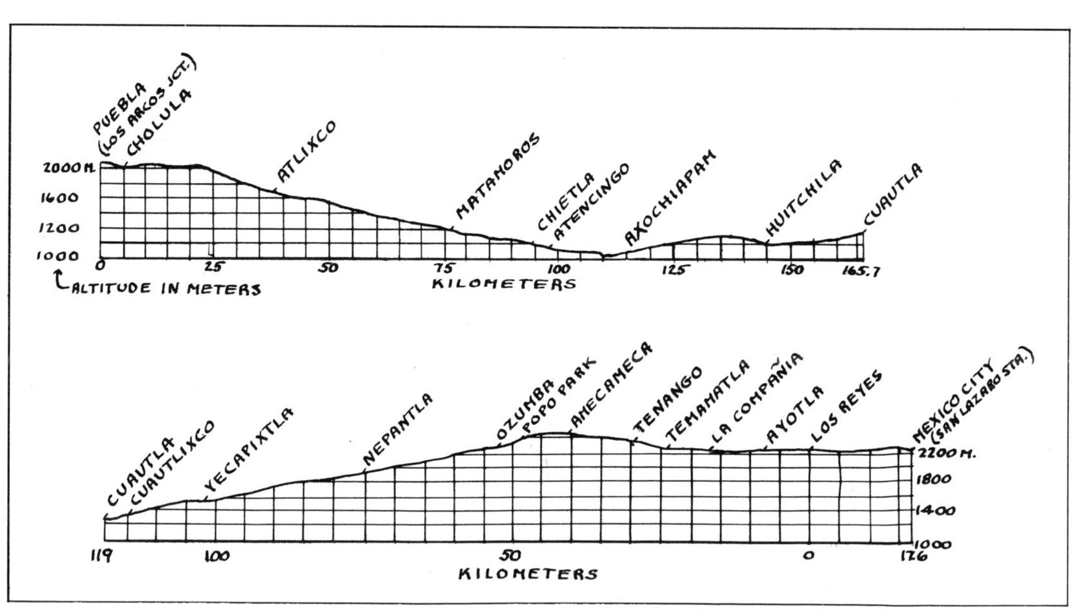

The profiile represents the Puebla-Cuautla-Mexico City main line which also appears on the map above, except for the southerly bend between Atlixco and Cuautla. Chalco on the map is near La Compania on the profile.

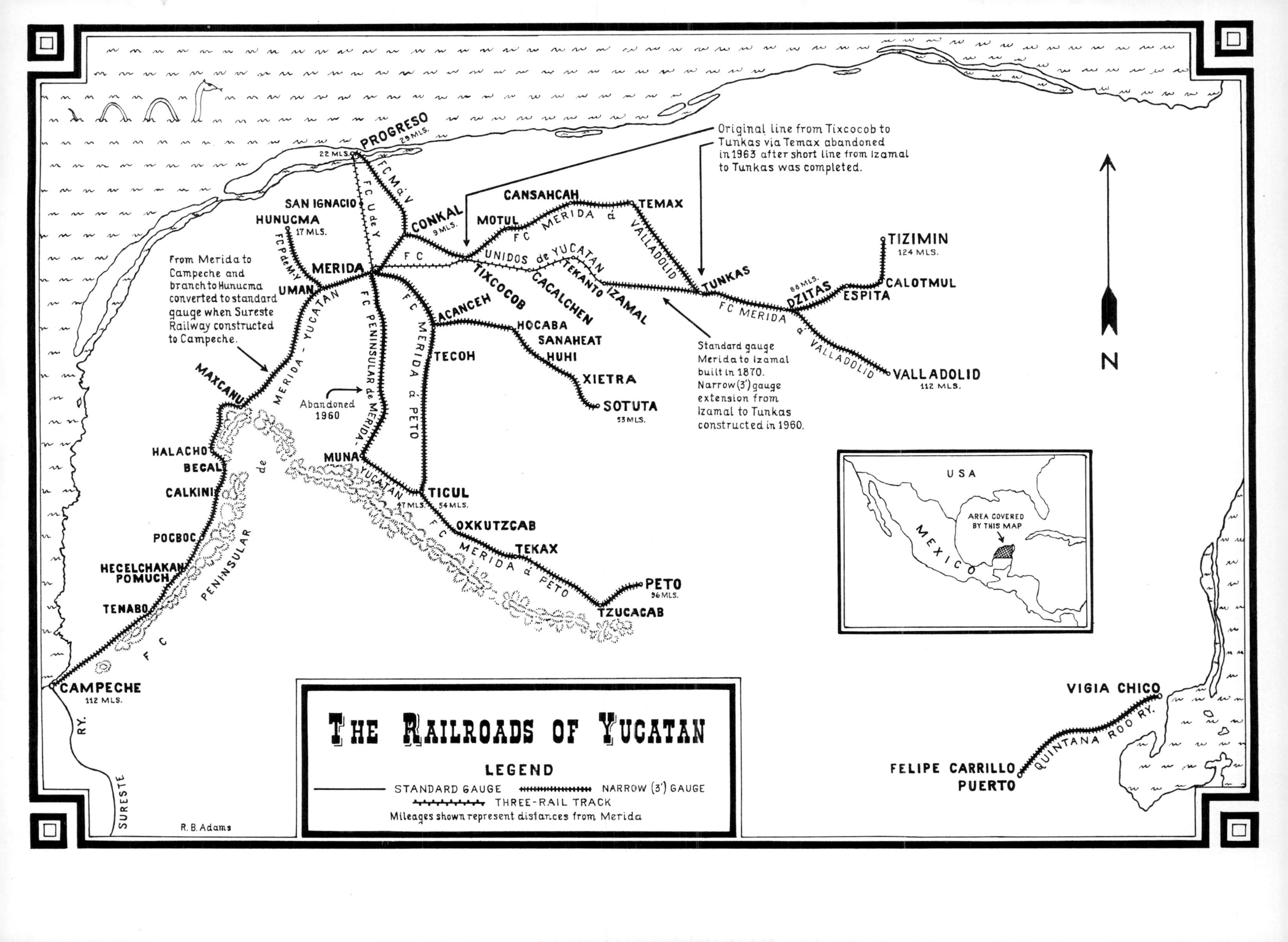

THE RAILROADS OF YUCATAN
LEGEND
STANDARD GAUGE
NARROW (3') GAUGE
THREE-RAIL TRACK
Mileages shown represent distances from Merida
PROGRESO 29 MLS.
22 MLS.
FC M á V
FC U de Y
SAN IGNACIO
HUNUCMA 17 MLS.
FC P de M-Y
MERIDA
UMAN
CONKAL 9 MLS.
MOTUL
CANSAHCAH
TEMAX
FC MERIDA á VALLADOLID
FC UNIDOS de YUCATAN
TIXCOCOB
CACALCHEN
TEKANTO
IZAMAL
TUNKAS
DZITAS 88 MLS.
ESPITA
CALOTMUL
TIZIMIN 124 MLS.
VALLADOLID 112 MLS.
ACANCEH
HOCABA
SANAHEAT
HUHI
XIETRA
SOTUTA 53 MLS.
TECOH
FC MERIDA á PETO
FC PENINSULAR de MERIDA-YUCATAN
Abandoned 1960
MUNA
TICUL 54 MLS.
47 MLS.
OXKUTZCAB
TEKAX
PETO 96 MLS.
TZUCACAB
MERIDA - YUCATAN
MAXCANU
HALACHO
BECAL
CALKINI
POCBOC
HECELCHAKAN
POMUCH
TENABO
FC de PENINSULAR
CAMPECHE 112 MLS.
SURESTE RY.
VIGIA CHICO
QUINTANA ROO RY.
FELIPE CARRILLO PUERTO
USA
MEXICO
AREA COVERED BY THIS MAP
N
Original line from Tixcocob to Tunkas via Temax abandoned in 1963 after short line from Izamal to Tunkas was completed.
From Merida to Campeche and branch to Hunucma converted to standard gauge when Sureste Railway constructed to Campeche.
Standard gauge Merida to Izamal built in 1870. Narrow (3') gauge extension from Izamal to Tunkas constructed in 1960.
R. B. Adams

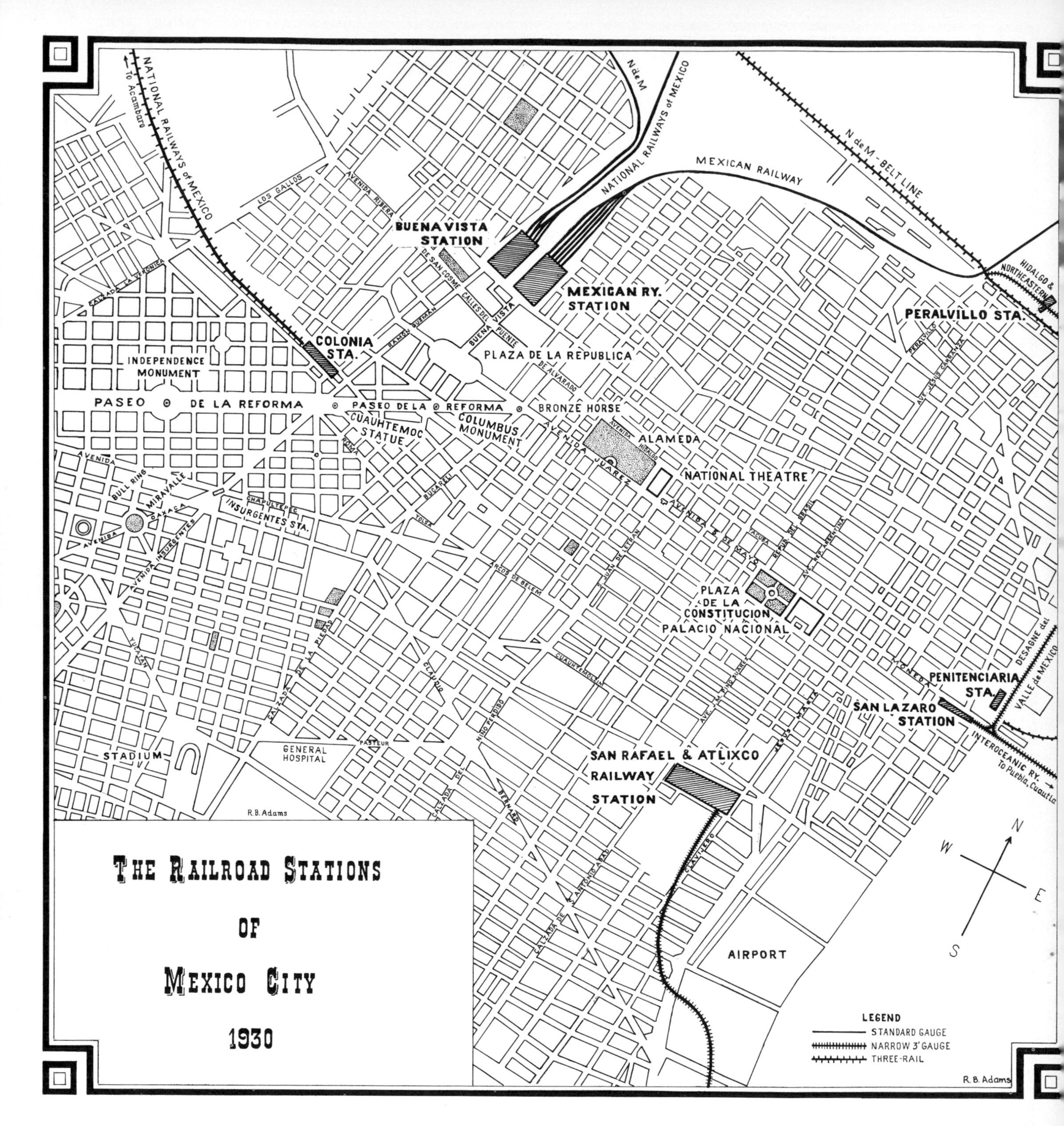

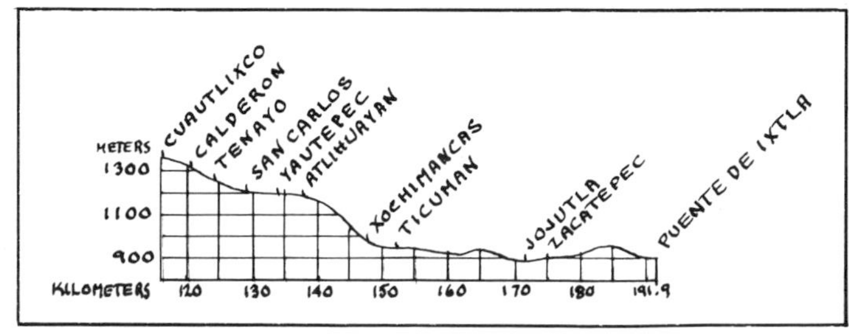

Of all Mexico City's rail terminals in 1930, only San Lazaro remains. The N. de M.'s new station is north of old Buena Vista. The profile, left, depicts the branch line linking Cuautla, south of Cuautlixco, with Puente de Ixtla on the standard gauge line south of Mexico City.

Index

263
N. DE M.

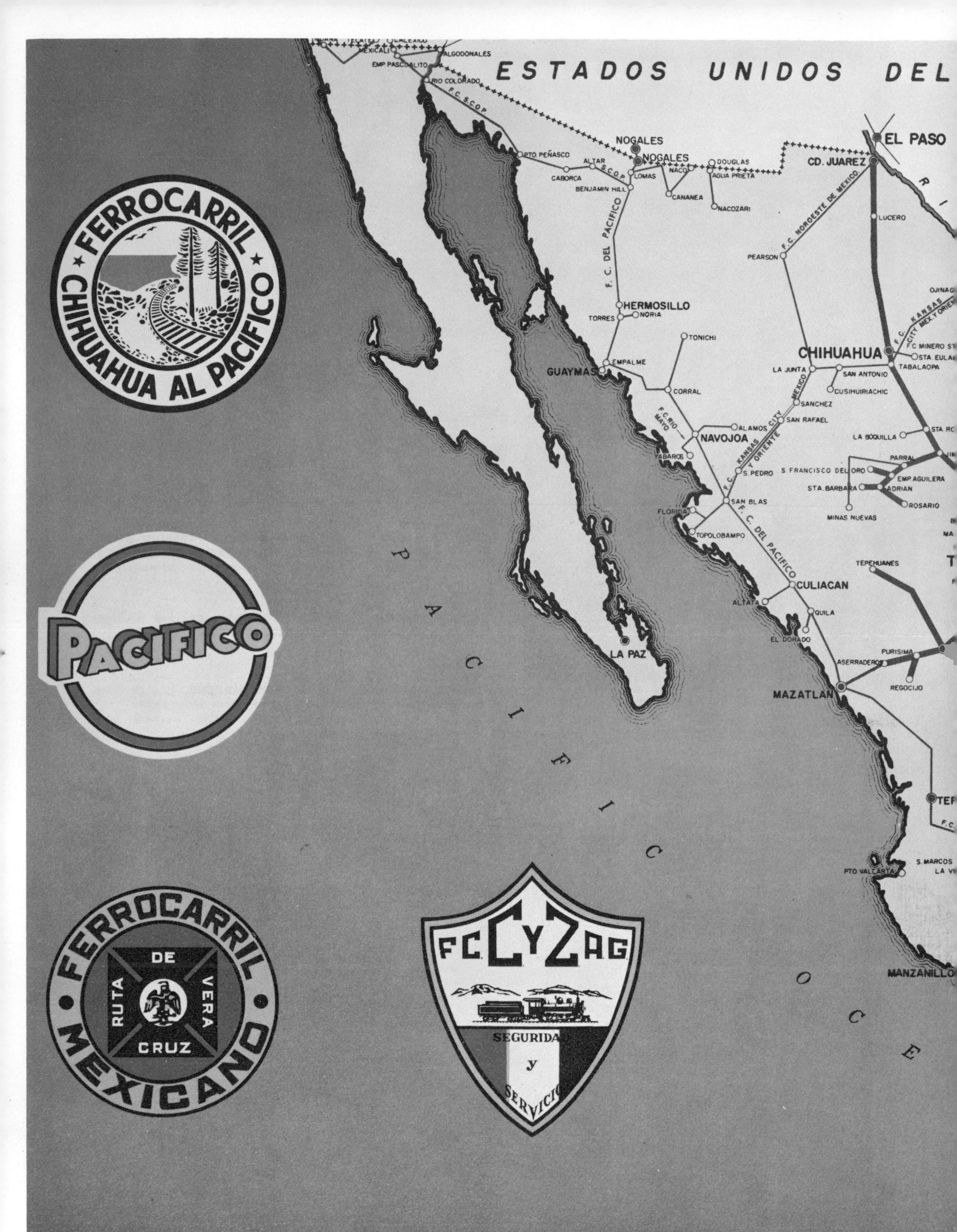

ESTADOS UNIDOS DEL
MEXICALI
ALGODONALES
EMP. PASCUALITO
RIO COLORADO
F.C. S.C.O.P.
NOGALES
NOGALES
PTO. PEÑASCO
ALTAR
CABORCA
S.C.O.P.
BENJAMIN HILL
LOMAS
NACO
DOUGLAS
AGUA PRIETA
CANANEA
NACOZARI
EL PASO
CD. JUAREZ
F.C. NOROESTE DE MEXICO
LUCERO
PEARSON
F.C. DEL PACIFICO
HERMOSILLO
TORRES
NORIA
TONICHI
OJINAGA
CHIHUAHUA
F.C. MINERO
STA. EULALIA
TABALAOPA
LA JUNTA
SAN ANTONIO
CUSIHUIRIACHIC
GUAYMAS
EMPALME
CORRAL
SANCHEZ
SAN RAFAEL
F.C. RIO MAYO
ALAMOS
NAVOJOA
F.C. KANSAS CITY MEXICO Y ORIENTE
LA BOQUILLA
YAVAROS
S. PEDRO
S. FRANCISCO DEL ORO
PARRAL
EMP. AGUILERA
STA. BARBARA
ADRIAN
ROSARIO
SAN BLAS
FLORIDA
MINAS NUEVAS
TOPOLOBAMPO
F.C. DEL PACIFICO
TEPEHUANES
CULIACAN
ALTATA
QUILA
LA PAZ
EL DORADO
PURISIMA
ASERRADEROS
REGOCIJO
MAZATLAN
P A C I F I C O
O C E
PTO. VALLARTA
S. MARCOS
MANZANILLO
FERROCARRIL CHIHUAHUA AL PACIFICO
PACIFICO
FERROCARRIL MEXICANO
RUTA DE VERA CRUZ
F.C. C.Y Z. A.G.
SEGURIDAD y SERVICIO